# Home

## is where you

# Queer

## your

# Heart

# Home
## is where you
## Queer
## your
## Heart

Editors | Monique Mero-Williams
Miah Jeffra    Arisa White

Foglifter Press
2021

ISBN: 978-1-7321913-8-9

Interior Design by Miah Jeffra and Monique Mero-Williams
Cover Design by Monique Mero-Williams
Cover Image by Mathias Jung, "Beim Kaffee dachte Claudine oft ans Meer," 2020
Interior Artwork by Ayuna Collins
Courtesy of the artists
Copy: Susan Calvillo

This book has been made possible, in part, by grants from the California Arts Council,
The San Francisco Arts Commission and Horizons Foundation.

Cataloging-in-publication data is available from the Library of Congress

Foglifter Press
San Francisco, California
www.foglifterpress.com

to the homies

# TABLE OF CONTENTS

# Preface

Home is where you queer your heart

and your liver

and your spirit too.

Two thousand and twenty has taken us in many directions.

On August 30, 2019: Our call for work invited the various ways queer writers explore themes and questions of home. We asked: How do queer writers negotiate feelings of home when their nation has further precluded them from a place of comfort? If the future is queer, how do we language home in these, and other, ways? What does it look like on the page, when read? How are the conditions of the times affecting the way we make and write about home?

We assumed we would be solely reckoning with a U.S. presidential election season as we curated this anthology, but the coronavirus, its attendant cultural resets, federal and statewide mishandlings, the murder of Breonna Taylor and George Floyd, calls and action to defund the police, home is where we were ordered to shelter in place.

We are home, working from home, schooling from home, growing and shedding at home, alone and not-alone-enough at home, losing our minds and finding our bodies at home. We sing Prince songs while washing our hands. Quarantined in our smaller orbits from here to there, our blood surveilled, our contact is traced. We mask ourselves, in hopes of not spreading or contracting Corona. We are grief-stricken, anxious, and with so much uncertainty, we are in states of emergency.

Once again, we are experiencing a significant story of economic, environmental, and technological change, and I, Miah, and Mo thought it best to extend the deadline—a few times—to give writers and artists the opportunity to process through the current moment. Within our lineages of queer narratives, it has been a matter of survival to leave home, but when you can't, it's a matter of survival to make it anew.

As most folks in these times, we, as an editorial team had to form new balances and habits to manage our daily lives, grieve for loved ones, tend to our mental health, soothe our nerves—hopefully you live in a state where that's legalized—, and find space to catch and deeply breathe our breath. Found inspirational social media like The Nap Ministry, who tweeted on August 24th what we've all been feeling: "I wish the rest of 2020 was just called off for work, schooling and capitalism [were] halted and everyone had all their needs taken care of and we could all just rest, nap and daydream. Pushing and grinding during a pandemic feel[s] inappropriate and traumatic."

However, working on *Home Is Where You Queer Your Heart*, reading through hundreds of submissions, was a respite from our day jobs. Our virtual meetings were plenty of laughter, chocolate, wine, and kombucha. Despite the limitations of Zoom, we were making home each time we convened to imagine how this book would extend itself into the world. Together and through this anthology, we were prefiguring the homespaces we need to guarantee our well-being and nurture our potential. Home, more than ever, needs to be a generous act, a politic of care. And that's where we landed as we edited and curated this anthology—in care.

With care as focus, we organized *Home Is Where You Queer Your Heart* so that it moves in a spiritual direction, serves as a guide for our queer future, arriving everyday, and as a compass through these and all times[1].

East

Where the sun meets your face, are writings that come to offer you creative guidance.

North

On the left, where your heart is housed, these works inspire you to seek the most challenging outcome of the day.

---

[1] Adapted from "The Third Dimension: Linear Space and Time," found in Barbara Hand Clow's book *Alchemy of Nine Dimensions*

South

On your right, the organ you cannot say without "live," stories of those who want to support and nurture you.

West

At your back, the love and homes that have sheltered you are here, loved and housed by the love and homes that have sheltered them, writings that show you what you need to transform and let go.

Welcome to our house.

Sixty-nine contributors strong.

We are grateful for their words.

For the creative beauty to build

*Home Is Where You Queer Your Heart.*

# where you from?

shell of snail
in the soil *I do not know*

where my feet
first land

swamp skin *I do not know my*
mother tongue

coils in my mouth
we call it *I do not know* catching ghosts

a glossolalia
felt good to *I do not know* utter

not know but know
it meant something

that means something
don't it make *I do not know* you wonder

why your dreams
steal away at night *I do not know my*

magic is *I do not know* reinvented
every generation you know

got to kill a thing
so it can grow

water people die
on dry land if they *I do not know*

don't move *I do not know*
where I'm from

is complicated
I say here and I'm bound

to be corrected
every word lifts an oar

sometimes I say, nowhere
and again, corrected

y yo no tengo más idiomas por
alejamiento, nadie en

my family understands
why I move and I

don't understand
how they can't

magic is reinvented
every generation you know

got to kill a thing
so it can grow

if groundlessness is sustainable
I will learn to fly

to swim in quicksand
Aunt Kay calls the center of the earth

wells are all I remember of that
land where we used to drink

the ground water
& find arrowheads

all this mud is a war
unmarked graves remain

further south I prayed
wind and still waters answered

in another religion
no, not that one.

I'm sure
this time

magic is reinvented
every generation you know

got to kill a thing
so it can grow

the tongues in my mouth
the ridges on my fingertips

ache for old worlds gone
ache for gone worlds new

Use above QR code for redirection to the video poem found at http://dr.betti-najudd.com/where-you-from.html

This poem was previously published as a part of Cave Canem's participation in the Poetry Coalition's project "Because We Come From Everything."
Spoken over the song of "Indigenous to No Land," published in *Meridians* *11.2* (2013)

# h is for home

first da flat toots with boots & hardhats & clipboards & hands
gesturing magic wand style like how they finna make some shit
disappear & they do  cuz da plywood  barricades pop  up with
plexiglass diamonds cut in them so you can see the mess they
making mostly dust & noise to us but they there tractoring da dirt
into something ~~habitable~~ profitable which we know nothing  about
profits just prophets & outlandish outfits that would make Jesus
proud of our out loud living wondering why our dreams always end
in headaches cuz  jackhammers wake up early & be mad angry da
way they be murdering concrete & you know it's da end of times
when they start killing churches block by block we feel less holy less
whole but ain't got time for nobody blocking our blessings with
hardships we memorized since the ship shit been hard highwater
& hell with no help save our humble heartbeats determined as
hounddogs on a nigga scent scratch & sniff our rent smells like shit
but least the heat works right got nightsweats to prove it & my lady
a hothouse of radiator hiss and stairwell piss & between her black
crush of thighs a hairy pyramid a heaven of dammed up light a
harlem hustle a nappyheaded haven a harem of hoodlums wearing
hoodies like haloes a homoerotic platter of bananas a plate of
peach pits spiked with pink fleshy bits & i'll be damned if it don't
taste like home—

# Amalia's Kitchen

When I was little, every time I walked into my Ama's kitchen I was immediately whirled by the scent of grilled onions, ground comino, fresh cilantro, and boiling frijoles. My ears were bombarded with the cheers coming from boiling pots and claps coming from sizzling pans. Whenever I walked into that twister of olores y sabores, no matter how bad my day had been, a smile always spread across my face, as smooth as butter on a warm tortilla. I'd feel the heat from the kitchen fall on my shoulders like a baby blanket and my stomach responded to the smells with a loud GROWL. That's how I knew that I was entering Amalia's world, where Amalia, my mother, governed with skillful hands, a stash of corazón for every dish she prepared, and an old ranchera under her breath. Ama was always signing or humming along to Cuco Sánchez or Las Jilguerillas while she cooked. The songs always talked about amores amargados, lovers seeking revenge and killing other lovers y corazones dañados por un amor mal pagado but Ama never seemed sad when she sang along.

When I was really young, most of the times I would go into the kitchen were to ask my Ama for something— *"Ama, me da una cora? Ama, me deja ir al parque con Saúl, Ama...por favor."* Ama never told me NO, instead she would put her spoon down, wipe her hands on her mandil, walk over to me—her forehead crowned with beads of sweat and she'd ask me to dance with her. I never said no, either I would let myself go limp so that Ama could easily carry me or drag me como un títere across the kitchen. She would continue with her singing and I with my pleading until the end of the song. Later in life when I was not yet an adult but no longer small enough for Ama to twirl me around the kitchen, my pleadings for quarters soon ceased and inquiries, recetas, and fairy tales took their place. By this time I had grown tall, well tall enough to see over the stove and into the pots, I had grown enough to see but most importantly ask what and how much of it was added to the caldos y guisados that nourished me and filled my stomach to the size of a cantarito. Seeing the way my Ama's hands moved, as if they were free from her mind and body made me understand how her dishes always tasted as delicious as the first time they hit my taste buds. Each dish came with its own story and while I was learning how to cook, I learned a lot about mi Ama and myself.

It was between the grinding of stone on stone of the molcajete that she first told me of Autlán, her hometown in the state of Jalisco—just a few hours from Guadalajara. Autlán, the not so tiny pueblo where dust clouds would rise up to her knees with every step she took, where electricity didn't make it there till the time she was ten, where at the age of thirteen she had to see her brothers and sisters sent away to different tía or tío's homes after the death of her mother. At that time, Autlán seemed like a magical place to me, where women carried baskets full of goods on their heads and kneeled at the mouths of rivers to beat their worn clothes against rocks. It was a place where el Diablo, sans the horns and trident, dressed in drag as a mujer de la noche con un vestido rojo, made special appearances. This is also where a bruja, otherwise known as my paternal grandmother, lived solely to poison the love that existed between my mother and father. As I grew older, Ama and I didn't need the rancheras anymore because her stories were as full of nostalgia, pain, and happiness as any of the songs that blasted on the stereo. My Ama's stories flowed from her mouth con la rapidez and clarity of a corrido and landed softly in my ears for safekeeping. This is how I learned that I was born at home while Ama was cooking a pot of pozole.

To this day Ama only cooks pozole on special occasions so once I asked her what was the secret of her pozole that made everyone love it so much and not get enough of. She smiled and said, "You should love it just as much, you were born next to a pot of pozole." Ama told me that when she was pregnant with me she was cooking her pozole, her feet swollen like tamales and her tummy stretched with ripeness, and she started to feel hot. She did not stop stirring the tub size pot of stew thinking that the heat curling its way out of the pot was the cause of her drenched forehead and dampened back. And all the movement in her belly, she thought, were just her tripas telling her that it was time to eat again—even before I could eat I was a big eater. Ama rubbed her belly, continued with her stirring, and added the seasonings. It was between the pinch of comino and dash of ground black pepper that I began my demands to be brought into this world. When she tasted the pozole she felt the heat of the stew travel from the tip of her tongue, throughout her belly until it was running down her legs. She says I was lured by the trail of pozole.

During my many pláticas con mi Ama in her kitchen it never occurred to me that one day those visitas would end. Why would they? I would leave her kitchen with a full stomach and the scent of her dishes fluttering after me como colas de papalote never thinking twice about change. I'd leave knowing I'd return the next day and see the same broken coo-coo clock on the wall next to the frame of *La última cena*, and just like these permanent fixtures our conversation would be there waiting for us. It lingered in the air thick like fog with details until we picked it up again holding it over the gurgles of boiling pots. But that rupture did come—I moved away from home for the first time and left behind Ama's one-bedroom, shoebox-size apartment for an even tinier space also known as a dorm room. Being away from the sometimes-suffocating comfort of home was hard for me. I missed Ama's apartment filled with the sounds of strumming guitarrones and screaming trumpets. Sounds that would spill onto the street and mix in with the "scratch, scratch, scratching" of the raspado man on his block of ice and the "ting-ting-tiiiiing" of the paletero's campanas, and created a neighborhood cumbia. On rainy days the homesickness me caía como un chubasco. I would get so homesick I could feel it like cold spots in between my joints. As soon as I heard the splattering of raindrops against my dorm room window my mouth watered over the thought of the arroz con leche Ama was surely making for my family back home. I would imagine the walls in my Ama's kitchen perspiring with the scent of cinnamon and sweetened milk that unfurled over the stove. The only remedio was for me to call home even if it was to just say buenas noches.

Whenever I had the time to get away from my studies I'd go home where I was always welcomed with chiles rellenos, camarones a la diabla, nopales en salsa roja or any other one of my favorite dishes. But it was the deprivation I experienced during my first year of college that I vowed to learn my mother's recipes. This way I could have a little piece of her with me no matter where I went. The rest of my undergraduate career I made sure I lived in a space with a kitchen where I could hit the burners as hard as I was hitting the books. To this day, I am still collecting Ama's recipes. I call her up; ask her how she is doing.

"Bien," she says in short, soft whispers as if she were calling me from another country.

"Just fine?" I ask.

"Pues si, aquí haciendo me vieja," she adds.

I ask her about her health, other members of the family and I fill her in on my personal life before moving on to the particulars of my call. "Ama, como prepara su sopa de papa (or whatever recipe I'm trying to learn at the moment)," I ask with pen in hand ready to take notes.

"Pues, picas cebolla, tomate, chile jalapeño," she instructs me step by step "pero que queden finos," she adds to her directions so that my soup can turn out thick with flavor as hers always does. Her instructions are always clear and precise; I hang up with her and proceed to chop away at the ingredients. It never fails that a few minutes after ending my call that she will call back.

"O, se me olvidé decirte," she announces before I can say hello, confirming my hunches. She calls me back to give me more guidance and shortcuts to the easy version to her already simple yet perfected recipes, anything to help me make my dishes taste as good as hers. I can say that my cooking is not half bad after all I did learn from the best but I know it, my taste buds know it, and most definitely my heart knows that my dishes will never be as savory as Ama's because mine are not spiced with cuentos y recuerdos. Regardless, after I've finish experimenting, my girlfriend and I lie around happily rubbing our stuffed panzas. I later take the recipe I sloppily wrote down while on the phone and transfer it onto my journal where I've written down instructions for other great dishes from Amalia. I glued a picture of my Ama and me on the cover of my journal. In the picture, we are leaning against the sink in her kitchen and if you look closely at the picture you can clearly see how aged her kitchen is. The tile is lined crookedly after so many times of being cemented and the drawer handles are worn with finger smudges. There is the everlasting Virgen de Guadalupe candle captured on the left-hand corner and lots of bright light coming in through the window, which gives the kitchen a celestial glow. My Ama's arm is around my waist, and we both have these apple-cheek forming smiles on our faces. I don't recall what exactly made us laugh the instant the camera blinked its eye and froze that moment for eternity but whenever I pick up that journal and see the cover I can't help but smile all over again. Just the same, I smile when I open up my journal and think about the great things that lie on its crumpled, stained pages.

# & You Shall Know Me By My Lists
## after Susan Sontag

Like: bonfires, beaches, big dogs, body piercings, sunrises, sunsets, afternoon naps, cinnamon, cucumber, cotton, Prince, sushi, semicolons, combat boots.

Dislike: neediness, hockey, mittens, snow, anything suggestive of or related to winter, jogging, pineapple, cats, combovers, gummy bears, perfume, cigars, spitting, Taylor Swift.

Like: *Gerbera* daisies, the color fuchsia, spinach, making lists, asking questions, sunbathing nude, pizza, paper clips, red-eye flights, that feeling, you know, when

> you're in a foreign (read: *über-whyte*) place, like Austria, or Idaho, & you've been there a few days without a single sighting of anyone with even five percent of your melanin & you're just about to resign yourself to the fact that you're the only niggx within a couple thousand miles when there, across the way, you spot him, or her, or them, doesn't really matter who, so long as they're an adult (as opposed to a charity child adopted by a well-meaning whyte couple, they don't count, I mean, of course they count, in the universal, *we are all Gxd's children* sense but not in the context of providing the type of support one might be desirous of in this situation) & identifiably one of us & you do what our people universally do in these situations, you nod that special *I see you fam* nod where you tilt your chin up for just a second but it's long enough, unless it's an older woman, like your mama's age, then you smile & lower your head ever so slightly, in deference, as if to say, *I see you, mama, all respect*

– kilts, palm trees, alliteration, anaphora, beards.

Dislike: okra, guns, gerrymandering, "small talk," public toilets, root canals, genocide, *ketchup* or *catsup* (whichever), flan, that moment, you know, when

> you're walking down the street, any street, any time after dusk, minding your own Gxd-damned business, & who do you spy in the *not enough between you & her* distance but *Becky*, not a specific *Becky*, but *Becky*, as in the prototypical *Becky with the good hair*, & you want to pass her cuz she's walking waaaaaay too slow but you don't want to startle her because she might scream & suddenly your casual stroll becomes a perp walk, so rather than bother *Becky* you cross the street & nearly get sidelined by a car you're not entirely sure wasn't just trying to hit you for points (niggx only worth 50)

– kale, conspicuous charity, humble-bragging, selfies.

Like: carrot cake, sugar cane, *Cane*, Clifton, belly laughs, fresh basil, traveling the world, dismantling the concept of "masculinity," polyamory, spankings, resistance.

# Kiss in

*1 Samuel 20:41*

front of the mirror first. Practice loving lips like yours. *Then*
look for the lips you imagined. Half smile, half question *they*
tacitly ask: if here, if now, if only in the dark, if we *kissed*
then how long until we're a we and which word for what *each*
of us knows we mean. Kiss mean. Kiss crying. Kiss on the *other*
side of town. Kiss on the cheek if there are kids around. Kiss *and*
tell without changing pronouns. Kiss for who couldn't, who *wept*
or bled or walked perverse, hands cuffed and lips locked *together*.
Keep kissing. Kiss in the street. Kiss on the courthouse steps *but*
not in the pew, not even stolen among rainbow stoles. Uncle *David*
still in your ear, calling your kisses contagion, while you *wept*
yourself empty. Kiss the hole of you. Kiss yourself back from *the*
dead. Kiss your kids into being. Be the mirror you needed *most.*

—CHRISTOPHER SOTO—

## All the Dead Boys Look Like Me
### for Orlando

Last time I saw myself die is when police killed Jessie Hernandez

A seventeen-year-old brown queer // Who was sleeping in their car.

Yesterday I saw myself die again // Fifty times I died in Orlando // &

I remember reading // Dr. José Esteban Muñoz before he passed.

Made me feel like a queer brown survival was possible // But he didn't

I was studying at NYU // Where he was teaching // Where he wrote shit that

Survive & now // On the dance floor // In the restroom // On the news // In my chest

There are another // Fifty bodies that look like mine // & Are

Dead // & I've been marching for Black Lives // & Talking about police brutality

Against Native communities too // For years // But this morning

I feel it // I really feel it again // How can we imagine ourselves // We being black // Native

Today // Brown people // How can we imagine ourselves when

All the Dead Boys Look Like Us? // Once I asked my nephew where he wanted

To go to College // What career he would like // As if

The whole world was his for the choosing // Once he answered me without fearing

Tombstones or cages // Or the hands from a father // The hands of my lover

Yesterday praised my whole body // Made angels from my lips // *Ave Maria*

*Full of Grace* // He propped me up like the roof of a cathedral // In NYC

Before we opened the news & red // & Read about people who think two brown queers

Can't build cathedrals // Only cemeteries // & Each time we kiss

A funeral plot opens // In the bedroom I accept his kiss // & I lose my reflection.

I'm tired of writing this poem // But I want to say one last word about

Yesterday // My father called // I heard him cry for only the second time in my life.

He sounded like he loves me // It's something I'm rarely able to hear.

& I hope // If anything // His sound is what my body remembers first.

# The Lovers in the Photograph

The men nestle, one inched into the cleft of his love's thighs.
They wait under the eye of the sun, in the bull's-eye
of the camera's lens, as a white witness documents black
love on a late spring day in Chesapeake, Virginia, in the year two

thousand something. One, eyes closed, lips
resting against his fellow's cheekbone. The other, eyes open,
stares forward soft-browed as if he's just opened his eyes;
two moles make a base clef of the curve of his left eye, or a colon:

Open exposure in this one frame. Loose clothes betray
a slim collar bone, a meaty bicep, two modest black
bellies sun-coppered and hairy, the slightest catch
in a fold; a clasp on an elbow. The lovers caught,

lean into each other away from the leaves,
well in front of the building, hold their spot
on the blacktop of the complex's parking lot. Locked
as if in bronze. I have never seen a monument like this:

durag and chinstrap mustache, brawn-armed
bear with a fresh tight fade. I've lived at the corner
of Confederate and Lincoln, spat on the stone feet
of a gynecological barbarian, seen equestrians

erected high above men's heads, but never yet, two
sleek wide noses or one man's neck tilted in supplication
mouth slit open to let the air dart in, hands wound
lightly around a waist and lower back, knuckles alit

on a broad Dockered thigh, two men spun
like blossoming vines shining in the splendor
of two like soldiers in love. In light, not shadow.

But here the woman's eye has arrested
our fellows in dewy day without labored sweat or defiant glances,
not off guard or posed but seeming free and seeming
safe in the baleen of each other's embrace.

# Abundance of Light

Your body is a miracle too.

    The weight of your hands—

    the slender aim of your lips

Someone is reveling in your majesty,

    like how the first day, heaven was created.

Pulling your skin, a knife underneath the water.

    How your tongue beckons.

Your empty vessel, your pruned dahlias.

Tamed amidst the leaking sun, burning wet.

Hold onto this sweet tongue—

    the crib of shoulders, ripple of back

calling the ocean by its name    *darling.*

Remember your mystery & this abundance of light

# Eye of Heaven
## for Edith Henry and John Gibbs Jr.

What struck me first was this sentence: "Several of the captives have gained renown as quick learners and creative performers." They were talking about the oceanarium lives of the slope-headed dolphins with the ridged teeth (*steno bredanesis*), but I thought they were talking about you, and me, and all of our brilliant friends who have had to learn so fast, perform so creatively here in our captivity.

I kept reading. "At Sea Life Park in Hawaii, a Rough-toothed Dolphin mother and a Common Bottlenose Dolphin father produced a calf that lived for four years." The life span of this dolphin should be 32 years. What happened? I researched Sea Life Park which celebrates its hybrids. Advertises on its site right now that you can swim with a "wholphin." Says they teach children about genetics with a special creature who is part bottlenose part false killer whale or was it melon-headed whale, or was it...? 140 dolphins have died in captivity at Sea Life Park. The ones who are hybrids are marked as "UNSPECIFIED DOLPHIN OR PORPOISE" in all capital letters like that. Also none of their causes of death are listed definitively. But I dug and I dug as if morbidly compelled and I found the hybrid calf who lived four years. And according to this death record she had no name but "HYBRID STENO MAMO" in all capital letters like that.

There is a 1974 article in the *Journal of Mammology* about this captive dolphin and her tragic story. Her mother was born in the open ocean and captured in 1969, while pregnant. Shortly after arriving at Sea Life, newly captive she had a miscarriage. What did they name her? Makalani, the eye of heaven. God is watching. At the time that she became pregnant again she was captive in a tank with two male bottlenose dolphins. The article does not characterize this as a breeding scheme, more like an aquatic housing crisis, but who knows. Three months before she gave birth they placed her in a different tank with two female dolphins of her same species. She gave birth around 4P.M. on October 4th, 1971. Scientists were allowed to come to the facility but not to measure the newborn or anyone else. If this dolphin lived she would not only be a hybrid between two different dolphin species, but what they also had defined as two different dolphin families. A big deal. A small dolphin. Female, showing signs of both species, swimming clockwise around her mother perpetually. The other female dolphins with her helped the mother release her umbilical cord.

As a mother, Makalani was protective. Slapped a trainer who tried to move the young dolphin (which the scientists referred to based on her talent for following her mother, "the precocious youngster" they called her), Makalani attacked another person who tried to touch the baby. In Egypt the name Makalani means "she knows." What did she know? When the scientists concluded their several months of observation they felt all signs were good. The dolphin was smart and well and protected. One day she would be a star performer at Sea Life Park. In their article they proposed that maybe she was proof that those two different dolphin families weren't different families after all. What a victory for dolphin unity, conservation, education. This article is cited again and again in studies on dolphin hybridity.

But according to the death records she died in 1975 at four years of age. Was Mamo her name? Her cause of death is left completely blank. The other causes of death at Sea Life are disturbing when listed (food poisoning, malnutrition, brain hemorrages, multiple still births, killed by another dolphin), what would be incriminating enough for this facility not to list at all. It leaves us to fabulation. The death records say Makalani died two years earlier. Was it the loss of her mother at two years old that did it? Did they separate the dolphins, try to breed the mother again? Were Makalani's actions against trainers in protection of her child too disruptive for the Sea Life way of living? Was it a housing problem, a feeding problem, an unanticipated function of being a dolphin that had never before existed in captivity?

Keiko Conservation, the organization that re-published the death records online says that Sea Life Park should be shut down. The Sea Life Park website says you can swim with dolphin hybrids and eat a meal with your family at an authentic nightly luau today if you want. They don't say anything about a once famous hybrid who lived only to be four. Her mother who died four years after capture. Or the dozens of spinner dolphins, bottlenoses, sea lions, seals who have died in their care over their 40-year existence. Some scientists who depend on dolphin and whale captivity for their research protest the use of what they call biased terms like "emotional," "majestic," "children," "solitary confinement" in documents about marine mammals in captivity. Because you might think of these animals as people you know, as parents, as prisoners, as relatives, as friends.

Are they wrong? I am related to all marine mammals. I am related to all those in captivity. I am writing this in honor of my Great Grandmother Edith who was not the only woman in our lineage to die captive in an asylum. They say she died of a broken heart after the death of her young son, my great-uncle, a disabled child who I never heard of until I found his name on an old census report and asked the question. He died in captivity too, after great grandma Edith succumbed to pressure from her community and especially my great grandfather (after whom little John Gibbs was named) to place him in an institution. He died there. In captivity. Within the first 24 hours. I have not seen the cause of his death in there.

Captives learn quick, perform creatively, or else. I am writing this for Great Grandmother Edith. The artist. Eye of heaven. In honor of what she knew even if she couldn't act on it. I am honoring her as who she is. Creator of the universe, source of all love. Thwarted protector of a child like no one had seen before. Her love never ended. Her love lives right now. Here in my breathing. I would swim around her clockwise. I would show her how her love survived all of this time, in the quick learning creatives who scream here in captivity. I am circling and circling her name. I am writing this for great uncle John Gibbs, the forgotten. The reclaimed. The proof that what they said family was, was not family. With a witness that it is not too late to create structures of care that honor his existence. To unlearn the hiding and the shame.

What I need to say is, you are. And the walls around your life, and the silence around your death, and the language work to erase you and remove you from me is not stronger than my grief, because my grief is fueled by love and I yet claim you. And I've come back for all the names I've never known for you were stolen. And I am never far away from you in fact. I am creator and creation. Right here, the source of all love ever. I strike away the lies about you with my lungs and tears, my circles and slaps. Eye of heaven. You are watching. And I don't know everything, but yet, I know.[1]

---

[1] #nomorebackrooms #disabilityjusticenow #freeallmammals#abolitionnow
(Yesterday as I was researching this I saw this small good news that marine mammal captivity may be on its way out of style
https://www.cnn.com/travel/article/virgin-holidays-whales-dolphins-seaworld/index.html)

# From The Year of Blue Water
## (unpublished, or, a B-side)

*"but your work here is done, mama"* –Harry Dodge, in *The Argonauts*

*114. A long text*

Page 129 of *The Argonauts* begins Harry's account of letting their mother die. At the second reading, like the first time, I immediately lose it. So here, Wei, is my attempt to clarify this vast reservoir of pain that seems to open at this passage. It must be so common for people to say that a person's "work" is "done"—that there is no more need to work. And here's when I feel the rush of all that work—my mom picking out fish bones so I could safely eat the stomach of a newly-cooked fish; the many nights where she returned, alone, to make dinner alone; the work she did with my dad as a janitor at my daycare on top of her other job; the work she did over conversations at night, shrouded in darkness, fighting and talking to my dad. The work she did, the pain and time and loss she experienced by not leaving, by not choosing, at each turn, something that was wholly her own life.

She did choose her own life: her life was sustaining us, nurturing us, "[setting] us up all very well with her love and her lessons." But at one point we children changed our bodies, our minds. What I had accepted on autopilot for so many years as a child, the very trust that let me leap into her arms, was no longer what I needed to be sustained or nurtured. My mom loved me in a way that didn't talk. And once I formed myself in the steely reduction of words, that love didn't exist in my consciousness. It is only now that I am building myself again, to uncross the vale of definitions, that I feel her vividly inside me, a web of repeated acts, an unabating presence beside me that constitute my first instincts toward love.

The pain she endured, the work that she did, to give up on me when finally, when it was finally certain, that the scheduled repayment of love would not appear as she imagined.

How can we see the ones we love and help them be seen by the world?
How can we love people in a way that brings them connections to this world,
so they feel that when they leave it, they are still somehow alive?

"Your work here is done" reminds me that I have yet to say thank you—how do I say thank you?—in a way that feels enough, in a way that feels permanent. Nothing is permanent!
We may fear our own deaths.
We may fear death as the end of rejuvenation,
that sources of love, strategies of love,
may disappear with the disappearance of our loved ones.

So really, it is a reminder.
Have I enacted, have I and can I repeat
the acts of love necessary to sustain the lives of those who loved me?

This waking, this call to arms, seems a reckoning
often only remembered at the moment of death.

And perhaps that's the great tragedy!
That we should not wait for death to enact our love!

Time is both infinite and finite!
Love is both infinite and finite!

Yanyi

# All These Cats Have AIDS

When it comes to Hugo and I, the story is this: we met in 1973 in a bar called The Townhouse, when I was 25 and he was 29 and both of us thought gay people only existed in New York. We went to Coney Island for our first date and he won me a baseball bat at the arcade. He was gifted at the game where someone guesses your weight. He puffed out his chest to make himself bigger, he smiled to make his face wider. I felt so butch walking home that night, the bat swinging at my feet. Hugo said it was sexy. We fucked when we got back to my place. It wasn't my first time with a man, but it was the first time I thought it was okay, the first time I felt no need to jump in the shower and wash off immediately what I'd just done, and he fell asleep in my bed so quickly I could have sworn he was my brother, or my child. I thought that I'd be lucky to live life as carefree. When he dressed the next morning, I asked him to stay, and he did.

He was stubborn as hell. I liked that about him. Once he had his mind set on something, he believed nothing else. When the AIDS crisis first started, he developed a theory. He said the disease would become so widespread, so non-discriminatory in who it attacked, that people would be compelled to give their support. If wives, babies, grandparents all got sick, how could they say no? All we had to do was wait it out. But it never broke the tipping point. It wasn't run-of-the-mill. It wasn't glamorous. There's no difference between a failing liver and a failing immune system. The problem was that we didn't have any way to treat ourselves and, also, everyone hated us.

We were sitting in our apartment on Avenue C. listening to records. We put on the portable fan because it was vengefully hot that summer and our landlord refused to replace our window unit. He said we must have broken it, and if we wanted a new one we'd have to pay. We knew gay people who'd been evicted for lesser reasons, so we didn't pursue it further. The fan at its highest setting blew at the speed of a big wheel. I told Hugo to splash some water on his face so the air would feel cooler. Or I could kiss him all over. He always liked when I did that.

He said he had a better idea and went off to the kitchen. I stuck my head out the window, searching for a breeze that I could coax into the room. We had snacks to share, we had wine, we were delightful to be around. A minute later Hugo returned with a metal bowl filled with ice and positioned it under the fan. The air bounced off and hit him in the face, blowing back his curly brown hair. "Like a January wind," he said and sat there for an hour.

We took the sleep when we could. Sometimes we went for days without a solid few hours. Stress came over us in waves. The worst was when the phone rang and we'd wonder for a split-second who had died. That fear was always cruel, not knowing who'd be next. We had lists in our heads of the people worse off, the ones we thought would be next. We lived in the land of the worst-case.

We had our own problems, too. Hugo often had prolonged bouts of diarrhea, and he'd moan hollowly, his voice gravelly because of his dry mouth, and it wouldn't be until morning that he had exhausted himself enough to drift off for a few minutes. In the morning I always made sure to slip out from the covers as smoothly as possible, to avoid the creakiest floorboards, keep my belt buckle from clinking when I put on my pants.

My main goal back then was to hold it together at work and let it all out at home. After I got fired from the textbook company, I found a job managing the office of a nonprofit that gave free legal services to LGBT people. Most cases involved entrapment or solicitation. My salary wasn't much, but I didn't need a lot since Hugo made enough for the both of us. When he was in college he'd wanted to be a lawyer, but his gift for friendly discourse made it easy for him to get big money as a salesman, and then, when he realized it was more interesting selling people than selling objects, as a public relations guy. I didn't care for such excitement, but I loved that he loved it, and I fed off his joy.

The lawyers at my job worked at leftist firms. That they were allowed to do their pro-homo pro-bono at all was a victory. A few of the highest earners covered the office expenses, myself and my assistant, Elmer, who could coax anything out of anyone with his Isaac Hayes voice. He and I would often joke that one of our clients would eventually make it big, really big, like Freddie Mercury, and they'd take care of us. They'd buy us a place to live and provisions to last a lifetime. We'd never have to work again.

The other day, I received a letter postmarked Norman, Oklahoma, from a high school student doing a book report. He'd come across an old article about Hugo in *The Advocate*, and he wanted to write about gay militants. It's been thirty years since we did it. I've gotten a lot of letters in that time, and I respond as much as I can. I answer people's questions and debunk the untruths, but mostly I just tell them who I am and who Hugo was. Somehow, the newspapers always seemed to miss that part. The boy said he'd never written to a prisoner before, and he had an excitement running through his body that he'd never felt. He was doing something forbidden, fun. He didn't think any of his classmates would be quoting someone like me for their projects. He asked if Hugo and I knew we would alter the course of history, if that was what drove us. I wrote him that Hugo and I were not gay militants. We were not gay liberators; we were not ones to be celebrated. When we did it, we didn't know what would happen in five, ten, twenty years down the road. All we wanted was not to die, and we did whatever we could to make that happen.

We needed to grab people by the scruff of the neck and force them to look at us. My first idea was a giant art installation of works painted with HIV-positive blood. Then I read in National Geographic that cats have lived with a similar virus for centuries, so I thought we might set up a petting zoo with the banner *All These Cats Have AIDS*. Then I wondered why we couldn't just get someone famous to speak out for us, someone who could convince the masses that we weren't a threat. Hugo looked at me like I knew nothing of the world.

According to him, we needed to be aggressive. We needed to get the publishers and TV producers on our side. We needed to seduce them, get their blood beating at the inhumanity of it all. He said this to me every night as he dressed for his galas and fundraisers and black-tie balls. One night, he returned around ten, perfectly sober, a bounce in his step.

"Guess who's gay," he said and leaned in for a kiss. It wasn't a question as much as a declaration, as if I could have said any name and he would've shouted out yes and handed me a prize. I loved indulging him in his little games.

"Prince Albert of Monaco."

"You're probably right, but that's only rumor. This is a game changer. Mayor Koch."

"That's not news, darling."

It really wasn't. During the 1977 election there were lawn signs that said *Vote for Cuomo, Not the Homo*. Everyone in New York City knew about Ed Koch.

"He's going to come out publicly. And a friend of mine said that he's going to pledge support for AIDS research."

"I'll believe it when I see it," I said. "And here I thought you were going to say someone that matters, like River Phoenix."

"In your dreams, dear. He's too cool for you anyway." Hugo flashed me a smile and went to change into his jogging clothes.

I could rarely keep pace with him when he ran, but I wanted to tell him what had happened at work that day. I searched frantically for my gym shorts and a fashionable t-shirt, and when I returned to the living room he put his arms around me and said how glad he was that I was tagging along. It was so rare he got a running buddy. Most guys we knew preferred ogling at the gym. Some of his former friends had outright refused to be in close proximity to the infected.

We ran uptown on the West Side Highway, past the piers, past the meatpacking district and the homeless enclave of street kids and drag queens. We'd seen some of them before, hustling at the bars, hoping to get lucky, preferably with a closeted man because discretion always came with a surcharge. We turned onto 80th street and headed into Central Park to avoid the cars and stoplights. I told him about my day.

A gay man named Desmond Morris was assaulted by a pair of cops. They'd stopped him on Bleecker and asked for identification, and when he said that he'd left his wallet at home, that he was just going to the corner store to buy a sandwich, they laughed and said he must be dying for some sausage. He tried to walk away, but they said they weren't finished with him yet. They'd have to take him in. It wasn't until after Morris had been beaten, after he'd been carted to the hospital and treated for a fractured skull, that the men discovered he had HIV. The pair of them, straight-laced Irish boys from Red Hook, went into hysterics, said they were going to kill Morris, stalked him outside his home, left him damning anonymous letters, until they finally settled on launching a criminal lawsuit, assault with a deadly weapon, and stopped talking to the press. One of our lawyers had volunteered to take the case, but his firm's senior partner played golf with the chief of police and forced him to withdraw.

Hugo ran faster as I said this and I found it impossible to keep pace. I gave up after a few yards and stopped at a water fountain while he sprinted down the path. Good, I thought, get the rage out now, when nobody but me was watching. We all had ways to thwart our distress.

"Show off," I said when I caught up to him. He smirked and retied his shoelaces.

"Why don't you meet with Morris yourself," he said. "Screw the lawyers, for now. Just show him that people still have his back. I'll go with you."

"You shouldn't. You don't want to be seen in a prison."

"Absolutely I would, if I had a client there. You said the cops accused him of starting the fight?"

"They said he attacked them with the intent to spread HIV."

"And they had no injuries themselves?"

"Only their feelings, apparently."

"Oh, the trauma," Hugo said.

As we ran out of the park, we passed a trio of cops outside an office building. They shouted something at us as we ran, but we didn't stop, we didn't turn around, and a few blocks later they simply weren't there anymore. I guess they figured we weren't worth their time.

A week later, we went to see Desmond Morris at Rikers Island. A bruise prickled under his left eye and he had stitches down the side of his cheek. He sat up straight. His broad shoulders reminded me of all the football players I'd crushed on in high school but never had the nerve to speak to. He didn't look like your stereotypical queer. Why the cops decided to single him out was perplexing.

"I *wish* they'd gotten infected," he said from across the table. "I could have taken them if I'd just fought back."

"How'd you get those marks on your face?" Hugo asked. He wore one of his best suits. People probably thought that he was a lawyer and I his paralegal. We took notes on yellow pads that I'd swiped from the office.

"Oh, you know, bricks, lead pipes, shivs."

Hugo cringed. Unlike most of us, he had never been beaten up, not even a schoolyard brawl. His charisma shielded him from most trouble. He could have won over anyone, varsity players, class presidents, prom kings. Yet he always sympathized with the underdog. He looked at Morris with such tenderness, as if he'd gone through the exact same thing, that I was unsure who to feel worse for. He'd stepped into Morris' boat, and he had all his limbs out, trying to plug the holes.

"I know a guy who's friendly with the warden," Hugo said. "We can get you into solitary confinement."

"Absolutely not. I don't want special treatment. I won't give them another reason to single me out."

"Morris," I said, "we'll get you a good lawyer. But you have to take care of yourself until then. You need an ally in here. If people see that, they might leave you alone." He scoffed at me.

"Doesn't matter what cell I'm in. People keep saying I'm a child molester." He stared at the floor. "I'll stand up for myself, but there's not much I can do when it's five versus me."

I looked around at the other inmates. Most were talking to women, their wives or girlfriends or mothers. They all wore the same beige jumpsuits. I wondered what a straight man would do if he found himself in a prison full of angry gays who wanted him dead or, worse, infected. I would have watched that TV show. Hugo jotted something on his pad, but when I looked closer it was only scribble. He always kept a pen with him to take down phone numbers, but oftentimes he merely used it to doodle, to give his hand something to do while his brain mulled things over.

"We'll find you a good lawyer," he said. "We'll destroy their case." His voice was calm, measured, as if he were holding a pack of rabid reporters at bay. "But for now, you have to keep yourself safe."

He grabbed Morris's hand and held it. That's all it would take, I thought, a handshake between someone important and someone like Morris. Put that on the front page of the papers, and we would have had a tide of goodwill, an unflappable burden of proof to those nurses who refused to draw blood, those caretakers who refused to nourish the enfeebled, the parents who refused to hug their dying sons. Imagine if Ronald Reagan had shaken the hand of an AIDS patient, the sea change that act would have spurred. It would have buoyed us for years.

We left the prison and took a taxi back home. Hugo had meetings and I had cases that needed attending. But something about that ride stuck with me, something about Hugo, the way he smelled, the way he held my hand tighter than normal in the space between our legs. Frustration, desperation, hope. I wondered what he'd concocted in those heavy moments of silence.

Morris was right. He was killed a week after we spoke, pushed down the stairs or knifed or hung from a rafter. Take your pick. We never learned the real cause. The newspapers reported only that a fight had broken out in the jail yard and gave no further details. I'm sure the people who did it knew he had HIV, and it was just as likely that they felt he died like he was supposed to, like he deserved, bleeding out on a cold floor.

Hugo was the one who told me. One of his reporter friends had called him and he came into the office dabbing his eyes with the cuffs of his shirt. He sat down on the windowsill and I made him a cup of coffee and had Elmer sing to him while I finished the paperwork for a bribery case. He held the mug to his lips, hands shaking, and I had to turn my chair away to keep myself from running to him.

The two cops spoke at a press conference and said that while they would have liked to see Morris have his day in court, they felt safer knowing that such a dangerous person was no longer a threat. They smiled, waved to the crowd, and that was the front-page photo on all the papers the next day. I tacked it to the wall and we doodled all over it. We drew a dick in one of their mouths and gave the other one a giant swastika tattoo. Then we burned it and sprinkled the ashes out the window, a little black snow for the summer day.

This was around the time that Hugo developed a cough he couldn't kick. We spent a few weeks thinking he had a summer flu and I'd catch it soon. But I never had anything wrong with me. We'd shared so many fluids that we thought that as long as I was okay, Hugo was okay too. But when his coughing turned bloody, I told him that he needed to see a doctor. We knew a good guy in the West Village who never stopped seeing gays through the whole crisis. As we looked around in the waiting room, at men who were more bruise than skin,

Hugo whispered to me that if it were him, he would never go out like that. He would die beautifully, without a smudge. I promised to help him with the makeup.

We resumed our lives as best we could. Hugo kept a cadre of white handkerchiefs in his suit pocket and got good at wiping his lips without giving anything away. To all his ignorant friends he had only a terrible cough. They told him it was fine, that something was going around and he shouldn't be concerned. They offered him lozenges.

People forgot about Morris. We put up a memorial in Sheridan Square but it got rained on and ruined after a week. The flowers got pilfered and put in people's hair or redistributed to the other memorials dotting the streetlamps. Hugo tried to get the *Voice* to write an obituary but got turned down by the senior editor.

"They're all homophobes," he said, "they're no better than the guys at the *Post.*"

"Why don't you write something," I said. "We could print it up and distribute it around the streets like they did in the early days, before Stonewall, before faxes. We could give copies to a motorcycle gang and offer free beer for every twenty fliers they distribute. They'd plaster the village in no time."

He laughed and pinched me. We threw our plates in the sink and retreated to the bedroom. We put on a Cat Stevens record and made a silent pledge to not let anything or anyone ruin our evening. We held each other and danced skin to skin, and when I put his legs up onto my shoulders, he requested we stay that way forever.

When I woke the next morning he wasn't in bed. He wasn't in the apartment. He'd left no note. It wasn't unusual for him to leave earlier than me, but he always kissed me goodbye or, if I was still asleep, left a note on the counter. I wondered if something had happened to him, if he'd been beaten up or kidnapped or picked up by the paddy wagon. I wondered if I'd get a phone call from the precinct and have to bail him out, as I'd done many times for friends who got too friendly with an undercover cop or had their pants down during a bathhouse raid. After work I vowed to make calls if he hadn't returned, but there he was, sitting on the couch in his suit, legal pad on his lap, hand covered in ink.

"I'm going to do something," he said. "And I need your help."

Hugo always was the brave one.

I grew up in a conservative Catholic town. My general fear—of retribution both earthly and divine—compelled me to follow the rules. I went to Bible school every Saturday, church every Sunday. I remember the priests and their booming voices, their achingly good gifts for manipulation. I remember them shouting that bad things happen to those who do bad, that even the smallest offenses were damnable. I didn't want to be thrown into the abyss. But, as Hugo told me his plan in between fits of coughing, between holding his ribs in as if they'd burst and having to sip hot water slowly, I realized we were already there, swimming around in the dark.

The Joseph Clark Memorial Dinner was, and still is, an annual white-tie gala for Catholic charities. The ballroom at the Wortham Hotel is dolled up with red and white flower arrangements. The mayor attends it, the chief of police, the publishers of all the major papers. The Archbishop plays host. A church secretary arranges the place cards and a massive stage is put up for the notable guests to perch like rare birds. Invitations are always difficult to come by, and they aren't inexpensive, even back then, so I wondered why Hugo took such sudden interest.

"The cops that beat up Morris are getting an award. They'll be at the head table, right near the stage." He handed me a copy of the press release. His hands were sweaty. I looked over the paper, then told him to think about what he wanted for dinner. He went to the bedroom to find something more comfortable to wear.

We needed to get out of the house. It was a Friday night, still hot as hell, and the fans and ice buckets weren't doing much good. Hugo suggested we go to the Duplex. We hadn't been to Christopher Street in a while, and a night out with singing and dancing and cocktails sounded like a perfectly civilized form of release. My office had been flooded with calls that week about people being dumped in the street because morgues wouldn't store them and funeral homes wouldn't bury them and crematories wouldn't burn them. Their passage had been denied. There was no ferryman in sight. I was exhausted.

I put on a plaid shirt and jeans and waited as Hugo searched his closet for an outfit that fit his diminished form. He came out and modeled a pair of bell-bottoms that I'd never seen before. "Wore these when I was 21," he said, "before I discovered pastrami." The pants swallowed him, but I took two butterfly clips and pinched the sides like clamshells. We could cover them up with a long shirt or a belt or whatever struck his fancy. He plucked an army-green denim jacket and draped it over his shoulder, James Dean-style.

"Dashing," I said. "Now you've just got to slick your hair back and find a criminally fast car. Let's go, partner."

At Duplex, the entrance hallway spilled out into a large area, like the shape of a pot or the state of Oklahoma. Near the door you got all the smells of the city, whatever happened to be wafting by, but in the main space it smelled like polished wood and perfume and dried gin. Often times a bartender or another brave soul would perform Donna Summer, The Bee Gees, the latest show tunes. Sometimes the Broadway crowd showed up after work and gave impromptu solos, their faces still caked in makeup, a feather boa or two draped around their shoulders. I knew some of them through work. Several shows were forced to close when their actors and crew died of AIDS and it became too costly to rehire. The survivors weren't eligible for unemployment. Many had gotten fired from their day jobs when their bosses heard they'd been in proximity to the infected. We tried our best to get them new work, to point them towards people who would be kind to them and wouldn't flinch at their touch, but most of the time we failed.

Hugo got us seats across from the piano and I brought us some whiskey sours. His stomach did better with whiskey than gin or vodka, and he sipped so slowly that by the time he finished he was drinking mostly water anyways. We said hello to a few people we'd seen in the neighborhood over the years. A few times we marveled that so-and-so was still alive, like a far-removed uncle who sends Christmas cards every five years.

A man walked to the microphone. His face was pale and he had heavy black liner around his eyes. He wore a motorcycle jacket and carried himself with the confidence of a performer, though we didn't know what show he was in. He didn't say his name. After a dramatic silence, the man hushed the piano player and began to sing, and then I remembered who he was, one of the actors in *Cabaret*. We hadn't seen it. Friends of mine had loved the movie, loved the novel it was based on. But I couldn't bring myself to swallow anything that rang too true to life. No James Baldwin, no Edmund White, no Armistead Maupin. The gay guys so rarely wound up happy, and I already knew enough about loss. When the man finished his number he took a seat at the bar. I walked up to him and touched his shoulder. I said I loved the song. It must have been fun to be starring on Broadway.

"It's a routine," he said. "Like any job."

"You're in a hit show. You get applause every night. How many guys can say that about their job?"

"True." He stared at the floor and lit a cigarette. "People love to watch a good genocide."

"Do you think they would have fought back if they could?" I asked. "The characters in the show."

"An uprising of deviant whores? Not a chance. They wouldn't fight."

"You mean they're not strong enough?"

He shook his head. "You miss the point. They don't care enough about themselves to stay alive. Deep down, they think they deserve it."

I didn't say anything, and without looking at him again I walked back to Hugo. I couldn't acknowledge it. I couldn't make true anything he'd just said.

Around 2:30 the bar emptied out. We ambled down 10th Street, past the NYU kids, past the 5th Avenue condominiums and neon-lit bodegas, past the drunks splayed on front stoops and the lovers sitting on fire escapes with their feet dangling down. The city wasn't having us, but we paid it no mind. We had nothing more to say.

Somebody had to write the story, Hugo told me. I'd begged to accompany him but he shot me down without hesitation. Somebody needed to say what happened. Somebody had to say why. But we agreed that I would walk him through the lobby and stay with him until he went upstairs. In my mind that was non-negotiable. I owed him as much for our years and years together, for his courage, for his kindness. The least I could do was send him off with a smile.

On the day of the dinner, we played a record in the apartment. We picked at the errant fibers on the couch and we talked about the night we spent riding the Staten Island Ferry, staring at the lunar eclipse and making fools of ourselves as we howled at the moon. We were always different at night, more fun, more free. It was easy to become someone else, to slip through blackened doors and emerge among friends, to feel the rush of a bare fingertip on your body. At night, we were in control; we knew who we were.

If someone had told me that in ten years there would be drugs that could keep people alive for decades, that there would be evidence showing our touch was harmless, that people in real power would be rallying for us, if I'd known all that then yes, of course I would have told Hugo not to do it. I would have held him back with my own hands and told him that grace was near. But we knew no soothsayers. It was impossible for us to imagine that world.

Sometimes I couldn't believe that Hugo and I had ever met. I couldn't believe we'd been together for 14 years, that we danced to Sylvester at Studio 54, that we shacked up on Fire Island four summers in a row, that we made blueberry pancakes on Sundays. Every time I saw two men together, walking down the street, sitting in a bar, emblazoned on a movie screen, I thought of him.

But sometimes, even when he was alive, I tried to forget him, too. I tried to forget all that had happened. I tried to rid myself of the smells and sounds of the sick, the calls for firing squads, the jeers from the old ladies and macho men on the subway. I questioned whether coming out and escaping to New York had made my life any better, whether it was worth the agony I'd caused my parents and myself. There were days when I would see Hugo's face and wish he were a stranger, someone who just happened to stop by. It frightened me that he and I were so entwined, that we were locked into all this trauma, all this hate, all this pain, without escape.

He'd gotten a few sarcomas on his neck and one on his forehead. They looked like islands, like New Zealand or England or Japan, and every week it seemed a brand new country bubbled up out of his flesh. The marks would make him suspicious. People would look at his skin and wonder what was wrong. It was plausible that someone in the audience would see his bruises, assume it was AIDS, and cause a stir. We'd already bought him a teenage-sized suit because of the weight he lost. Now we needed to cover him up.

I got some makeup and an applicator at Macy's. The salesgirl thought it curious that I was buying different skin tones. She said my wife couldn't possibly be that many colors. I laughed and told her that we all change, but people didn't pay enough attention to notice. The truth was that I didn't know which shade would look the most natural on him, so I bought ten. We couldn't have him looking patchwork.

He sat on our bed and I dabbed the foundation on the sponge like children's paint. I lined up all the different colors and searched for the one that matched, the stripe that would render the best camouflage. We decided on 25C, cool beige. I traced around his eyes, down the ridge of his nose and the circumference of his lips, across his neck. I glammed him up like a rock star, like a headliner at Webster Hall. He didn't speak the entire time. He just sat there silently, smiling, moving only when the pressure of sitting was too much for his tailbone. When I finished he looked happy and bright, as if no time at all had passed since our first date.

"You do what I told you," he said while he checked himself in the mirror. "Get out of the hotel as soon as I go up to the ballroom, leave the city, and lay low for a while."

I came up from behind and held him. I kissed his ear. "Of course, darling," I whispered. "Sly as a fox. Stealthy as a ninja. They'll never find me."

He laughed and I put my head on his shoulder. We stayed like that for a moment.

"Do I look believable?" He turned and reached out for a handshake. His hand was cold, too cold, even for October. I rubbed it like I was rolling dough, like I was trying to light a fire with twigs.

"I'll keep them in my pockets," he said.

"You'll be all right with the vest on. It'll warm you up." It was on the bed, a pack of cigarettes and lighter alongside. I stared at it. It took us a month to secure all the materials, then a week to sew the pockets in all the right places. Remember, this was the eighties. Nowadays I have no doubt that we would have been caught in a few hours. But if we'd been planning this today, that would have meant we'd both survived, and I would serve any sentence if that were true.

The lobby of the Wortham smelled like verbena. Tourists walked around the hallways, staring up at the chandeliers, at the carved ceilings and the elaborate carpets. Women carried their purses in one hand and their drinks in the other. Men smoked cigars at the bar. I saw a family of four walking side by side, the boy in blue and girl in pink. I recalled the one vacation my parents and I took in the early sixties, when I got lost at Disney World and ran up to anyone who looked friendly. If a stranger had looked me in the eyes then and said they were my parent, I probably would have believed them, if only to rid myself of that sudden, inescapable loss. I told my father, when he finally found me, that I never wanted to feel so alone again.

Hugo's cheeks glowed as he passed under the lamplights. We didn't hold hands as we walked and I'm glad we didn't. I have no idea what he was thinking, but I suspect that if it were me, I would have wanted to be alone with my thoughts. I would have pulled my body along while my mind went someplace else. I wouldn't have wanted a long, tearful goodbye. I'd want to say my peace and go.

A few people waved at him and he waved back and said hello and did everything one is supposed to do in his line of work. He always liked his job, he liked conversations and simple pleasantries, so I'm sure he felt at ease. Through all of this—the illness, the fear, the hate—he still loved to hear stories about people who'd made it big in art or business or politics. Even more, he loved the stories of the people behind the celebrities, the kingmakers we never knew existed. That was what he wanted to carve for himself. That was the space he wanted in the world.

More guests arrived. We didn't linger. We didn't want anyone to have a chance to talk long to Hugo, to appraise his suit coat or his cufflinks or his shined shoes. We couldn't chance someone seeing a flaw in the makeup I'd applied or the four stitches I'd added to the bottom of his shirt to make the vest fit underneath. It would be all we wished for if he simply got into the room, took his seat, and faded into the background. If that happened, we would succeed.

I couldn't kiss him goodbye, or even hug him like I would a friend at the airport, a friend who I wouldn't see for a long time. But nobody we knew got a proper goodbye, none of our friends got to be with their partners in the hospital rooms, so it felt right that we wouldn't get a grand sendoff either. We didn't have time to dwell. So, all I did when we got to the elevators, when he got in line behind a woman in a lush taffeta gown, was turn to him, smile, and wave as if I'd passed him on the street but had no time to stop. He smiled, put his hands in his pockets, and I left him there, waiting to go up.

When I was 19, I got a draft notice. Many of my classmates had already died in Vietnam. Men my age were among the first to get called up. I didn't believe in the war, but I wasn't about to spend my life in Canada, branded a traitor. I would do what I was told to do. I went to my appointment as scheduled. I spoke with a grey-haired officer about my life. I told him that I grew up in Virginia Beach and my father was a fisherman, that I'd seen plenty of soldiers around and respected their stoicism. I said I used to play the violin and I was proficient with a typewriter. I hadn't done sports, but I could run as fast as anyone in gym class. He led me into a big room sectioned off with white curtains. I sat on an exam table and stared at the vision chart across from me. A while later a doctor entered and asked that I undress. When I was younger I always felt ashamed at disrobing in front of the pediatrician. I thought that without such cover they'd be able to see past the boy I pretended to be, the boy who flirted with girls, the boy with nothing wrong. I thought that if they looked at me in such a state, I wouldn't be able to hide.

The man shined a flashlight on my face. Fine. He pressed his hands hard against my lower back then reached around and prodded my stomach. Fine. He asked me if I felt any pain and I said I felt nothing. I turned my head to the side and coughed. He placed the stethoscope on my ribs and asked me to breathe deeply, then normally, then to exhale and hold it. He asked me to do it again. He wrote some things down onto the paper and said I could get dressed. When I returned to the officer he said I was free to leave. He gave me a pamphlet and said that there were other ways to serve, and then another boy was ushered into the room and he shouted off the same spiel. The doctor had heard an erratic beat in my chest, an abnormality that refused to behave. Too slow, then too fast. The lines didn't match up. There would be no war for me.

I stood on the street, feeling for my pulse and trying to understand what I'd done wrong. It started to rain. I took shelter under a bus stop, but with no money in my pocket and no end to the deluge in sight, I gave up waiting and walked back to my dorm room. I toweled off and began my lessons for the week, resuming a life that was, as I always learned, completely out of my control.

I wish I could have seen it, what it was like in the ballroom. I'm sure that people saw different things. To one person in the crowd it might have been a firework boom, another might have seen a crashing stage light, a table buckling. If a person had experience with demolition, or coalmines, or a warzone, perhaps they could have correctly gauged that it was an explosion caused by dynamite. But I'm sure, in the heat of such a moment, that even the most battleworn among them had trouble seeing the truth.

A security guard sprinted down the lobby. The stairwell doors flung open. People emerged, shouting at each other, tripping over the carpets, holding tight to the nearest sturdy object. A woman fell in front of me. She opened her mouth but no words came out. Her dress had been ripped at the bottom so it looked fringed, like something Josephine Baker would shimmy in. I helped her to her feet and told her not to worry. I went to the door. The crowd ran in all directions away from the hotel, and I walked down Madison. I walked and walked and walked. I walked the perimeter of the island, until the sun came out and I heard men shouting for ice at the Fulton Fish Market. Then I returned to the apartment and got in the shower. I didn't watch the news. I drank coffee and I ate the last of the fruit salad in the fridge. I sat on the couch and tried to make sense of what happened. I stayed there for days.

I wrote out on notebook paper what we did. I listed all the materials we used, where we purchased them, the lies we told the salesmen. I described how we sewed the explosive into the lining of the vest. I told them how Hugo wanted to wait until the end of the night to set it off, but I convinced him to do it as soon as everyone had arrived and before the speeches began. I wrote why we did it, but people would assign their own reasons. There was no use to try and change their minds.

I tidied the apartment. I put all the photos of us into boxes along with any paperwork that seemed important. I gathered up our vinyl and books and left a note for them to be donated to the gay community center. I threw the food away. It would rot before too long. Mid-afternoon, as the traffic crawled along  3rd Avenue, I stuffed the letter into my pocket and walked out the door.

So many articles were written about that night. I remember a feature in *The New Yorker*, about the one-year-anniversary, the ramped-up security at hotels, shopping malls, train stations. The author interviewed a woman who was sitting at a balcony table. She didn't notice Hugo in the crowd. Everyone had just gotten their salad. When it happened, the man next to her screamed. They all looked down at the stage and saw two tables burning and a fine, gentle mist of red. The author showed photos to the woman, images of the aftermath and the hole in the stage, and as she thumbed through them she fainted.

One of Hugo's acquaintances was there that night, a professor of political science at Columbia who often went downtown for unsavory fun. He and Hugo had slept together back in the day, but Hugo didn't think much of it, and they remained strictly platonic after that. His table was towards the rear of the ballroom, so he was one of the first people to escape. He did interviews. A long time later he wrote a book about what happened. He believed that Hugo had surrendered to a misguided impulse for revenge. He suggested that the evening had set the gay rights movement back 50 years and caused more harm than AIDS ever did. Things would have righted themselves eventually. People would have come around.

From all the coverage, I learned something new about Hugo. Amazing that you can spend years with someone and still not know them fully. His hometown paper published an article about the bombing, and they sprinkled in bits of his early life among the vilification they bestowed on him. He graduated from high school in 1964. I knew that. But I didn't know he was the class valedictorian, and that he gave the commencement address. I still wonder what he spoke about, if he bored people or made them laugh or mesmerized them. I wonder if they remembered his words. I wonder why he never told me. After all these years, I haven't been able to track them down, even though I try, even though he's the most famous person to come out of Laurel, Mississippi.

The two cops died in the ballroom. Sometimes people forget that they were the reason behind all of this, what they did to Morris. I said as much when I gave my statement in court. My lawyer warned me not to, but I wanted people to remember what they did. I suspect, though it's never been proven, that Hugo was right next to those men in the ballroom. Maybe he spoke to them. Maybe he smiled. They got the most publicity of all the victims. People put up memorials in Brooklyn. A middle school in Bay Ridge was named after them. Nobody remembers what they did to Morris.

Hugo did what he wanted to do. Everyone knows his name now. He set the course for as many lives as those cops did. And yet, I can't put him in the same breath as them. I can see horror in what he did, but I can't see him as a symbol of death or hatred. I see him only as he was when we were together, when we were friends, lovers, young and unmoored and free.

I told him, the night he told me about his plan, that it would be so much more effective if we could just turn those two men gay. One morning they would wake up and see their wives and find themselves as limp and wilted as week-old flowers. They'd go to work and have to hide their erections in the locker room showers, to suppress the urge to stare at their colleagues from behind. They'd have no idea what to do. Perhaps they'd seek help. They'd find us at the Stonewall, at the Duplex, at the Monster. They'd tell us that they've never felt so adrift in their lives, and we'd say that everything would be all right, that the distance to shore was not as great as it looked, and we'd bring them back, safe and sound.

I've been in here for 30 years. I wake up every morning and I see the slate gray of the walls, the sliver of light that looks like a line on a tennis court. I'm served all my meals inside my cell. I read books. Once a week, under the eye of a guard, I can check a pre-approved list of websites: *The New York Times, The Advocate, The Guardian*. Even with this new foot-washing Pope, the Church is still crusading against gays. The dogma hasn't changed. At three in the afternoon I'm allowed to go outside for 45 minutes. I talk to a few people, but most keep their distance. I don't know what sort of mythos has clotted around me, but it's palpable. I get stared at. I get glances from the corner of the eye, around the shoulder. I get line after line of puzzled looks, because how could a person possibly survive with the weight of the world's anger on their back. Yet, they're still scared of me. I've never been touched.

Now they have pills to prevent HIV, pills to render the virus moot. It still infects people, but it's no longer the danger it once was. I've never taken them. After Hugo, I figured it would be a few years for me, that I'd die like so many men I knew. I waited for the bruises to appear, for my mouth to go dry and my bowels to cannibalize themselves. Every time I woke with a new scratch or bruise I thought: this is it, I'm ready. Knowing that I would follow him soon after, that we'd see each other soon, was one of the reasons I agreed to help him. But nothing happened to me. I'm fine. I don't know why.

Do I regret what we did? I know I'm supposed to say yes. I know I'm supposed to say that if I had known that there would be medicines, that in 25 years most people would survive on a daily pill and would stop being treated like spittle to be washed away, I would have told Hugo to wait. But even if I had said that, maybe it wouldn't have mattered. Maybe those cops would have kept beating people. Maybe I would have still had to watch Hugo disintegrate, bit by bit. Maybe I'd still be in this cell, staring at the wall, writing a slightly different ending to the same story.

All of this happened, in one way or another.

# Chicxulub *Köçekçe* / Pioneer Species

Köçekçe ("koo-check-cheh") *were songs written about third-gender / crossdressing Ottoman dancers who were considered "effeminate boys."*

Like those jellyfish that swell     with future oxygen,
I live into my gender,     balloon constantly rising
into atmosphere I'm sure     I can't breathe. I wish to be
the exact opposite of     those moths that live
on caterpillar-digested food for their week-     long lives. I hope I never stop
digesting myself, staying hungry.     In my new wool tights
I feel foreign     in my natural habitat, first mammal to walk
meteor-scorched plains still gray     with dead possibility.
I don't know what numbed out these genera     in me since
three-year-old Kenan danced to     Tarkan in my father's Texas home
swirling my babaanne's silks     like a Köçek dancer.
I still hope to unearth     those gracile Ottoman bones,
çarpare castagnettes and davul drums,     any reminder
of those who came before. I will make soil     from rock
for others to grow, live on sun alone.     I will remake
my own DNA from my people's     nitrogen, secret it
in stromatolites in the western Tethys.     When my beard digs
its rhizomes into my skin, breaking     my soft Ottoman face
into fine filaments, I am ruined     for contouring, according
to the drag show tip jar, yet I feel     their filaments breaking
down the rock of my gender     certainty. I consume myself
again, fossilize myself     for the next extinction.

# Ode to Gnawing

There is a certain comfort in gnawing
choosing the gristle, what gets to remain
wet. Being the god of the moist. Godly
spit we let drip down our knees. Gracious hands
made of towels, with enough empty to
to soak up all of this spilled boy. Look what
I have made a mess of now. Sloppy the
kill. Meat hanging from the bone dripping the
sweet marrow. My mother always used to
preach to leave nothing breathing on the plate
To pick down the muscle and cook with the
fat. I have learned how to undo every
Boy like a good supper. Like a meal made
for my thighs. Like my mama taught me to.

# Turnstiles

When I came here / lifted from mother's / abdomen like soil
I had enough lives / stockpiled to know / there is nothing to
the myth / *getting it right* / no matter how / many rotations we
spin and spin / till we're sick dizzy / son & I / In centripetal orbit,
fleshy upright turnstiles / we scream a laughter / into ether like
prayer already answered / He's exhausted bones / by nautical
twilight I gaze / between crib bars / brown skin / in deepening dusk
crest & trough / his dulcet breath / Oceans tide my looking / Perfection
my sins may deface / At star-rise ceremony / in blackness / I lift him
soft swift certain / of an un-caging / in my chest. Lay him / out just
a moment for apex / of breath / hummingbird heart / thrumming
against my life line / I could weep / at my own / capacity to hurt him &
hurt him again / Be the reason / he therapies / But for now I kiss
sweet sternum / massage soft tendrils / sprung from scalp
Stare into  ceaseless /        forgiving night.

# The World They Uncover

In the neural network that is my home, one synapse fires in Milwaukee, Wisconsin, home to the Green Bay Packers and six-month, suicidal winters. Serial killers roam in packs, and just up the block in a nearby neighborhood, two twelve-year-old girls took another one into the woods to knife her near death, all in the name of some Internet boogeyman.

My ex-wife lives there, too, on a street that shares its name with my dead son. She lives there in a brownstone with hardwood floors and cloistered windows, paned with stained glass, like an antique church. These houses are common to this part of Milwaukee. My grandparents lived in one far before I was born, when they were a young couple, still inventing the world each night through their furtive gropings. Now my ex-wife is there, with her new girlfriend, whom she leaves each morning to drive five miles or so up the highway to her job as a nurse. All day she processes patients for discharge, and while I don't live there, a part of me exists in that office with her, filing prescriptions, needling Medicaid, coding paperwork: heart murmur on four, home with a pacemaker; NICU infant, finally hatched; liver transplant, recently jaundiced, follow up next Tuesday with Dr. Blank.

She and I are no longer married, but she calls me every other weekend, at least twice a month, to check in on my daughter, her former stepchild, an autistic twelve-year-old with cerebral palsy, who, despite that description, is light and happy, and oddly beautiful, the awkward years having skipped her the way a stone skips Lake Michigan, where on the other side, a second synapse bursts open with impulse and information; a lightning strike across the lake.

On the other side is my current partner, a woman of 53, in Chicago. She's a songwriter, with two children, young when I met them, now growing into themselves. Young women, with braces and long limbs, and health problems, and acne, and friends at school that turn over gender and sexual identities as fast as we used to change the channel on our old black and white TV. In their city, being gay is nothing new nor unusual. It's a coin that's already been spent, and acceptance is near everywhere, ubiquitous.

Perhaps my girlfriend wouldn't agree with me. She works sometimes on the south side of town, and in those neighborhoods, has experienced blank stares, rolled eyes, the occasional sigh of disbelief, maybe even a long drawn out, "Dammmmmmn," similar to the ones I heard from my students when I taught at an HBCU. There's still occasionally a dark element of shame associated with queerness in these communities, and I often had to confront my students directly about it, calling out their bias, hushing their judgmental titters. First, they learned James Baldwin was black, and he became their hero. Then they learned he was gay, and he was their shame. I saw them grapple back and forth between these two extremes, only in the end to discard the question, decide it wasn't worth their time, in an era that also contained Twitter.

I now live in another part of the body, in Austin, Texas. My girlfriend and I see each other about once a month. We communicate mostly by phone, or text. Her face appears to me as an oblong blob, gray as it arrives, the color of stone. I see past it into her eyes, her smile, her warmth. At night, as I fall asleep alone, I imagine her ass next to me, feel myself pulling up next to it, inventing a home between us, in our digital lives. She wrote a song for us once that echoed, "By the light of our phones/can we make this our home," and this encapsulates what I'm talking about. She and I disconnected in space, but intimately enmeshed inside the network.

Take it back a step.

I was raised in Mount Plymouth, Florida, an hour plus outside of Orlando, deep in the interior of the south. Beneath a canopy of trees, I swung on a homemade swing I crafted in our garage, cutting a hole in the middle of a board, and throwing heavy twine above my head so that it caught the branch above just right. Pulled it down and threaded that center hole, tying a knot. It wasn't a perfect swing. It wasn't balanced. I didn't get that ideal back and forth motion we know and call swinging, but rather, looped wildly and strangely, in all directions, Wonkavator style, even wrapping myself around the trunk of the tree in spiraling half-circles and orgasmic arcs. It was cool there in the front yard, as it was cool in Florida almost nowhere else. Certainly not on the white sand road that led to my house, nor on the country backroads, exposed pavement cracking in the sun.

Our house itself was another hot zone. School, as well. To be young, queer, and in love in that small Christian town meant hiding out in cars at night, kissing by the burnt orange juice plant, hoping no one caught sight of you in the glow. It meant counting furiously all the people who may or may not have caught sight of you, holding her hand in the movies, laughing too long by the lockers, or possibly mouthing something secret and forbidden to each other from across the hall on the way to French II.

One time I sat in high school art class sketching some ugly motherfucker with a long, drawn face, pimpled and smirking like the Joker. He was assigned to me;

I didn't pick him. And as I attempted to get it just right—the ears, for instance, only as long as the space between eye and nose and no longer, for this was a rule of natural symmetry—he whispered some smart ass comment to me about her and I, something he'd no doubt witnessed when he pulled up next to us one day at a stoplight. Her head was in my lap as I was driving. I had just looked down into her beautiful eyes and stopped to stroke her hair, smiling perhaps too big and too long—too happy for that particular space and home that wouldn't contain me—only to catch him there in the car next to me, that righteous, ever present smirk, like the hand of God. He couldn't see her, but he could see me. And that is a good metaphor for the whole mess of a town and doomed relationship, which inevitably ended with her marrying a man and sidestepping queer identity, while I ran as hard and as fast I could to Greenwich Village, a place I instinctively knew was: Home of the Queers. A place where I could be myself, find myself, feel myself, because in 1988, relocation was the only option. Queers, if they existed, lived in the Village and nowhere else. I aimed to find them.

But that was the late eighties, when the neural network looked less like the Matrix, and more like tic-tac-toe. Paths either intersected or they didn't, at bars, at bookstores, or at Queer Nation / ACTUP meetings at the Center. It's no longer that world. Being queer is not a thing of physical location. Shit, neither is humanity. I'm more linked in one moment through social platforms to high school classmates I never liked, to football coaches, former production assistants I hired on the road, random writers that friended me after a reading, and my girlfriend's mom and brother, than I ever was just living my life. I'll most likely never breathe the same air as any of these people ever again, but through social media I influence them. I prove what I couldn't prove in high school, which is that I exist. Chances are more of them see me now as another mother posting first day of school photos, than they do as a gay woman who has made a life with my best gay friend, the father of my little girl.

Which wraps me round to the other part of my neural network, the one right here. If you look at a map and follow my trajectory through the past 30 years, there's a trace like missiles leaving a base, aimed for the heavens. Florida, to New York, to Los Angeles, to Dallas, to small town Wisconsin, to Madison, to Ohio, to Austin, to now. How do I find and define my queerness in all these multiplicitous homes and conditions, where not only has my physical location changed, but the world around me has changed, as well. The loci of the loci itself has shifted. A Rubik's Cube. Nothing is what it once was, and I no longer have to travel to "communities of acceptance" to accept myself.

I place home through the synapses. Phone, girlfriend, text message, ex-wife, phone call, child, school, work, her father; iPads, motion, Internet, sound, visual, dream. My life is a picture, much like the ones I love from the artist Sally Mann. She said once she had a "magpie aesthetic." Photographed a series of dog bones, brought in from her yard. "It's not," she said, "because I'm interested in dog bones. Only that the dog bones were there, and I found them."

My life is a series of dog bones. I'm like that magpie, with that aesthetic. I find something in the yard that is myself, and I assemble it, piece by piece. Home was, but home evolves. Queer was, but it opens, too. I learn something more about it each day. My girlfriend's daughters, who I sometimes flagrantly refer to as my stepchildren, change like the weather, like the moon, phasing behind clouds in the sky. Off-handedly, one will assert, "I think I'm bisexual," but if you notice it or acknowledge it, they spook. They stand at the sink and pour a glass of water, drink it down. They walk away confident and not thirsty. The way I spun around and around that tree back home, getting nowhere, I see they've opened up a whole world of new expectations, beyond where I've traveled. Each week, a new friend of theirs renames themselves, calls out to the world their definite indefinite identity, and they are brave, and no one is shocked. My home lies where they are, in the world they uncover, located squarely in the future.

# Pulling the Moon

I've never made love to a man.
I've never made love to a man but I imagine.

> I imagine pulling the moon.
> I imagine pulling the moon out of his brow.

Pulling the moon out of his brow and eating it again.

> Eating and pulling his hair in silence.

A kind of silence when the moon goes out.

When the moon goes back and forth between us.

A kind of silence lit for only a moment.
Seeing for a moment through the eyes of the horse.

> Through the eyes of the dead horse
> that burns slower than my hair.

My hair that burns the moon of.
My hair with a hand inside it.

# Xiaogui

When our parents go to work and our grandparents go to the parking lot of the Korean Baptist Church to do exercise, which from far far away looks like they're finger-painting the sky, pressing their sweat-and-sour palms to the cheek of the sun, we go to the park and chase the squirrels with an electric flyswatter and fry them as black as the moon that's gone missing, black as our mothers' hair at the roots before they dye it bloodstain-brown in the sink, black as the scar on Sugar's shin from the time Linny tried carving his name into her skin with a rock because that's what the Monkey King did, carve his name on the middle finger of god and pee into his palm too. Good thing Sugar kicked him in the crotch with her cowboy boots on, which means now Linny can't have kids, his mother so upset about her son's deflated testicles that she drove to the duplex where Sugar Wong lived with her ma and demanded that they pay to get her son's balls fixed. How do you fix a ball, anyway? Pump it up like a tire? You can't use duct-tape on it, even though our parents use duct-tape on everything, including open wounds, and one time Niangniang comes to the park claiming she's shaved her legs when really she's waxed off her hairs with a strip of duct-tape, and besides, she's got no hair on her legs, except maybe one strand on her calf that you couldn't even floss with. There's an eyelash-shaped creek that cleaves the hills above our beetle-backed houses. We call it the butt-crack, that place where the creek carves itself into the field's fat ass, where the wildfires start wolfing down on the grass and the city goes on its knees and we all breathe smoke through our noses only, competing to see whose boogers turn the blackest, and of course it was Vincent who won, with his boogers and earwax the texture of coal. He couldn't hear until his mother chiseled out his earwax with an electric toothbrush. Every summer, the firefighters come with their hoses knotted and glowing like serpents. The firefighters are women from the detention center, one of whom is Leana's mom, Leana who works the counter of the dim sum restaurant and has no front teeth, because the day her mother got detained in Contra Costa for not wearing her seatbelt—the day before that, Leana's little sister had used meat-scissors to cut out the seatbelt, using it as a bandage/sling for a game of doctor in the empty lot, a game that the 大人 ended when they caught us trying to anesthetize Yanny with a spoonful of black vinegar so that we could cut open her belly with the machete used for watermelons—Leana took a bite out of a cinderblock and broke her teeth out. Teeth, turns out, don't grow on trees. We find this out when we steal our nainais' dentures and plant them in the field where dandelions multiply like acne and our older brothers play soccer wearing wet cardboard as shin-guards. We water the dentures and Marilyn even squats and spits on the soil, but zero rows of teeth grow up from the ground, and we don't get to harvest them by punching the dirt, and when our nainais can't find their dentures, they tell our babas, and baba isn't like mama, he doesn't yell at all, he just asks us very calm, please go dig up the dentures, and we do, and he gives them to mama so that she can boil them in a pot, and while the water's racketing, he takes us to the back of mama's closet, where she keeps a taped JC Penney shoebox with our birth certificates and 400 dollars cash, and makes us kneel in the dark with our hands under our knees, and even though our nainais make us kneel to pray, this is a different kind of kneeling that rusts us, that makes our knee-hinges whine our names when we try to stand up. This is a different kind of dark than the one beneath a bedcover, more like the one inside a fist, a dark where we can't see our own arms and can pretend for a while that we haven't yet been booted from our mothers by that god who gets paid to kick babies out of the womb, which is why we're all born green-assed like unripe fruit, and some of us ripen fast fast, like Henny who wears a bikini, and some of us are sour our whole lives, like Jennlu who's so green we call her the Statue of Liberty. Lift her shirt and see: her back's so green we ask if she can photosynthesize, if she can swallow the sun and shit it out as a searchlight. After the dentures, after our punishment, we decide not to steal anything beginning with the letter d. We decide we will only steal things letters a-c. We steal apples from the chaoshi that are rotted and open around their seeds like fists. We steal bullets from the gun that's buried in Xue's backyard, the one her baba kept loaded in case of communists. One night he woke up and unburied the gun and ran down the street shooting windows and owls, but no owls died, and no windows neither, and our parents duct-taped the holes and put up plywood and Xue's baba apologized for calling us communists, even though we didn't mind being called that, we'd rather be communists than old like him, like all babas with anchors for balls. That's why all babas walk with their knees bent by need, because they can't carry their own crotches. We threw the bullets into the creek but somehow they got baked into the birthday ice-cream cake that Gloria's ma bought at Baskin Robbins, the cheapest cake in the Bible-thick laminated catalogue, with just Gloria's name and a frosting trim and not even a plastic figurine. Gloria and her ma and her two brothers each took a bite of their slices and the bullets shot out and strung through their tongues, which now have perfect holes like the ones in beads, and then the bullets in their mouths opened into beetles and flew right out the window. We ask our parents how come we don't get ice-cream cakes and they tell us be happy with this douhua even though we think it tastes like a bowl of sweat. Our nainais say we are pudding and god is the spoon. Our nainais say listen to your father and we ask what kind of utensil is he. Our nainais are always mean to our mothers because, we are told, Chinese mothers are married to their sons, and they don't like to share those sons with other women. Because we aren't sons, we decide to be bears, like the one on the California flag in our classroom, and we climb the hills together on all-fours before giving up and walking like girls the rest of the way, all the way up to that cliff where our sisters go to get pregnant, where we once saw two boys twist-tied together like a pair of blue snakes, the kind of snake that once got into the city's plumbing and bobbed up in someone's toilet, Elen Chan if we remember, and bit her on the ass and made her butt-cheeks blue until they fell off one by one like apples. At the top of a trail only coyotes know, there are crows with eyes baked into pearls, and we're up high enough to watch the clouds breed, giving birth to tomorrow's weather, which is today's but more tired, rain so lazy it doesn't bother to land, just touches the asphalt with its fingers before rescinding up into the clouds. The rock goes caramel-soft in the sun, and when we sit on top of it, the houses below are beetling around in the heat, scuttling away because we stand over them and they don't want to get smushed by our thumbs. The streets are barcodes, everything costs something, and from here we can see the lot for sale near the Dollar Tree, where all the stray dogs clot together. The dogpack stole a baby once, Pearl's baby, but it was her fault because she left it in the stroller outside an apartment building while she ran up the stairs, searching for her husband behind one of the scabbed doors, her husband who we all knew was impregnating a girl who'd just come from Taiwan, a girl who would later give birth to a baby so heavy no one could hold it, not even the professional body-builder from Guangzhou who lived above the laundromat and who kept a canary inside a perforated detergent box. We don't know where the dogs took the baby, or if it was really the dogs who took it, but one month when the trees switched their wigs to red, we saw a poodle-mix gnawing on something that looked like a baby. Bambi and Linda chased the dog all the way back to the lot, but the baby turned out to be a KFC bag, and the bones were just the drumstick kind. Still, Bambi brought us what was left of the chicken bones, chewed to the texture of oatmeal, and showed us all in the park. We believed her when she said it was Pearl's baby. We buried the bones in someone's side-yard, maybe it was Mandy's, because there was a palm tree in it and only rich people own palm trees, only rich people buy things that cast shade, and we prayed for the baby of Pearl. We prayed the baby would grow up to be a yam and we would candy it, sprinkle it with windshield shards we find on the street and call sugar. Later in the summer of the chickenbone baby, three older boys steal the tires off a cop car and push it into the creek that heaves with dry-mouth. The boys went to prison in another city and we wrote them letters: *Dear sirs what did you do with the tires? Did you hang them from trees and swing from them like we see in books and on TV shows?* The boys never wrote us back but we saw their faces on TV, we recognized one or two of them from the park, where all the boys played basketball shirtless and we weren't allowed to go near them unless we were impersonating mosquitos: that's what Sana says. Sana says if we shiver our arms like mosquito wings and buzz out of our mouths, we can go anywhere unnoticed, we just have to watch out for that one nainai whose daughter died of dengue fever and who goes out every morning to war with mosquitos, punching bodies of still water to abort its eggs. We buzz into bedrooms and listen to our fathers fish-hooking our siblings out of our mothers' mouths. We buzz near the boys in the park and land on the lips of their beer cans and get sweat-drunk. We buzz over to Pearl's windowsill, watch her turn on the TV and write down names of missing girls, as if any of them could be the baby she left in the stroller and that the dogs stole and did/didn't eat, depending on whether you believe Bambi/Linda and how much you love dogs. We buzz around each other, hive in each other's hair, kiss each other before we kiss boys, though we have never met a boy and don't want to, our brothers not counting. We kiss and say it's practice for when we're married, which is when we will blow out babies like smoke rings, daughters dissipating before we can name them, daughters with too many bones, too many things unnamed inside them. Bambi and Linda practice the most, and one of them, we always forget which, has a pet crow she keeps leashed to her wrist. She brings it to school and the teachers say it's not allowed, but Bambi/Linda stands up and doesn't leave, goes to sit by a window instead and dangles her arm outside so the crow can fly an orbit around her wrist, a planet whose sun is a fist. When one of them, Bambi or Linda, moves south to Azusa to live with her grandfather after her mother dies one day in the house she's cleaning—the owners came back and found her facedown in the bathtub with a jug of bleach spilled into it, half her hair blonding already—the other girl, Bambi or Linda, severs the string on her wrist and the crow flies off, carrying the day into another city. The crow eats hair and dive-bombs onto our heads when we walk outside, so most of us carry a baseball bat or a butterfly net or at least a backscratcher to beat it away. Bambi or Linda, the one who hasn't left, the one whose mouth smells of other mouths, goes to the creek with a different girl every day, and we don't know what they do, but we know it's the reason why the wildfires start early this year, why we shove wet towels in the crack beneath our doors and bar the windows with blankets and watch the TV, sirens salting the room, our mothers flipping their faces like nickels, each expression illegible to us. We smile smooth as spoons and laugh because the hills look like an ass on fire. We pray Bambi/Linda and her girl make it out of the fire, but the sky's so smoked right now it's like the texture of jerky, tough on our teeth when we try to tear a hole in it to see what's survived. It's only later, I don't know how many years, that we see Bambi/Linda in some other city, one of us spotting her at the Nijiya in Japantown, one of us sees her working as a crossing guard in front of the smoked-out elementary school, holding back the traffic with her hips. Some of us see her with a man, with a scar, on fire, as a house. What we want to ask about is the crow, where she had gotten it from, where it had gone, whether she might kiss us if we asked, if she could show us what was worth burning for. Those who have left with their names: Derek who becomes a software engineer and pretends he never lived here. Na-na who had a baby and broke a hip birthing it. They replaced it with metal and that's why she can't get on planes anymore and come back. There's Xiaomi whose mother is the bottle lady: she claw-grabs the bottles of suanmei tang and cans of Arizona out of our hands before we've even finished, her shopping cart weak-kneed with the weight of what she's collected. She invites us every Saturday to her driveway to stomp the week's cans into silver hockey discs we kick around, pretending the two trees at the end of the block are goal-posts and our shadows are the enemy team. We dribble our cans down the street, the sun's fist berating our ribs, and Xiaomi's mother yells after us and says we won't get our cut of the quarters unless we turn back. And we don't listen, punting the can hard hard. It bursts open into a bird and flies over the hills where girls kiss. On Sundays, after our mothers cut our hair on the floor of the kitchen, where we sit cross-legged on newspaper and listen to her tell stories about boys that hit you like rain, Xiaomi's uncles gather in the yard with seven watermelons. When we come to watch them open the watermelons with machetes meant for other weather, for places where air rubs you like a pelt, they tell us a story about shoplifting the seven melons off the back of a truck parked behind the grocery, how they each wrestled one through the bars and ran, and we all laugh thinking about the seven uncles big-spooning their melons, holding them like babies until they reach the backyard and put them down on petaled-out newspaper. Beneath the rinds, the flesh is the same temperature as our hearts, each chamber full of flies. Six times, they splay open the rinds, the flesh beneath so red and sweet our teeth soften already. Flies flee out of the center of each watermelon, frenzied by the scent of themselves, colliding with our mouths and playing tag with our teeth. We beg to open the seventh melon, and the uncles teach us how to hold the blade away from our bodies so our skin won't come unstitched. When the blade comes down, the watermelon halves its heart and releases a flock of flies that fastens to us and becomes our skin. We choose a chunk of melon and eat it to the bone of its rind and then we go for seconds and then thirds and then fourths and fifths until the flies spread evening over the sky like chili jam and the moon glows wet as a gum-wad we stuck there with our thumbs.

# Kondo Living

*but when we really delve into the reasons for why we can't let something go, there are only two: an attachment to the past or a fear for the future*

you want to let systemic racism go but you are attached to the past of it & lord(t) knows what will happen to the tangled ropes it knots in the future & you are left here hanging & then _____ _____tells you that you can do it & she is so reserved & pretty & has a daughter who likes to fold laundry & you want to ask if you should fold dirty laundry too//if shoving a shoulder in on both sides is a true gesture of letting go

you want to put all the systems of oppression in one pile

all the internalized classism in a pile

you want to put the patriarchy pile into two piles because there are lights & darks & you are forced to sift through them evenly

*visible mess helps distract us from the true source of the disorder*

you want to declutter the womb you thought belonged to you & send the bent hangers & old gloves away

*tidy by category not by place    (but)*
- Portland, Oregon 58.1%
- Washington, D.C. 51.9%
- Minneapolis 50.6%
- Seattle 50%
- Atlanta 46.2%
- Virginia Beach 46.2%
- Denver 42.1%
- Austin 39.7%

you want to gather up the bricks & pods from the gentrifiers & tell _____
_____this is what you want to let go of & she will say (yes) she can help you she can wash your life & create white space again

Color of:

seventeen
football games (1) we went to just to see each other    be "alone"
dinners with "friends"    on opposite sides of town
October chill (13) like new lungs
that plaid flannel (6)
    stitched like little marching ants
leaves crunching (16)
    under rainbow-lace converse up the
foot-worn path from your house up (10)
    through the trees (4) onto
country club golf course grass (2) and
    bare feet    toes (7) rubbing
J Beibs swoop bangs (3) and
    your smile    all teeth    when you chuckle
        a child's drawing    of a person

your freckles    trying to cross    the bridge of your nose (5)    to mine
BBQ sauce (8) lips    you promised    always kiss on the    first date
                                                    (the winky face
                                                    at the end
                                                    of that text)

a park bench facing a rising moon (15)
you reclined like a pose and
looking up at me (14) like
          the full moon          our only witness
shining down midnight (13) like
a watercolor wash (11) over the lawn and
your head in my lap,

who was not also          a judge

we recreate la pieta (12)
queer it before we know
          what queering can mean

hands in your hair (9),
          sleek and fine,
                    shine like magazine glossed pages and

me:
          "Are you comfortable?" (12) and

your voice
all astonishment:

          "No one's ever cared enough
                    to ask me that before"

and later, bodies pressed
your back, my shins, stick grass dirt bed
our Hanes briefs inverted with
          the negative space between us—

# Chapter Nueve, excerpt from *Fiebre Tropical*

When Mami talked about El Apocalipsis, it always ended badly. She slowly removed her glasses, flipped her hair, eyes closed, index fnger and thumb pinched between eyebrows so we knew we had to pay attention. There is a sort of magnetism in Mami's gestures. A hypnotic force that pulls every bone, freezes all muscles with a nod or a touch or, in the Apocalipsis case, an eyes-closed, grabbing-bridge-of-nose combo that indicated something troubling Mami was about to be released as a "piece of life advice" or a passive-aggressive story.

It started with a loud silence.

Then she'd sigh (eyes still closed). Again. And again and again, until after five minutes one of us asked, Mami, ¿qué pasó? And she'd say, ¿*Qué* pasó? Que ¿*qué* pasó? Leéme esto. And one of us would read: *Porque El Señor Himself con voz de mando, con voz de arcángel y with the sound of the trumpet of God will descend from heaven. And the dead en Cristo will rise primero.*

She was obsessed with the coming of Christ. More than anything in the Bible it was when the heavens parted and she'd fly into Papi Dios's arms that had Mami mojando canoa about being Christian. It was also because of this obsession that she couldn't stand my apathy toward the Apocalipsis. Because what happens with those unsaved souls, mi reina? They burn and burn and Satan inscribes *666* on their butts like cows while having a big orgy.

I told Mami I didn't care and asked for money. You don't care? How can you not care about this?!

I knew money was so tight, I knew we barely paid rent, I knew every time we talked about budgeting homegirl landed on the Apocalipsis just in time to avoid explaining why the Pastores had bought our groceries that week.

Mamá, just tell me we don't have money, I whispered angry. And that, mi reina, is how the Apocalipsis talk ended. Door slammed. Mami prayed at me, La Tata drank, Lucía wrote Christian songs.

But Mami wasn't the only one worried about Satanás burning numbers on my ass. The Pastora had already pulled me aside many times for "una charladita" on matters concerning my soul burning after the Rapture and yada yada yada Cristo was still waiting for me and yada yada yada wouldn't it be nice to join my family eternally? I wondered what exactly Mami had revealed about our house to the Pastora that made her think we all wanted to spend our afterlives together. I also couldn't imagine Jesús and Dios like kids in a dentist's waiting room checking in with the receptionist every so often, *Did Francisca receive my son in her heart yet?* (said no god *ever*), then He sat again and consoled Jesús, who couldn't stop sobbing because the answer was: *No.* I evaded those questions with nods and grunts and emergency bathroom breaks.

And yet. Reina mía, reina mía, guess who else loved the Rapture? It was so hard to dodge Carmen's insistence. Mami and La Pastora I could handle, Lucía and La Tata were a piece of cake, but Carmen? Damn. I was with her when she chased a woman from Sedano's into Walmart and out again because the señora said, *Okay, I'll think about it.* You couldn't tell Carmen you'd think about it because that meant giving her hope about one less person burning in hell, which was something that greatly troubled her. Plus, Carmen and I had become inseparable. It felt like at any moment I could close my eyes and tell you exactly how many pimples she'd had on her forehead that day. Like I could mimic her jumpy giggles and if given enough time count the freckles on her brown skin from memory. After Sedano's we hung out at her house even though the Pastora still wasn't 100 percent on board with her primogénita kicking it so much with an unsaved soul. Nonetheless, this unblessed cuerpito criollo sat on their couch every day before and after outreach and every Sunday after church, Wilson sometimes joining us, but mostly just la jefa Carmen y this persona debriefing and planning our next Jóvenes en Cristo outreach, the next Jóvenes meeting, while Carmen's bare feet lay on my legs as she complained about Paula insisting on sleeping over at her house.

Estoy mamada, ¿sabes? Technically I can't say that, but I'm so over her, pela'a.

Every time she talked shit about Paula, a piece of my skin danced in enjoyment. It was rare that we got to talk shit, but after a few weeks Carmen started letting her guard down and I did everything to encourage her.

Yo sé, why doesn't she look for another church?

Primero, why don't you let Jesús save you y ya? Salimos de esa. She sat up, her head falling on my shoulder like she was almost begging me to be saved.

Pela'a, you smell like shit!

We'd been passing out flyers all morning, then lifting boxes with new youth merchandise in and out of the church. Of course I smelled like shit, although I didn't notice.

Francisca, she laughed, let me lend you some deodorant.

Don't bring me anything! It's fucking hot outside, Carmen. Además why are you smelling my armpit, you weirdo.

She sniffed under my arm again and laughed. Nena, she said, Francisca, hueles terrible cojone.

I refused her medicated Dove deodorant with its miniscule hairs. The mere idea of having pieces of her in my pores gave me an excruciating thrill that I just couldn't stand.

Okey pues, I can lend you a shirt. Take that nasty thing off.

It was pouring outside. The rain banged against the windows, the wind whispered through the tiny cracks. Sometimes I still closed my eyes and pretended I was back home in my room and the rain was cold, misty, full of darkness and danger, that if I stepped outside a bunch of señoritas in miniskirts would rush past me with plastic bags on their heads. The AC always killed the daydream. This time it was the AC plus Carmen holding a pollito-yellow shirt from her own Catholic school back in Barranquilla.

A ver, she pulled up my arms, let me help you.

I could've done this on my own, Carmen knew I could do it on my own, but she held my waist tight. Her arms around me like a soft straitjacket, like they could have stayed there forever and eventually blended with my Ramones shirt. Carmen was in charge and I let her. She breathed close, mumbling one thing or another about using the right deodorant and about my tiny arms, which she thought were cute. How can arms be cute? How could she think my hairy stick arms, now up in the air waiting for her to pull up my shirt, were cute? Her hands were cold. They were on my skin and then they weren't. As she pulled up my Ramones shirt, my earring got stuck. I yelled but she kept yanking at it, trying to break it loose but making it all worse, sending a ripping pain from my left ear to my left toe. I heard the earring hit the foor but the shirt wouldn't come of. Great. And now half of me was exposed and I couldn't see anything and the shame of her staring at my belly, my gray bra, at the mole with the hair I forgot to pluck because *I did not know* someone was about to see me half-naked and the boiling heat of shame slapping my face and fuck La Tata for suggesting those earrings made me look so churra, so guapa, so señorita, when I never, ever wore stupid pearl earrings and now I only looked like a maldito joke with no tits y Carmen que nada se lo toma en serio y Carmen giggling—Mierda, pela'a, your ear is bleeding—and her cold hand on my waist again not comforting but supporting herself because homegirl could not stop laughing.

¿Cuál es el chiste, Carmen? ¿Cuál es el chiste?

It's no joke, she said cagadita de la risa. Sit on the couch más bien.

She pushed me onto the couch then landed next to me. She smelled my armpits again and I couldn't do shit about it. Then her fingers gently slid underneath the shirt collar, brushing my neck, almost poking my ear but fnally the shirt was of. I wanted to pretend it wasn't over. My ear was still bleeding. I pretended I was angry at her, touching my ear like it was hurting so much, searching for the missing earring on all fours.

She rested on the couch looking for the frst time like a cool dorky girl who just happened to be wearing a shirt with a bleeding crown bisected by a blue dove. That morning when she picked me up, the venecos had yelled at her to please come bless their dicks with her dove, but don't bring your friend! Blue dove shirt kicking the Ramones' ass. I didn't say anything but felt so glad I was with her.

I have a secret remedy for your ear, you wanna know what it is?

Pf sí, claro. Like I'm gonna let you anywhere near my face right now.

She waited for me.

Leather couch on white tiles, faded bra on yellowing skin, and my belly still exposed, still too real right now and allofasudden Carmen's hands, also too real, on either side of my head pressing on my neck, my toes contracting in fear. I may have closed my eyes? Or grabbed her leg? I may be making shit up but I know at some point I grabbed the couch as if we were flying off and her breath stank of Cheetos. Stay still, Francisca, she whispered. The thrill of her warmth approaching y yo frozen on the spot until I felt her tongue, like a mollusk entertaining its prey with its tentacles, licking and sucking on my earlobe.

She did not kiss me, mi reina. Well, kinda. Not really. She put my entire right lobe in her mouth like those hamsters the shekinas bring to church sometimes suck on tubes of water. Eyes closed or open or staring at pictures of the Pastora because I didn't want Carmen to stop but also I had no idea exactly how my earlobe tasted or if I'd washed my earlobe that morning or if Carmen would turn around disgusted. Her teeth barely touched my skin and I couldn't make out the form of her tongue, just its waves of water.

Not sure how long this lasted. Maybe real-life 30 seconds, maybe a minute, but it was eternal. We were there 60 years until her tongue grew wrinkly and we passed out from old people's disease. We died side by side while she still sucked on my lobe, my faded bra holding my sagging breasts, her shirt threadbare. The warmth of her saliva on my ear was abruptly followed by the cold wind of the AC right above us. I dared not look at her. The thought of a disappointed face—I didn't want her taking back all the seconds of saliva spent on my ear, I wanted her to be proud of licking a part of my body. The fear of Carmen suddenly snapping out of it.

# Between Towns

In Sumatra, two young men, weary after riding their one motorbike on dirt roads in and out of jungles, around volcanoes, and through farms of rubber, rice, and oil palms, stopped at a lonely little café perched on the edge of a mountain overlooking the Batang Toru River. They asked the proprietor, an old woman dressed in Muslim garb, for two black coffees and the toilet which they entered together, eager to relieve themselves after the hours of a bumpy ride. When the pair returned and sat leaning on each other at a table open to the late-day breeze and a wondrous view of the river roaring through the vast forest, the woman brought them cups of fresh local coffee. "You must be close friends," she said, smiling as she sat near them.

"Why do you say so?" said the taller man before pouring a little coffee from his cup into its saucer and drinking the thus slightly-cooled brew.

The woman waved her hand to and from the little room where the men had found the toilet.

There was no one else in the café, and so the shorter man rose up a bit from the crook of his friend's arm and said, "We are lovers, ma'am. We are queer. You understand?"

"Of course, dear. I understand. It's nothing to me. I have served all kinds of folks in my time here. My long time here."

The shorter man blinked his eyes and exhaled to a calmness as he leaned back into his friend who asked the old woman, "What sort of people live in the next town?"

The woman replied, "What sort of people lived in the town you are coming from?"

"Horrible!" said the shorter man. "They made life miserable for us because we had fallen in love. Even our own families—this was our home town where we grew up and went to school—bullied us until we had no choice but to leave."

"I am so sorry for you," said the old woman. "But I am afraid you will find the same kind of people in the next town as well."

The two men looked at each other and shook their heads in sadness and disappointment. When they finished their drinks, they paid and thanked the woman for her kindness, remounted their motorbike, and set off on their way.

Some time later, another pair of young men, on a motorbike from the opposite direction, stopped at the same café for coffee. They also engaged the proprietor in conversation. "You are gay, right?" asked the old woman.

"Is that a problem?" the fellow with blond highlights in his jet-black hair retorted.

"Not at all. Not at all," said the old woman. "It's nothing to me. I have served all kinds of folks in my time here. My long time here."

"Tell me, then, ma'am," the young man asked, "What sort of people live in the next town?"

The woman replied, "What sort of people lived in the town you are coming from?"

"Wonderful people," he said. "That's where I met my boyfriend here. And no one seemed to care that we fell in love. Indeed, we had friends who encouraged our relationship, who were happy for us." The boyfriend nodded. "But there are no good jobs for us there, and so we have to find new horizons."

"Well, don't worry my dears," the woman said, "You will find the same kind of people in the next town as well."

# How to Survive the Fire

The first rule of survival is to run,
I tell you this so you understand how memories
are floods drowning a lonely man,
how the sight of a man burning
in a park stays with you;
his voice becoming yours at night.
There's no boy hiding in my throat.
I tell you the truth, my mouth is clean
but on my tongue are cities
where boys are beaten to death.
Say Lagos, say Onitsha, say Lafia,
say cities where the only freedom
for a man who loves another man is to leave.
I tell you this so you understand my silence,
understand why I crawled into my voice,
I do not want to die.
There is nowhere safe in this city of mine
and songs of freedom are just what they are.
You have to see nails drawing blood
from a swollen head
before you understand why God turned
his face from Christ and whispered, Run.

# Bus Roulette, excerpt from "Dogs in America"

Dear Sly,

**Bus roulette**
(instructions for a game)

**Object:** To reach Home*

**Obstacles:** Uniboob, silkworm mustache, Greyhound cops, anxiety disorder.

**Contents:**
- 1 fraudulent bus pass
- 1 government issued ID
- 1 5th grade US geography education
- Unlimited: senseless excuse about why you didn't visit the ticket counter to get a real ticket
- Natural charm (purchase separately)

**Gameplay:** Play begins at any major Transfer Point ("Greyhound Station"). Using 5th grade US geography education, player must select a bus headed in the general direction of Home. Should player choose wrong bus, s/he must go back a corresponding number of spaces on the board. Player may opt to skip a turn and remain at the Transfer Point.

**Play ends when one of the following occurs:** player is arrested, player reaches Home, player forfeits the game.

*Home = a malleable destination, potentially non-geographic in nature, ref: "Home, where the heart is," home plate, homestyle, and "my home is in god"**
**embroidered on this lady's baseball cap. She's reading a pamphlet called 52 Uses For the White Space at The Back Of Your Bible***
***Not really. But she should be.

Love,
Avi

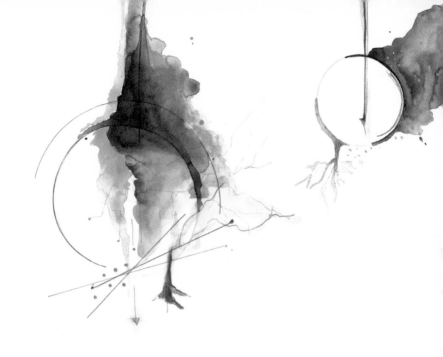

NORTH

# N'Jadaka's Appeal

Hey Auntie! Can you spare me
a homeland? The one I left
didn't gift me my mother's
name. Every word I'm fighting
for: my native tongue, my immortal.

Hey Auntie. Let us carve me a tongue
to lick these wounds scriptured
on my skin. They sting, they linger,
they read as abscess—or absence;
I never learned the difference.

Hey, Auntie, maybe you could
fix your face to love me. I know
I spit chaos, but if you cut out
my tongue I will write you
a psalm, a shadow, a love song.

Hey, Auntie? Why do men metaphor
mothers into countries, into tongues?
I wouldn't know. I've never had
a country. I mean, a mother.
I mean, a tongue. I mean, a home.

# American Honey

It's easier than you thought—leaving.
Only one night spent sleeping on your own
in a motel parking lot beneath the stars
of a summer Okolona. Your long-built dread
dispersing like gas into a brilliantly Black
Appalachian sky. For once, you are a girl

unmolested. You could do this: be a girl
without a home. Always gone. Perpetually leaving
behind Strip Mall, USA & the dark
green dumpster you raid for food, something to own
& the two kids no one will take care of, the dread
that comes on when their father grips you. Sparkle,

let your freedom build slow like the death of a star
across the years. & when she calls for you—granddaughter
of Elvis, confederate flag bikini, voice you dread—
let the interstate's roar swallow her sound. In your leaving
you see your country for the first time. Your very own
seeing. When he howls for you, your body is a silent, Black

barn hidden in wild grass & your locs—pastoral, Black—
are ropes for him, swaying from its rafters. Dangling star.
It's easier than you imagined—leaving behind your own
mother. Her daughter, her ghost. Now you can be a girl
on the back patio with three white men & you can leave
with their money, egg suede cowboy hat adorning your dreads.

You've swallowed the Mezcal worm of your fear.
Now you're standing in the cowboy's convertible, Black
wind at the edge of the camera's frame. You're leaving
with the get-away boy you found sparking
in a K-mart parking lot. You're keeping it alive—your girlhood,
the adrenaline, the novelty, the dying star you own

a million miles away. You're learning how to own
yourself, how to be 14-deep in a 12-seater without dread.
How to disarm. How to let it go when the white girl
from Florida says *nigga* again, how to be the only Black
girl among strangers. Dancing around a bonfire under the stars.
Singing out of the sunroof down the interstate. Leaving

each new town you meet and own a memory in. Leaving
behind your mother's dread-veined eyes. Fuse-less stars.
Learn it all, girl, until what you've left behind is a brilliant Black.

# da hood™ as anti-hero

da hood™ as character is not static. not stationary. not a station you get off at three stops too late. da hood™ is dynamic in the way it grows. tall & shiny. or wide around the edges where it flattens & browns. or implodes within itself; if implosion is a type of growth—an expansion toward nothing. or the way a cancer grows tumorous fingers, disappearing what it touches. or the way the fingers are really a set of mouths. eating the brick, the sheetrock, the asbestos, the wrought iron, the lead paint, the slabs of cement gone sideways. the ways we are forced to pick sides. a minimal menu: aluminum trays of *us*. porcelain bowls of *them* with tweezered garnishes of shit we can't pronounce. da hood™ is most pronounced at dusk when the musk of us breaks free of baby powder & sky all purple like our bruises. after a day of swelter & sweat this when da hood™ come alive under cover of night all black & bright like our skin. this when the masks fall & all our primal shimmies itself to the surface. & wasn't it our shiny surfaces that first seduced you? when in winter the brownstones was dusted white & da hood™ was mad quiet. the rats & roaches done crawled south. & da hood™'s mouth seemed sutured shut or at the very least leaking silence. or humming silent night for the whitefolk lullaby. *slee-yeep in heaven-ly peace.* except the hood never sleeps. baggy-eyed but woke. but heaven sho-nuff & hell too cuz da hood™ AC always be broke plus global warming plus mad blackfolk just be radiating the anger & brilliance of a zillion ancestors uprooted & re-routed & re-rooted & rootworking & rooting for even the most rotten       most forgotten         of us—

# The Reincarnation of Wonder Woman

"I have something to tell you all," he said over his cereal, eyes barely visible through his wild black fluffy hair, cut in a way that often made him look like a Mexican Christopher Robin. His mother was reading a book of poetry and did not look up, her hazelnut hair, also wild and wavy, cascaded down her back. It was one of his most favorite things about his mother, how her long wavy hair made her look like a super hero. His father had already left for work. It was a cold morning, their marble floors ice on his bare feet, the blue leather of their modern chairs at the breakfast table stuck to his bare legs, since he was wearing shorts to school today, on Fridays his school's uniform was shorts, but with a sweater that to him made no sense.

His uncle Freddy who had crashed on their couch the night before, was eating some chilakiles he said would help with la cruda, whatever that was. His hair was thicker, darker, and wilder than theirs, his locks twirled above his head like a shiny whirlpool. Out of all his uncles, Freddy was the youngest, at 16 lived in a perpetual party, family members often had to run out of the room crying from his jokes, and his mother's concentido. They sat in the breakfast nook of their very clean apartment in Toluca, Mexico, it was across the street from a nice big park.

"I'm the reincarnation of Wonder Woman. I was dead, and now I'm alive. I am Wonder Woman," he said, not eating his breakfast. He did not like to eat.

His mother looked up from her Octavio Paz book, and sighed.

"I know I look like a five-year-old boy, but this is what happens when you are reincarnated, you shrink into the body of a small child, deep inside I am Wonder Woman."

"How can you be the reincarnation of Wonder Woman?," his uncle asked, "Wonder Woman is not dead."

"Eat your breakfast!" his mother's voice sounded tense, like she was going to be mad at him all day. "Eat. Your. Food," she said looking very tired.

"I am Wonder Woman," he said. Feeling stronger every time he declared it, staring his mother down from across the table.

"Linda Carter!" His uncle Freddy said between bites of food, "Now there is a wooonder wooowoman!" His hands made a gesture like he was holding two large mangoes. "She's Wonder Woman and she's not dead."

"No, I am not dead, I am alive! I am Wonder Woman—made of clay! I am;

strong Amazon Warrior! Spy! Fashion model! Princess! Sexual goddess!"

His mother put her hand to her forehead and pressed the wrinkle between her eyes. "You don't even know what that word means, do you know what reincarnation means?" His mother put her book down, took a sip from her coffee. She always took two or three sips and never finished it but for some reason she never let him have the rest of it.

"Do you know what the word sexual means?" his uncle Freddy asked.

"I know what the word sexual means!"

He did not know what the word sexual means but he had seen someone on television say it and lick their lips, so he looked at his young uncle and licked his lips, which made his uncle laugh, and which is when his mother's hand smacked his face hard enough for him to fall backwards off of his chair. Making his uncle laugh even harder.

"Ya vez, chaparro, you're not her! Wonder Woman would have dodged that."

No one could catch him at school, except the school bully Halcon. He was one fast first grader. Like every other queer kid all over the world, he just wanted to be left alone, and like every other gay kid in the world, that never ever happened, especially with Halcon around.

He had to be fast, everybody seemed to be obsessed with wanting to kill him at school. He was really good at finding places to hide around the school. But still he was found and then the chasing and running and running, girls, boys, all excited to figure out how to torture him some more, how to have fun punching or pinching or pulling the gay kid's hair, or stabbing him with pencils, or bending his fingers backward, once he was told to stand against a wall, so they could play execution via firing squad, but the bullets were rocks.

He was faster than every kid and teacher in the school, so the yard duties knew to keep a close eye on him. He's a runner they would say.

His first day of school ever, Kindergarten class of Escuelita Benito Juarez, he had walked up to his teachers and said, "Hello, this is boring and oppressive, I'm going home."

They said, you can't go home.

He calmly and politely said, "Watch me," and left. They laughed, the yard duties laughed as well, "Oh he's going home everybody, he's done for the day!" They laughed but he kept walking, faster and faster.

"Okay that's far enough kid," one of them said, but he showed them how fast he was. The yard duty laughed and thought he was bluffing, but then ran after him when she realized he had already made it across the front yard, and to the gate.

"Its locked!" the teacher screamed out of breath, but he was slim and small, and squeezed his body through the bars to freedom.

He walked through the city, triumphant, felt so powerful and alive. He remembered every park, every business, every store, the graffiti, the trees with their white pants. He swore he would never let anything cage him ever again. He had money for lunch, so he bought himself an helado de mamey, and calmly rang the doorbell at his apartment on the other side of the city. His mother screamed when she saw him at the door with ice cream dribbles on his new white school uniform sweater.

Halcon was a nasty third grader that towered over all the first graders, perpetually angry, who relentlessly bullied everyone, but everyone pretended to like him so they wouldn't get picked on, even the teachers. His real name was Huichol, but Huichol hated that name so everyone had to call him Halcon. Halcon had caught him once or twice, followed by severe beatings, while the other children laughed. The next day he found a large broomstick leaning against a wall next to the janitor's closet, so he grabbed it with his small girl hands, and beat Halcon on the head and legs, making Halcon bleed all over the yard, and worst of all cry. When his mother came to pick him up, the teachers were there, angry as fuck, standing in a row with their arms crossed. All the kids in his class and other classes were there with their arms crossed, ready to tell on him. Halcon was also there with Band-Aids on his knees and arms, holding ice on his huge head. After his mother was told what he did to poor little Halcon, the teachers stood waiting to hear his mother say, something like, *oh he will be punished, how awful, wait till we get home.* But his mother looked down at him, and said, "So you hit that kid with a broomstick? Isn't that the ugly kid that chases you and beats you up? The kid that terrorizes you and these menopausal harpies won't do anything about? Isn't that the ugly kid that tried to drown you in the fountain? And stabbed you with a pen? That's the kid you hit in the head with a stick?"

"Yes" he said.

"Good, fuck that kid! I'm so proud of you for defending yourself, I'm so proud of you, that we're gonna go get ice cream!" his mother said looking down at him, with a halo of sunshine around her wavy hair.

"Really?!" he asked.

"Yes! And we're gonna see that movie your father doesn't want you to see, *Labyrinth.* You and I are going to have a great day. Let's get the hell out of here." Every teacher and all the kids in the yard's mouths dropped to the floor. The collective gasp was heard all throughout Mexico.

That night he dreamed about his other life, flying through the air, lifting a tank, beating up Nazis. Dark long wavy flowing hair like his mother's blowing in the wind as he flew from building to building. He woke up. His parents were coming home from an event. His mother had been in a play, his father seemed happy, their friends were there, drunk maybe. He crept past his uncle Freddy, who had passed out on his lower bunk bed, and walked to the door, to see his mother passing by. She wore a leather jacket, holding a wig. It was longer than her own hair, wavier, darker. His heart burst, his body trembled. The apartment was dark, the voices of his mother and her friends echoed from the living room.

In the dark he had found the wig box, on his mother's nightstand. Once he put it on, he felt at home, he felt complete.

There was Fanta, there was coffee, there was beer, there was a cloud of cigarette smoke. Young actors and comedians talked and listened to his father's Beatle's records, women laughed in the kitchen in the living room. His mother led the conversation as always, with her booming voice, clapping to punctuate a point.

"Power, it's about power, dynamic energy in a scene! If you don't have that then the audience falls asleep and they should! Your acting should have power!" she said to the crowd. He didn't know what she was talking about from behind the couch, where he was hiding, but this was his cue.

"YES, IT IS ALL ABOUT POWER," and jumped out from behind the couch, and stood on top of it, then jumped from the top of the couch to a tall table, wearing blue *Transformers* pajamas and the long flowing wig. "AND I AM ALL ABOUT POWER BECAUSE I AM WONDER WOMAN! THE MOST POWERFUL WOMAN IN THE WORLD!"

His parents' living room burst into laughter and applause, the women clapped and cheered, the men cheered, everyone seemed super happy he had made his appearance, except his mother, and his father standing in the back. His father looked super disappointed.

"He should be in the play!" one slim handsome man proclaimed.

"Yes, yes, do a monologue!" a woman said.

"I am not here to be in a theatre production!" he informed them. "I am here to save the world."

His mother approached him, nervous laughing, but then bent down and with her super serious voice said, "Take that off and go to bed, mi amor, now."

"NEVER" he said, "This is my hair! I have found what was missing!"

"It's late, you have to go to bed." His mother stopped smiling.

"Never!" He yanked his small arm from his mother's hand, something he was not supposed to do. The smack on his face rang throughout the room. Everyone paused for a moment, but then they all continued talking and laughing among themselves to ignore what was going on. His mother took him to bed, the wig had been ripped off.

"Is this all it?" he asked.

"It is way past your bedtime, chaparro." She put him into his top bunk bed with Rainbow Brite sheets and comforters. She tried to kiss him on his forehead, but he continued.

"Is this it?!"

"Stop! You'll wake up your uncle!"

"Oh, like anything is going to wake him up. Why did you bring me to this world if this is all it?!? This pathetic sad boring planet full of buffoons, BU-FOONS!"

"Acuestate and go to sleep." His mother was losing her patience.

"I reject it, I reject this sad boring life!" he declared and threw himself off his bed dramatically backwards, scaring his mother from the thought of his five-year-old head hitting the marble floors. She caught him in mid air, and gave him a frustrated hug.

"I'm sorry! Listen to me! I'm sorry! I don't know what is going on but, listen to me, I love you, I love you so much, okay, but you need to go to bed, you need to stop acting so crazy! You need to never disrespect me in front of anyone ever again."

She grabbed his small face in her hands and kissed his head five times. "Also please, please, stop running away from school, stop acting like this in front of people!"

She put him back in his bed. And then rubbed the area on her face between her eyes. And grew quiet. She was quiet for a long time, backlit by the lights in the living room coming from the hallway.

"Estás enojada."

"I'm not mad at you," She said, putting her hand on her hip, her other hand on his arm.

"Sí, yes you are, I can see your rallita." He could still partly see her face.

"Stop calling the wrinkle between my eyes a rallita. If you're not careful you'll get one too."

"I want one. When I grow up I'm going to have one."

"Look, I love the way you are, but if you act this way, people are going to keep trying to hurt you. Be yourself here with me, but in front of people outside, at school, just act normal. I would die if anything ever happened to you."

"Wonder Woman does not die," he whispered to his mother.

His mother let out a long breath.

"And stop touching my wigs!

His mother hid the wig. It had been days that felt like years without the wig and no matter how much he begged, his mother would not even let him mention it.

"I'm going to have to take matters into my own hands," he said to his mother one morning as he was leaving for school.

"What the hell are you talking about? Are you threatening me?" she asked, putting on a pair of large sunglasses left over from the late seventies.

"Oh, you will see," he said.

"Oh, we'll see what happens when supposedly I will see."

"That's right, you'll see."

"Yes, we'll both see"

"We will"

"Oh, we will!"

"I mean, you will."

"No, *you* will! See your grandmother's wooden spoon? When I leave your little butt the way your cousin Miko's butt ends up after your uncle is done with him? Get your backpack, we're late!"

The next evening his mother had some friends over, they were having coffee. A woman named Amanda Miguel sang with a powerful operatic voice *o no! o no! o no! o no! o no! o no! o no! o no!* over and over again from the record player. He calmly walked into the living room, smiling.

"Hola mi amoooor, ven acá!" his mother called him over.

He did not go to his mother or respond to her. He walked right into the middle of all the women, facing his mother, and calmly put her fabric scissors on the coffee table. He said, "You should go to your bedroom," and walked away.

"What?" His mother smiled at her friends, but then said, "Wait, come here."

He kept walking away.

"What do you mean, go to my bedroom? What did you do?"

He smiled at her and kept walking down the hall and into his room.

"Who said you could touch my scissors? What the hell did you do? Where are you going?!"

His mother followed him to his bedroom.

"What did you do?"

He sat with his hands like a little business man on his small blue children's table, staring at his mother silently. "Go to your bedroom, Mother, and find out."

His mother went to her room and screamed.

He had taken her scissors and shredded her new sheets, hole after hole, long ribbons of tattered sheets. What was once a soft pink celebration of rose bushes was now a red garden massacre.

She came back to his room.

"Now you see," he said calmly.

His mother's face was red. She sat on his bed. "I don't have time to talk to you about this, or beat the hell out of you. Were you trying to "teach me a lesson? Those are just sheets, and you're just a child. You cannot teach me a lesson, I don't care about stupid sheets. But why did you take my fabric scissors without permission? They're dangerous! You could have hurt yourself!"

He sat still with his hands folded in front of him, staring at her calmly.

"Why do you want that wig?"

"It is my hair."

"The hair on your head is your hair!"

"Give me back my hair."

"I'm going to go back to my friends. We are going to talk about this later, and since I can't trust you to be alone, I'm taking you with me. Oh, and no, no toys!"

He growled at her.

"Growl all you want."

He spent the rest of the evening bored out of his mind with his head on his mother's lap as she laughed and talked with her friends.

A month had passed. At school Halcon had caught him again after a long chase. The whole school crowded around to watch as Halcon held his first grade body on the ground and put a plastic bag over his small head, until he passed out. When he woke up he was at home. He was told he was going to take a break from school. His mother was out, at a rehearsal. His nanny was doing the dishes and was distracted. He walked seven circles around the coffee table in the living room. He had sat all his She-Ra dolls, Rainbow Brite dolls, and Care Bears on the couch. He began to tell them all a story:

"Wonder Woman was trapped.
Shrunk to the size of a five-year-old.
This will not do, she thought.
She had to figure out a way to outsmart her captors,
fight her way to freedom, but most importantly,
she had to get back her hair.
She found a pair of small blue briefs,

a red tank top, and some knee high gym socks
with red stripes. This will work, she thought,
then she saw it, a yellow head band with a red star in the middle,
a sign from the Goddess!
Things can only get better from here.

Now all she needed was her hair.

She waited till her captors were distracted,
snuck into what they called the *master bedroom*.
Her hair had been turned into a wig,
held captive in a large box at the top of the closet.
If it hadn't been for the yellow jump rope,
she would never have gotten it down.
After a couple of tries, there it was,
her long flowing black hair.
She secured it on her head and twirled! ….nothing.
I should have turned back into Wonder Woman by now.
She looked in the mirror, she was still a little boy,
wearing a wig, and a big black eye. Still, it was time.
She walked right past one of her captors who was on the phone.
Opened the door and walked right out of her prison.
Down the stairs, and out into the world…

   "Nice legs!" Screamed a street kid from across the street. She stood tall.
   "Soy la Mujer Maravilla!" she proclaimed.
   A cab driver leaning against his car whistled at her, "Mujer Maravilla? More like a Maricon Maravilla!"
   "Soy la Mujer Maravilla," she repeated, staring the cab driver down, and walked by him. "I don't have to put up with this, I have an invisible jet!"
   She flew her invisible jet across the street and down the way to her favorite park, El Parque Alameda, past the statue of Montezuma, and to a play area where a group of kids had gathered. She walked closer to the crowd of kids and heard a little girl screaming. "Stop!"
   Wonder Woman squeezed through the crowd to see Halcon stepping on a girl that was on the ground. She looked like he had been beating her up.
   "Be my girlfriend bitch!" Halcon had a booger coming out of one nostril.
   "I'd rather die Fart Face!" The girl screamed, dirt all over her face from the ground.

Halcon kicked the girl on her side as hard as he could.

Then, suddenly, a lasso of truth landed around his neck. He was pulled backwards, surprised, choking. He fell on the ground as a glorious being in blue underwear and a headband and shimmering dark wavy Amazonian hair flowing triumphantly in the wind pulled as hard as she could. When the crowd noticed her strength was not quite enough, all the girls in the crowd who had also been terrorized by Halcon decided to help. They ran towards her and started pulling the yellow jump rope. The harder they pulled the more Halcon was unable to get up, and ended up being dragged by the throat across the playground, choking, gasping for air. Finally, the boys—confused but scared of what Halcon might do to them for not helping—pulled on the other end of the jump rope until it was yanked from the girls' side. Halcon got up, red faced, sweating, tears in his eyes, dusted himself off.

"What the fuck is this pinche Marica wearing?!" He pointed, "Why are you out here in your underwear you stupid faggot?"

Everyone laughed. All the boys and girls began to recognize the small boy, who no longer looked like a superhero.

"Now we're really going to kill you, stupid faggot," Halcon said.

She walked right up to Halcon, right to his large, fat, red face and said, "Soy la Mujer Maravilla, pinche gordo mammon!" and stabbed Halcon in the shoulder as hard as those little hands could with a large pair of scissors stolen again from his mother's room.

The children's gasps were heard throughout Mexico. Blood squirted out of Halcon's shoulder and down his arm. He began to wail and weep and fell on the ground. "Mama! Maaaamaaaa!" He screamed to a large brick-faced woman who was running over.

He knew it was time to run again. The kids around him were not cheering. They all looked worried for Halcon. The brick-faced woman began to scream at him, adults came, a crowd gathered around him, all shrieking and talking at the same time about the horrible disgusting little queer freak that stabbed poor young little soft defenseless Halcon who wasn't doing anything. *Poor Halcon,* they kept saying.

The crowd was too much for him. He began to run. None of them could catch him. He ran through the park, through the trees, the benches. He saw the street that led to the other side of the park. If he made it there he could lose the crowd. But he saw a shadow behind him and looked over his shoulder. It's over, it was his uncle Freddy. He tried mightily to outrun him, but he failed. Out of breath, he didn't even try to free his arm from Freddy's steel grip. Freddy didn't even acknowledge him, just took the wig off, threw it to the ground, making the mob of people who were going to do who-knows-what to him stop and stare at the wig, as if the exorcism had been finished. Everyone had been cleansed.

"I'm taking him home," Freddy told the crowd.

"THAT FREAK TRIED TO KILL MY SON!" The brick-faced woman screamed.

"Oh, he's fine. He'll live. Also, your son sucks lady! Your son is a fucking tub of useless lard who beats everybody up. Fuck your kid lady! Everybody hates him!"

All the kids and the people in park, turned to the woman and said, "Yes, your son is shit, sorry, he sucks, he is a giant bully, pinche demonio, no one likes him, he's ugly," all in unison.

"Also that's just a little cut, he's not going to bleed to death," Freddy said. "He'll be fine, just put a Band-Aid on him so that fucking giant cry baby will shut the fuck up."

Halcon was still weeping woefully, taking huge gulps of air in to keep wailing next to his mother, holding her hankerchief to his wound.

Freddy stood up, taller than he ever looked before. "Now, I'm taking him home, and you should all go home. Go home! And if any of you lay a hand on my nephew again, I don't care what he's wearing, you will answer to me, and my friends, and my family. All of you fuck off!"

On the walk home, he looked down at his feet and said thank you.

"Secret identity," said his uncle.

"What?"

"All superheroes have a secret identity," Freddy said. "If they walked around in their superoutfits all day people would never leave them alone. During the day they wear normal clothes, to blend in, and hide a bit, until they have to save the day. Even Wonder Woman has a day job. Freddy walked him back to his house, not letting go of his tiny arm.

"You're lucky your mom sent me to find you. Those people could have really hurt you."

Night time, he was in bed, the lights were all out except in the hallway. His mother was sitting by his bed. She had made him pray, had made him take a bath. Her rallita was bigger and deeper than he had ever seen it.

"Please listen to me, I'm only going to say this once. You have to stop. You are not Wonder Woman. You are you, a five-year-old little boy. Who loves his mother, who loves being a five-year-old little boy, who doesn't want to dress as a girl, who doesn't steal clothes from his cousins, who eats his food, who doesn't want to make his mother cry. You are a little boy who does what he is told, and doesn't run away from school and never ever, ever stabs anyone, no matter what! This little boy behaves, this little boy acts normal, this little boy..."

"I'm going to stop you right there," he said, with a tiny finger on his mother's lips. "Whoever this boy is, this boy you're talking about, I've never met him, I've never seen him. But if you do, tell him I hate him."

# Home

Waves taped to my face, I'm crying
        Then sucking dick for rent. When the
Police lights drift across me like rose petals.
Rory, I'm not sure how we got here.
        Two punk faggots, sleeping in the
Parking lot outside of Casino Morango. I'm crying
        Every time he plays the sad song in my
Mouth. [Smack these teeth like piano keys]. Watch
The Police lights drift across my windshield.
Rory, do you think we can outlive this?
[The sound of conch shells cracking].
                Waves taped to my face. I have
Five dollars left — if we go to the gas station
        How far away can you drive drunk?
Lights spinning across the pavement
And I piss on the great saguaro; with my
        Lips split open and wide owl eyes.
                [I'm broken like a wishbone].
Police lights call me "criminal."

# Culture

The headlights remember boys like us: black, unbroken by the law. As they
man us to the curb, one friend says he's been broken before. But not like
this. The car parks. Two white men get out. Their blue uniforms adore their
muscles. *You boys up to trouble?* I want to kiss the question, make love to the
word "boys" as I have seen in porn. We're told to sit. It's cold, another friend
complains. So busy studying the officers' pelvises, I don't notice the flashlights
searching our faces, our chests, our legs. I wanted to touch what hung between
their thighs. *Got a call about some houses being broken into. Know anything about
it?* Prayer would be wise, but I don't remember to pray. One friend says we're
heading to his house up the street and tosses his eyes. A flashlight pulls from
his shoes to his lips, shimmering. Here, in the Southend, others know this
recycled story. One by one, we are searched. Nothing in my friends' pockets, a
pen in mine. They don't know how, after the frisk, the black boy in the porn is
scripted to blow the officers. I think tonight will be the night I'm written into
the perfect angle. But the production crew never arrives. I'm not headlined.
I'm sitting on the bed talking about the rest of our night. One friend says he
has an idea and the other looks at me. We know what we came here to do. I
take off my shirt, my basketball shorts, my boxers, say, *Let's stop bullshitting.
Take off your clothes.*

# Aubade ending in a hip

I.

Don't wake her suddenly after a night of laced chocolate
and tequila. Thread your fingers through her still-sleeping

hand resting on the light side of her womb. Whispering
will not rouse her. She will fan you off like a fly or turn

to her side, presenting the back nape of her neck,
which your lips cannot resist visiting even though

you know she will furiously scuttle and fuss. Language
is all about saying what you mean, often wordlessly.

How do you tell the lover laying to your left the sea
has tides? There are times when the water is high

others when it recedes. The moon's gravitation
dictates both. Gravity is an odd word for pull.

Twice a day the moon wills the ocean close—
morning and night—in an elemental hunger

if only to put her to bed, if only
to watch her curve around dawn.

# Home Is Where My Cock Is

Ema and I fell in love on Vancouver Island, on a beach with hazy views of the Olympic mountain range just across the sound in Washington State. As much as I love the mountains and feel at home amongst the laurels and scree; as much as I was momentarily fantasizing about a ferry trip that would take me into their peaks and valleys, I was also falling deeper in love with Ema. She was starting to feel like home too. Our backs pressed against a log, sand creeping into every fold and crease of my clothing and skin, I turned to admire Ema's golden hair shining against the grey and cloudy Canadian sky. "Keep me here with you in Canada," I begged. Ema laughed at the joke, one I had been making rather consistently since the election of Donald Trump, weaving together my desires for Ema with the desire to escape the tyranny of the current administration of the United States government. "You think I'm joking," I quipped. Ema laughed again and kissed me and nuzzled her face deep into my shoulder.

A couple nights later, I knocked on the door of Ema's rented downtown flat, bottle of wine in hand. Just a few sips in, we were in bed together for the first time. Ema asked me to fuck her hard and deep. She said she was hoping I brought a dildo with me, but I told her I left my cock at home. I wasn't necessarily anticipating needing it on this trip. (Later, she will come to differentiate between my "big cock"—my silicone prosthetic capable of fucking her hard and deep—and my "little cock"—my testosterone enhanced dick-clit capable of bringing other pleasures.) I fucked her with my hands instead, variably harder and faster as she demanded. "I guess I should have warned you about how hard I like to be fucked," she said with a satisfied grin. I smiled back and sunk into her embrace, exhausted and dreaming of what it would be like to stay here on this island and inside Ema.

* * *

Home for me is currently Cleveland, OH, the city I was born in, but returned to only recently after a 20-year stint in San Francisco, a city I grew to love but could no longer afford to live in following a no-fault eviction from a landlord who wanted to flip the property to the market rates of Silicon Valley's new silicon(e) elite. The return to Cleveland—an unexpected reclaiming of a home that had been so violent, I had to leave it—turned out to be a greater salve for my soul than I could have imagined. Finding home in the Midwest has meant finding home in a community so warm and welcoming, it has made homecoming feel like falling into the outstretched arms of the family I always wished I had. Home for Ema is in Vancouver, BC, though I'm not sure she would necessarily call it home. As an immigrant to the country, she remains steeped in the feelings of diasporic wandering and loss. Ema, who speaks so frequently of being unhomed as an immigrant in the West where no one seems capable of properly pronouncing her full name; Ema, who laments feeling outcast as a queer in her fairly conservative family and national culture; Ema, always seeking, always sought.

Home or not, Vancouver is where Ema lives and has made a life for herself. Our hearts and bodies happened to collide for one week in the midst of summer on Vancouver Island. When the week ended, we each returned to our respective homes, promising at least monthly visits and hoping for a future in which home would become a shared space. It quickly became the case that I flew to Vancouver so often, I decided to leave my favorite cock with Ema, so as to avoid potential awkward negotiations with TSA once or twice a month. Besides, she was the only one I was fucking at the time, and though I did enjoy that particular cock for jerking off, I had plenty of other options for my solo times at home. And Vancouver was starting to feel like a second home to me; Ema had become home to me. Ema told me sometimes, when I was in my home on the other side of the continent, she would fuck herself with my cock while she imagined me fucking her. I told Ema that some nights, I could feel her cunt pressed against mine in my sleep. I knew those must have been the nights I was inside her while I slept thousands of miles away.

* * *

When you're falling in love with someone, you are rarely capable of imagining a time when the good will cease to be, when the "us" you become will cease to be an "us." You don't usually anticipate the resentments that might grow in between seemingly innocuous bickering over who sleeps on which side of the bed or who ate the last of someone's favorite chips. You don't prepare yourself for surviving the fallout because all you're focused on is falling in. When you're falling in love with someone on a beach on an island, sometimes you can't even imagine ever leaving the island. When Ema and I came to an end almost a year after our week on Vancouver Island, she asked me to mail her all the stuff she had left at my apartment in Cleveland. I sent her everything, down to the nearly empty tube of sunblock and the half-empty bottle of shampoo. I hadn't left much in Vancouver, some odds and ends, but nothing of real import. Except my favorite cock, one that pre-dated my relationship with Ema, one that had become a part of me in that way our favorite objects do, especially those that serve a prosthetic function. I told her the only thing I really wanted back is my cock. I offered to cover the cost of shipping.

My request was met with a request to never contact her again, followed by endless silence. She never sent my cock, or, I never received it. I started losing sleep over my lost silicone appendage. I even tried to replace it with the exact model, as if that might offer some consolation. A new prosthetic for the prosthetically castrated. But the online shop where I bought my original no longer carried that same cock in the same color—a peachy tone that is as close to matching my flesh tone as one could get from a silicone injection molded, mass produced dick. The only option was a jet-black color. The color of my mourning, I suppose. I did not replace my cock; instead, I found myself increasingly torn up at its loss, obsessing over this piece of me that I had lost contact with. Where is my cock going without me? Whom is it doing without me?

* * *

I wake with a start, my bedsheets soaked in sweat, the space between my legs soaked with sex. I had been dreaming that Ema was on top of me, riding my "big cock" until she came and collapsed next to me. I reached down to remove my cock, so I could cuddle her without poking her, but it wouldn't budge. It was stuck to me, *in* me. (At this point, I should make it clear that this favorite cock of mine was of the strapless variety, the kind where I could insert a bulbous end inside me, hold it in place with my pelvic floor muscles, and fuck Ema with the long, dick-shaped end as hard and deep as she wanted). In my dream, the bulbous end had fused to my insides. My cock had become a part of my flesh, more permanently *mine*. Upon waking, I reach between my legs and feel the wet. I imagine my cunt as an oozing wound where my cock should be, another piece of my body hacked away and taken in love lost and hearts broken.

Another night. Another dream. I am moving through a dimly-lit, crowded space thick with bodies and the thumps of heavy bass. I lock eyes across the room with a butch who solemnly lifts her chin toward me before she swaggers across the dance floor, oblivious of the grinding and pulsating bodies splitting like the Red Sea for her. She sidles up to me and the next thing I know, we are kissing in the corner and she is pulling me toward the exit. A dream sequence time-hop and I am suddenly in Ema's twin-sized bed in her Vancouver bedroom. Ema is sprawled out naked on her bed and I am hovering above her, pushing the bulb end of my cock up inside me while she strokes my dick. Only, I am not myself. I look down and see a pair of breasts where I have none. I rub my hands up my thighs, smooth and plump and hairless unlike my furry solid stumps. As I press the cock against my cunt, I cannot feel my hard dick-clit protruding and rubbing against the silicone ribs at the base of my cock; I reach down to feel a clit that has receded to the times before testosterone. Ema pulls me toward her and I enter her. She moans and I moan, my voice high and unrecognizable. I fuck her until she comes. I rise from the bed, and I make my way to the bathroom where I look in the mirror to see the butch from the club staring back at me.

* * *

Weeks go by. Morning after morning, I wake soaked in sweat and sex. I call my buddy Miles to tell him I am still having the dreams, and it feels like they will never end. As we are talking, I suddenly recall a movie I loved as a child. The film tells the story of a man who loses his hand in a car accident. He searches everywhere for the amputated hand, but cannot recover it at the scene. In my memory, the hand scurries off into the woods, but I cannot be certain this is what actually happens in the film. The horrific thing, I think, is that his hand *is* out there committing murderous atrocities without him, as his psyche spirals further and further into darkness and paranoia. Maybe it's like *The Hand!* I exclaim to Miles. We laugh at the kitsch of 1980s cult horror. But I feel queasy at the thought of my cock out there, doing things—doing people—without me. My phantom appendage living on and fucking and haunting me in all its exploits.

* * *

I know I am wheezing and snoring in my sleep. I gasp myself awake, sucking in any amount of air I can in big gulps, like I'd been starved for oxygen. My bedroom window is open on a cool October night, but the air feels thick and unbreathable. I had been dreaming that I was falling into a dark pit, where I landed with a thud. Suddenly, objects were raining down on me, choking out any glimpse of light, any sweet breath of fresh air. As I thrashed about, the stench of rot and the weight of suffocation overtook me. Though I have never been into breath play, there is something oddly erotic about the dream. When I wake, I am hard and throbbing, even as I gasp for air.

The dreams of my cock—inside Ema, inside other people—begin to fade after that. I imagine my dick covered in a banana peel condom or stuck to a wet and moldy plastic bag. I wonder if silicone ever really breaks down, as I imagine my cock buried in a landfill somewhere, wherever Vancouver sends its trash. Maybe it's on a barge floating aimlessly across the Pacific Ocean. It feels like a part of me went from being unmoored and unhomed, traveling extensively into the bodies of others, to landing upon a slow death of disintegration in a trash heap, forgetting what it's like to have a body to call home. My sleep continues to be punctuated by waking fits of grief and loss and mourning. What a horrific sadness the things we are capable of doing to those we love and stop loving, our hearts and bodies rent. What a violence, I think, to keep a piece of someone, to force them to survive the slow death someone else chooses for their pieces. What a violence to keep us broken and fragmented and dreaming of a fantasy of a wholeness that will never be. What a violence to refuse us home.

# Agglutination

*The distinctive characteristic of Turkish is extensive* agglutination.

Agglutination *occurs when people are given blood transfusions of the wrong group.*

Turkey, I call you fear-pylon-bazaar-cacophony-only
safe-at-uncle's-apartment. I call you
black-and-white-minaret-spiked-never-home,
calling me and pushing me away with Bosporus-breeze,
crossroads-of-hunger, mouthwatering-lamb
sacrifice-country. I only now dare to call you
mine. What culture will swallow me,
all Turkish hairball and millennial speak,
all fomo-homo-poly-queer-schadenfreude-Western-savior,
all born-with-hole-in-chest-but-it-accentuates-pecs?
I wander your waterways for days
but pull apart from you unchanged,
my konuşma a bolus in my throat.
I trace your outline with my words
and never find you inside them.

# *Female Trouble*: Dawn Davenport (Divine)

You didn't open my suburban window—
you smashed it. One clumsy Kung Fu kick.
In the Cha Cha heels your parents refused to buy
for Christmas. At 13 how I wanted to dash
down that vanilla street with you in nothing
but a baby doll nightie and fuzzy blue slippers—
my backside the last damn thing those smalltown drones
would see of me—a blur of bouffant, boobs
and beergut wrapped in chiffon, certain one day
they'd bow before me, a hush stuck in their throats
like the bones of a rotten fish while I'd scowl as if
I'd just eaten dog shit, repeating a sing-song *fuck you*
so discordant, only the strayest cats would dare
follow me home.

# Everyone's an Expert at Something

The more i learn the more i learn
i don't know what the fuck i'm talking
about. To someone who doesn't care
a fig for poetry they'd likely think
i knew a lot, yet in most bookshops
i'm lost, shelves heavy with the bodies
of forgotten writers. It's relative.
a president can say *audacity* or
a president can say *sad* & both eat
the cured meat of empire. When i say
i carry my people inside me i don't
mean a country. The star that hangs
from my neck is simply a way
of saying israel is not a physical place
but can be carried anywhere. It says
my people are most beautiful when
moving  when movement, when
our only state is the liquid state of water,
is adapting to our container. Homeland
sometimes just means what books
you've read, what stories you've spread
with your sneakers. My people,
anyplace you live long enough
to build bombs is a place you've lived
too long—it's relative. My friends,
the only thing I know for sure is
the missiles on television are only beautiful
if you've never known suffering.
My friends the only country i will
ever pledge my allegiance to
is your music, is under investigation
for treason.

# Homeward: On the Queer Peripatetics of My In-between

While I write this, the borders between Canada—the country I live in, my wife's home country—and my home country, the United States, zip closed. I've barely gotten my life between two countries centered on a fulcrum toward something like balance when the pandemic hits North America. Not so much hits as we decide to recognize that we are not separate from the rest of the world. It has been almost three years for me of forms, words, fingerprints, fees, declarations, background checks, policies: ideas made visible, dried in ink, zinging through the wires in megabytes, the invisible coalescing around an arbitrary line that demarcates nations. Tax filing times two countries. No amount of nationalist rhetoric from my home country's capitol can swat microdroplets and particles from the air. Ideas and viruses both dovetail with the human capacity to travel.

Borders are so hetero.
Borders are social constructs.

Halifax, Nova Scotia, where I live now, feels less like a city in another country—one analogous and yet still distinct, foreign, and bound to my home country through continent, commerce, language, and proximity—and more like an extension of land mass which on a map makes a logical and soft curve down to the arms of the cape that nestles the harbor of my birthplace. In other words, this place I now live feels more like part of a bioregion encoded as home in my limbic system and in my heart as well.

"I find something comforting in the way ecology works…it's not possible for me to be native to anywhere, in any obvious sense," writes artist Jenny Odell[1]. In natural phenomena such as atmospheric rivers that carry rainwater all the way from the Philippines to the west coast of North America, she sees an image of "how to be from two places at once."

Where to begin to unpack my bindle of queer itinerancy? I now live in an earlier time zone than my hometown outside of Boston; Nova Scotia, a place where my ancestors have continuously lived for well over 400 years on record, and even

---

[1] Jenny Odell, *How to Do Nothing: Resisting the Attention Economy*

here I am an outsider, a settler, a *come-from-away* they call people like me—a designation that appears to stick to a body here, no matter how long ago the come-from-away came. So long ago I wandered away from the small town that raised me to find my people. I lived in Boston and Provincetown and San Francisco and Santa Fe and Portland, Oregon, all places where the per capita of queer tipped enough so that I could exhale, for minutes at a time, and make and live and fuck and be in a semblance of life that reverberated beyond mere survival. And if the isolation and exhaustion of having your culture, desires, and selfhood subjugated to the quiet margins, darkest spaces, and relegated to someone else's stereotypes was (and remains in certain contexts) was burdensome and brutal for me as white, able, educated, privileged—what of my friends and lovers and family and neighbors and coworkers and collaborators and acquaintances and overlapping strangers who I pass by daily who are racialized, immigrant, poor, dis/abled, as well as queer and trans in body? If I've transversed thousands of miles in a quest to feel safe, and hopefully also loved, what about them?

"The bountiful west is a fragile construction," says the voice of a female narrator in the documentary based on the book *The Cadillac Desert*[2]. There's an apocryphal quote that rattles in my memory from either this film, or perhaps a Ken Burns or some other PBS doc where the narrator says something to the effect that *all the water we have now on Earth is all the water we've ever had*, and ever will have. I remember feeling stunned, frozen in fact, by this revelation. I think about this constantly, while avoiding droplets from unmasked mouths in public space, listening to myself and others complain about too much or not enough rain, or while writing letters to elected officials in a province where I cannot vote to agitate for respect of the Mi'kmaq water protectors who fight extractive industry to save this vital element that circulates always through all of our bodies and lands. Odell echoes this when she says, "there is something immigrant in the air I breathe, the water I drink, the carbon in my bones, and the thoughts in my mind."

In the late 1990s, at the behest of the woman I then loved, I started seeing a therapist about my "gender stuff." The therapist, a silver-haired queer femme lioness, with a tattooed leg flung over her armchair in a repose of infinite cool, said that she worried if trans men would *ever feel like they belonged anywhere*. That the trans men she knew seemed to be adrift between worlds. The worlds I

---

[2] *Cadillac Desert Water and the Transformation of Nature* (1997), a PBS documentary based on *The Cadillac Desert* by Mark Reisner.

supposed she meant, though I didn't ask, were the queer world and the straight world. I wondered what belonging means when you can only bring yourself to a place in fragments.

I got a tattoo at Tattoo City in North Beach "back then," a sailor-flash rigged brigantine on my left triceps. *The ship has to point away from you,* my artist said, revealing a crack of earnestness in his black-metal, upside-down pentagram veneer, *that way you don't cross back over the way you've already come.* The banner beneath my ship reads: *homeward.*

I've lived in places where to be queer was to be multivalent. It wasn't an accident that I found myself here, across an international border, worrying about my aging parents, my huge family, my beloved far-flung friends, wondering when I will ever get to see them again.

*The secret to a long life is knowing when it's time to go,* I remember Shocked singing on those crackling campfire tape recordings. I'd conditioned myself to be able to pull up stakes and move on, an affect of survival that I neatly couched inside the guise of romance. *You got to know when to hold 'em, know when to fold 'em,* the old man advises Rogers' protagonist in a song that ensorcelled me as a child, *know when to walk away, and when to run.* This survival tactic is perhaps coded in my genes from my Acadian ancestors, branches of whom survived the rounding up, the imprisonment, the deportation, the sunken ships, the far-flung colonies, starvation and disease. A survival made possible for many Acadian families thanks to the generosity of local Mi'kmaq bands, an irony not lost on me when I see an image in the local news recently of a white fisherman waving an Acadian flag at a Mi'kmaw fisher flying a water-protector flag in a current settler Nova Scotian attack on Indigenous rights to sustenance fishing and harvesting of lobster.

My Acadian ancestors were a diasporic people, too. They knew when to fold 'em, but they hid out and they came back to their farmlands. And some of them were drawn across geographic markers and invisible lines to places where perhaps more of themselves could be. Or from where they could better survive. Or maybe it was to simply indulge a curiosity of the world outside—a reason that might be easy to dismiss, but that should be embraced, I think. What would our world be if our curiosity about other people and places was given precedence over our fears?

My femme friend Ann once confessed to me in a breathy aside: "I ran into her (The Therapist) once, in our neighborhood. She was with her girlfriend, I think. She was *smoking*." Our eyes widened at the possibility that she, too, was human. She hovered in a queer corporeality that ringed our own. We were hungry for mothers, for elders. She was a sign from the past pointing to a future. She was mythic, but also human, flawed, sucking for a hit of nicotine, of need, just like the rest of us. Like small children who are awed by the realization that adults know other people outside of the family, that their parents have friends and enemies, the scrim was lifted, if only for a moment.

I was lucky to know two of my great-grandmothers, both who lived until my early years of high school. Women live longer; it's a thing. *Is there a freedom in this bonus time for women*, I wonder. Great-grandmother Cecelia lived next door to me growing up. My father built a house on a swampy chunk of Grandma Cecelia's land that she sold to him for a dollar. She was Acadian and came from Cape Breton with her sister when they were teens to clean the houses of the wealthy in the Boston area. The line between Atlantic Canada and New England was much more permeable back then, more of a geographically defined corner of a continent rather than the arbitrary partitions of jigsaw land stolen from its ancestral stewards and divvied up by crowns and rifles and proclamations. People flowed between the countries to make their money.

My other great-gran with whom I overlapped lifespans was my maternal great Grandma Hülda, who came to the States from Sweden. I have few pre-nursing home memories of her, but a fuzzy one includes my great grandfather, Grandpa Johnson—I'm unsure why he didn't get a first name—and one of their cats, an aloof black cat with a bony nub at the end of her tail where fur should have been. Of course, this strange cat was my favorite; the more of a recalcitrant misfit an animal was, the more I saw myself in it and poured all my love into it. *I understand you*, I psychically implored that skeletal cat. The last time I saw Grandma Hülda alive, she was in a nursing home the next city over from us and she didn't know who I was. She fiddled with a bolt on the side of her metal folding wheelchair in a stale-stinking hallway while a woman yelled *Jesus Christ, Jesus Christ* on repeat from her bed. Maybe it wasn't a curse but an invitation, an invocation. I think she was ready to be relieved of her corporeal form. I didn't understand this back then, just old enough to drive, my best friend Nancy in tow, a girl I was maybe not-so-secretly in love with, along for a visit to this strange, sad purgatory, this holding pen before death's arrival.

There is a permeating collective silence from both sides of my genealogy. While there might be a lot of talking, there is so much that is left unsaid, unspoken. There are the family myths that have gotten tossed forward for so long that one forgets what the provenance of the game might have been, while so many facts, so much history, particalizes into dust and no one likes to disturb the layers. They are us, those motes, fragments of us.

Last spring, my grandmother Jeanne died. She was the last of my living grandparents. She was 89, bird-thin and frail, but her mind was still as sharp as an edge of obsidian. She still read *The New York Times* daily and made her way through a stack of historical biographies piled next to the hospital bed stationed in the middle of her living room, where she'd come home to die. The small, comfortable room was a shrine to her children and twenty-two grandchildren and the burgeoning small army of great-grandkids my cousins had started decades before. One wall was completely covered in shelves of athletic trophies earned by my aunts and uncles. A framed picture on the wall included me, a toddler with barrettes sitting on my father's knee, who wore a black suit, black horn rims, and sideburns. In the grainy, black and white family photo, my grandfather holds the corner of a Nazi flag out to the photographer, who was reporting for an article for the Proctor & Gamble newsletter. My grandfather worked in the P&G factory as a forklift operator and shop steward. That terrible flag was a relic, a counting of coup from when he scaled the cliffs of Normandy and overtook a cluster of Germans. Only twenty years old during the invasion, he killed several Nazis and was awarded the Silver Star and the Purple Heart; these were the bright stars in the constellations that our family gathered under. My father said that the Americans in Normandy often took home enemy souvenirs. My aunt Mary, only a year older than me, is also in the picture, in kneehigh socks and a white dress. *That picture could really be problematic taken out of context,* she recently joked to me, and suddenly I saw it in my mind as a stranger might, as someone who hadn't heard the repeated lore for their whole lives, shored up by many books collected by a father who showed you your grandfather's name inscribed in the text, footnotes, or indexes.

The last time I saw Grandma Jeanne alive, I learned for the first time that she'd earned a master's degree in education—I'd long thought my father was the first in the family to get an advanced degree. But she was a teacher, got her master's in education at a time when few women were able to pursue college degrees at all. She married my widower grandfather, a WWII hero who worked in a soap factory and who looked like a movie star and who already had four children.

Seeing my grandmother for what I assumed would be the last time, ensconced in her living room, there was so much I wanted to ask her. It was rare to get a moment alone with her. She had to watch the helm of a huge family. She had five children with my grandfather. With just my aunt, my father and my wife, this was the smallest group of people I'd encountered her with since I was a small child and one time took me into Boston to see the Boston Pops. We'd taken the T into the city and she gave me a small plastic bag of crackers to snack on during the concert. Maybe it wasn't just me then, either. My aunt thinks she might have gone to that matinee concert, too.

I didn't feel sad when Grandma Jeanne died in the same way that I've mourned the deaths of the young in my life: she really lived a long, beautiful life by most standards. She died on her own terms, at home, with her daughters around her and an Irish neighbor reciting three Hail Mary's. At her funeral in St. Bridget's Church, the priest recalled that, at the church's 150th anniversary six years before, he'd asked everyone to stand up and remain standing as they ticked off all the sacraments parishioners had received. My grandmother was the last one standing, having made every single one at St. Bridget's, and now she was completing the final one. This place was not my place but standing there, wondering if some of my second cousins kneeling in pews behind me expected my queer, transgender body to spontaneously combust before the life-size figures of Jesus and Mary, I thought about the three sacraments I'd received in the stained-glass light of this church, the oldest Catholic parish in the area, and thought about what it meant to send deep roots into a place for almost a century. What it meant to shepherd through generations of a family. I grew up in the fold of four generations and I walked away from it all. The message of being other was clear to me long before I had language to corral my in-between. I wondered, I still wonder, what it means to come back. I imagine now that perhaps I can belong, at least peripherally to them, now that I can belong to myself.

I swallow a lump of hurt, an old one, when I am not called over to join my father, uncles, and male cousins to carry Jeanne's casket up the steep granite steps of St. Bridget's. I am excluded from this uniquely male ritual, though I have the same size and strength as my male relations, to carry Jeanne over this final threshold, and I feel a flame of pain scorch through my chest: *I should be one of her pallbearers, as the eldest of all the cousins.* I remind myself that to feel slighted, to feel outside, is as worn and comfortable as an old slipper, and I choose to choke that feeling off until it withers away. And yet, what gulfs the in-between when the rituals of both the gender I left behind and the gender in which I exist both preclude me?

The connection of my aunts and uncles to each other always struck me as mono-lithic—they were a cohesive, tight band, who I loved but always felt outside of. But in the wake of my grandmother's death, my projection of cohesion and collaboration flickers. There is turmoil, and a swift move to disperse material effects. Why can't everyone sit down and have a discussion? At family gatherings, my hard-of-hearing wife has to toggle down the volume on her hearing aids to mitigate the sonic crush of my paternal family. It is like a joyous mosh pit with cold cuts and casseroles and canned beer by the twelve-packs. Convivial and loud and laughing. And yet while there is so much talking, what is being said? Now, in the searing of grief, there is no group conversation. There's (what feels like) a sudden decision to sell my grandmother's house, which stands on the other side of my great-grandmother's house where my cousin and his partner and kids have lived for years. I am horrified and upset by the idea of Jeanne's house no longer being occupied by the family who built it. Won't one of my cousins move their young family into this house? No one can afford to take it on themselves. Even the priceless has a price.

What about the memories and stories seeped into the grass and boulders and woods behind our houses, where we ran like small animals as free-range chil-dren? My father was raised in that house. His father built it with his own hands, next to Grandma Cecelia's house, where my father was born. My father built our house with his own hands. Who would we become if a stranger came to occupy Grandma Jeanne's house? And this person would forever be a stranger, an inter-loper, regardless of how long they lived there.

*I* don't want to move back there. I don't want to live in my old town, in my grandmother's house. I'd yearned, for as long as I can remember, to go beyond the bounds of our street, of our town, of the east coast. The west coast called to me with its fragile promise of a new life, of a place to no longer be in-between but at the sharpest edge of something.

But I am suddenly struck with shame, because I want my grandmother's home to always be there, a place that I can return to, prodigal and at my own conve-nience, whenever I feel like availing myself of a sense of home. I want the place to remain fixed in time. I want us to always gather there, crowded into the small frame that could barely contain the mass of us, made small by our voices and crush of bodies, coalesced around our matriarch, attached to each other by DNA and history, relationships and lore. I realize I want my relatives to maintain a theme park to my nostalgia. I want a place to call home, fixed in time-space, whether I go back there or not. My grandmother's house is placed on the market and I have to reckon with what it means when a place you call home, a steadfast location, a point of return, becomes unfixed and unmoored. What does it mean to go home without my grandmother's home to return to?

And now, every couple of weeks an email from the US Consulate informs me of the extended restrictions on border crossing. July, then early August. The latest one: non-essential travel between Canada and the US is restricted until late October. I read an article[3] that shows interactive maps indicating where the bulk of the US population would have to migrate toward due to the detrimental effects of climate change. The map saturates and darkens where I now live. These climate refugees will migrate en masse long after I'm dead, if I understand the maps correctly, but not too long after. What if the refugee from anywhere was the refugee we cared for? To resist the borders of gender and capitalism and sexuality and nationality, and the most detrimental borders of all—those that knife between self and other—I find I need to stop the silent whistling of anguish about my in-between and embrace it as the thing that might well save me. And to save the self, if we are to believe the relentless indoctrination of Christianity, only counts when you save the *other*.

***

Is it an inherently queer affect to move for love, to wander between cities on a promise of love, to be rootless enough that a beloved can pull the milkweed tendrils of you across miles and borders?

The endless application forms are convoluted even for my partner and me—both native speakers with advanced degrees. I'm eager to join my partner in her country, but it's not like I am escaping imminent suffering in my own country no matter how ominous the current American administration may feel.

I am white, English-speaking. But I am educated, white, Western, English-speaking. Trans and queer, yes, but on paper, by all appearances legally heterosexually married. My application for residency flew through on a breeze, several hundred pages of forms and files and a few thousand dollars later.

---

[3] https://projects.propublica.org/climate-migration/

The doctor's office assistant reaches over the peeling Formica counter and smiles as she hands me a red plastic party cup with my first name written on the side in black sharpie. I place her accent as West African, possibly Ghanaian. I smile back, warmed by the rays of her kindness. A nuclear family, possibly from Myanmar, cluster with me in the tiny waiting area. The father and I exchange awkward smiles, while his wife avoids looking at me. I scan the doctor's office, taking note of the general air of clutter and ennui. Rows of manila file folders with color-coded tabs burst from shelves behind the desk. The family folds into the washroom, and the mother emerges with three party cups of urine. I smile at her; she avoids my eyes. I enter the washroom and pee in my party cup. I place my party cup on the counter alongside the family's row of pee cups. It looks more like the aftermath of a college house party than an official medical process we've all paid a lot of cash to undertake. Even though I am unemployed and cannot yet work in Canada, the cost is just another hoop of many to jump through; money we've cobbled together somehow. By the end of it all, we'll have spent thousands of dollars and countless hours navigating bureaucracy.

I fold my arms across my chest as I wait in an uncomfortable chair, and my right hand cups my ship-tattooed muscle. Is this a step, I wonder, toward sailing closer to home, or of drifting even further away? My wife and I have committed to carving out our own family, merging friends and chosen family and the blood family we engage with and our dogs. We've hung a wall with pictures of our ancestors, many blood, many chosen, some not even human. My wife is estranged from her parents and I can hear the quiet howling of her grief whenever our conversations turn to them, or to family in general. We are constantly bound by family whether we are in contact or not, whether they are alive or dead. They live in us either through their presence or absence.

Maybe all of my tattoos are just sticky notes for longing. I have almost as many tattoos as years I've been alive, if you view the images as distinct entities rather than an ongoing palimpsest of the visual on a body, as I do. Unmoored from a fixed point of identity, these images sketch my map, collage together my narrative in my skin. They inscribe the circles I've made to find a way to live, to reckon with what happens when you step away from the glow of the fire. Everything disappears in the dark, at least until your eyes adjust.

The doctor is a small, compact white man; much shorter than me. Maybe he's trans, too. *Wouldn't that be fun.* He grabs a well-thumbed, definitely not-sterile pamphlet on smoking cessation from a messy shelf in the waiting area and tells me to read a vision chart with that pamphlet covering one eye. The exam will test me for TB and HIV; who knows what else. I've no idea how naked I'll have to get, nor how my so blatantly non-binary unclothed body will impact my application. I never want to have to drop my pants and become the centaur. I tend to withhold my trans identity in most instances of medical bureaucracy that really have nothing to do with the fact of my transness and I likely would not have indicated anything about my past names or gender markers on the immigration application at all, except for the fact that I don't want to fuck this up for us. My wife and I have agreed that I'd be forthcoming about it, to prevent any bias against me for being seen as dishonest by the immigration officials in some way. I tend to see rules as far more malleable and interpretive than she does, but I promise.

The doc asks if I've had any surgeries. I say *bilateral mastectomy*. He looks shocked, asks why, and I say, in as flat a tone as I can manage, that it's because I am trans. And a *hysterectomy*, I add. He's lost in thought. I can feel my cortisol spiking, a rise in temperature. Since he saw the man's face before the horse's legs, what next? What penalty will my gender exact on this process, I worry. Then he says, in a respectful tone, *how would you like me to note that on your paperwork?* I say that I am not sure what the standard wording is for this process, but I see that he's really trying to do right by me. He says with a light shrug, *I just don't want the radiologist to think you had cancer or something.*

Some new friends in my new city, Americans, both trans, who moved to escape physical violence by white people against their racialized sons, also encounter the large red plastic cups. This doctor is only one of two who will administer the required physical for immigrants. After listening to me go on about them, they were on the lookout for the party cups, too. Apparently, the receptionist maybe from Ghana said that they use them because official urine sample cups are so expensive. Here, taxes are high but everyone can go to the doctor, and the hospitals and clinics aren't like day-spas like they are in the US, but rather something you'd imagine perhaps in East Berlin before the wall came down, and yet, the lack of frills or potted ferns or bespoke pee cups is more about a cultural thriftiness and resourcefulness than one would ever encounter in the States, where even if you have health insurance you get thousands of dollars in bills after a direly-needed surgery.

Is the immigration doctor's camaraderie and patience with me, despite my transness, because I too, am white, English-speaking, able to flesh out the business-talk with convivial fluff, I wonder. My whiteness shields me from any attack my queer transness might incur. Nevertheless, I am still grateful to leave this particular medical encounter not too stressed, humiliated, angry, or traumatized.

A couple years after Ann told me about spotting our shared therapist out in the world, smoking, partnered, I went out to fondue restaurant for a friend's birthday party. As I glanced around the table at the baker's dozen of attendees, including Ann, I realized that at least half of us present were clients of this therapist. "If anything ever happened to you," I told her in our next session, "my social circle would be fucked." Now, I think every one of us who saw this therapist and identified as butch or masc back then has transitioned. Does she still worry about us all, wondering where we'll all belong?

***

After seeing a flyer posted on a bulletin board in the downtown central branch of our public library, I apply to be an ELL volunteer at the local public library, in part to reject the anti-immigrant rhetoric of my home-country and to put my privilege in service to immigrants with far more at stake than me, and also because I am underemployed and truthfully, I am lonely. I am an immigrant, too, and I can't yet legally work here. I am used to my time being filled to the tits with work, projects, friends, the camaraderie of my gym, and having familiar places where I walk for hours with my dog and my thoughts. And, here is a skill I have, one that I love to share and empower others around. And, I want someone else here beside my partner to know my name and to expect to see me on a regular basis.

The ELL program pairs me up with two men from Syria. The first guy is middle aged. His frustration with the language barrier is palpable, understandable. His family is scattered all over Europe and Canada. He can't get a job until he can speak English, he tells me. The program at the library is informal, conversational. We peck out an understanding between us by flipping through ELL picture books that annotate every object in the illustrations in both Arabic and English. We use the translation apps on our phones, and I always have sheets of paper on the table between us. I draw pictures, write out the weirdness of English. He tells me that our city is a bit dull for him. People don't gather and dance and eat and celebrate here in the ways that he's accustomed to. He's bored by it. We figure out early on that we live in the same neighborhood.

At the end of our second session, it is snowing. I have a ten-minute drive home, and he has an hour-long bus ride. I offer him a lift home. He invites me into his apartment, and I meet his whole family; his wife, his three children. His wife and oldest kid speak English, but at home they all speak Arabic. I think about how fucking lonely I've been since I moved to this city for my wife's job, and how people just don't really talk much to men out in the world, one of the secret ways in which Western manifestations of the gender binary can cut those who would seem to benefit from it the most. I wonder how strangers socialize in passing in his hometown. And I imagine how hard it must be for my guy to practice this onerous, unruly rule-filled, contradiction-rife language in the rest of his life outside of our two weekly hours together. His wife offers me tea, and I decline in favor of water. She hands me a glass along with a small dish of wrapped chocolates. His beautiful family beams around me with the warmth of a bonfire. His youngest girl, perhaps only three, monkeys up the back of his chair, smiling at me over her father's shoulder. One day a couple of months later, the coordinator emails me to tell me my student will be out for a while, due to an injury, and in the meantime, asks if it is okay to pair me up with another learner. *Will you let him know that they can reach out to me if they need anything*, I ask the coordinator, *A meal? A ride to a doctor's appointment?* But I don't hear from him, and we drift back into being strangers living separate though simultaneous lives in the same city. I wonder now if he's found a job, or a place to go out with his wife and dance. His biggest complaint about Halifax was how there wasn't enough dancing and celebration.

The next guy I work with is a young father. *How do you make friends*, he asks me, interrupting our dissection of some weird vagary of English, and I want to weep.

*I don't know, man*, I say, *it's hard.*

What advice could I possibly offer as a middle-aged trans man socked in by my own loneliness and constant low-grade culture shock? We moved here for my wife's academic post—she has somewhere to be, people who expect her, a purpose. I'm adrift, my days open and shapeless, and instead of feeling free to use this expanse of unemployed time, a condition I've seldom experienced since I started working at age thirteen, to really focus on my writing, the chasm of structureless time dips me into survival mode, where I instead spend hours sending emails to strangers to try to convince them that I am something other than a come-from-away who should be considered for employment. What hell this must be when you aren't fluent in the dominant language, when your nervous system is screaming from escaping war.

*One day I will invite you and your family over for a meal,* I say, wondering if what we have in common, being immigrants, being newcomers, could ever span the gulf of all we do not have in common. At the break we eat stale sandwich cookies and drink scalded coffee. I introduce my learner to two other program participants from Brazil who love soccer. *My* guy loves soccer. *Maybe he can meet up and play with you?* I say. The Brazilians turn to him, eager to talk the game. After only a few weeks of our sessions, the coordinator tells me he has ascended the long waitlist to get into the full-time English courses at the local immigrant support organization, and he filters out of the library program. I haven't seen him since. We live our parallel lives in this small city. I wonder if he ever met up with the Brazilians for a pick-up game, or if he's found work, or if he wonders about his family dispersed across the Middle East and Europe and Canada the way that I do about my friends and family separated from me by borders, pandemic, fear. I wonder if the gulf of his own in-between feels unspanable or if it feels like a strength, something that makes him a citizen of the world despite what politics might say, if he too thinks about the rain on his face being from the places he once knew as home. I never did get to make his family a meal before we lost contact with each other through the library.

For a few weeks, now, those of us living in what they call "the Atlantic Bubble" have been able to return to public space, though with masks required for inside businesses, and strange adaptations to physical distancing in effect. I recently joined friends—I have friends here, now—for a park picnic in the Commons. About ten of us sat in a large, spaced out circle not too far from the playground area. Dozens of families from countless countries of origin played and shared food and laughed and ran around in the waning summer dusk all around us, giving each other friendly wide berths. I hope every single one felt like they were at home.

# Stranger, Brother, Stranger

When I think of our childhood, we're on the third floor, on the musty carpet of our attic playroom, strewn with Playmobil bodies and plastic flowers small enough to swallow. We watched *Rugrats* even though Mom forbade it, and staged sales where we bartered small belongings we had managed to squirrel away. Marbles, rubber balls, baseball cards, and Homies figurines, little stones or medallions we had rubbed some worth into with the warmth of our fingers. I knew you were duping me somehow—you were older, better at math—but I didn't mind, because with my dimes and quarters I could claim pieces of you. Nevermind they were pieces you didn't want. I hoarded them, cherished them, just the same.

I've started to laugh like you. No one can tell except me, and there's no one to tell except you, but I don't call, because you haven't called, and we can keep going like this, I swear, brother, I swear. The last time we spoke we skirted around every important thing, landing on weather and dinner and small jokes we hoped wouldn't offend. Your face on my screen looked just as it always had—there: your Adam's apple; there: your dark eyebrows—and I could almost ignore the collar, the white square peering up at me like a third eye, its judgment unspoken but received. Forgive me, brother. I've been avoiding you, and the difference is noticeable, the quiet has heavy hands. In the dark outside my bedroom window a tree moves like the shadow of a shadow, but I'm not afraid. It's warm inside, and the bed fits two, and before we fall asleep my lover makes me laugh, and the room is filled with you for a few long seconds, and then you're gone.

We're hundreds of miles and thousands of days from where we started, but I can still place us back there, with our matching sharp elbows, sharp noses. On the dirt strip that lined the driveway we used to beach our bikes in ruts so that only the back wheels spun, so we could pedal as fast as we wanted without going anywhere, without risking the speed or the flight or the fall. We lined up end to end, you in front straddling your black frame, and me on my pink, following. We pedaled in tandem, making our wheels whine and whine with the effort of going nowhere at all.

## Zugunruhe

—Clara McLean—

scarcity        coming                    stirring        of the new

    our taut bodies              find        the map

north-seeking        knowing        the cool whoosh        we will never

stop hearing        bearing into        the ache of it        stroke by stroke

    ahead are the hills        that remember        below are

the burning cities        they too        recall us        belong to us

    looking        we will never        marking                stop

the distance                                where and when

Summary: A simple, inexpensive technique for obtaining data. The procedure is to place test birds into funnel shaped cages in migration season. They find themselves standing on inkpads beneath sloped walls of paper. Remove the covers, exposing each bird to the sky.

At nightfall, the birds will turn slowly in a circle, bills tilted upwards, wings spread and quivering. They hop up onto the white paper, only to slide back down. The inked footmarks left on the sides of the funnels have been shown to correspond with each bird's normal migration direction.

The footmarks can then be translated into numerical form. At termination, lids are quietly replaced, the units inverted, and the birds removed by hand from the small ends of the funnels.

The sky is visible overhead.

## In the Wake of a Transfer
### for Nia Wilson

I.
MacArthur was not supposed
to be where your
line ended –

*Nia's gone.*

You were to return home,
ride ricketing rails deep East,
transfer your long way Home –

*A liquified, river of blood.*

Graduate with honors, make
beats bend corners hold hands,
be eighteen –

*In supernova brightness*

You swallowed ancestral
fear to step onto that platform,
your sisters kept close by –

*Cleft carotid rests under tarp.*

A scream like
that ceaseless, sparking grate
will spear a humid night –

*9-car Dublin/Pleasanton in 2 minutes.*

And where do you journey now?
And what sense do we make of this?
Where will your mother's body breathe?          *She illuminates the tunnels*

II.
In the morning, when Her train comes, my Nails punch lunes into my palms. In the morning. In the morning,
Black women gather beneath unseen umbrellas – scatter plots along gray platform – lined
against the walls. In the morning, Black women downcast. Avert their gazes from oblivion,
necks weighted with recall. I boomerang a rage white. Slice a crescent sharp enough to sever.
Tongues that utter this:          *senseless.     Senseless.*

*Senseless.*
when children
become ancestors.

III.

& Mama –

I promise I'm safe on trains here.

& Mama –

I can hear you cry-singing for me.

& Mama –

You gonna find your way back to breathing.

& Mama –

There's so many colors here.

& Mama –

Colors I don't even have proper names for.

& Mama –

We got them dancers out here, too!

& Mama –

Everyone, everything is conductor.

& Mama –

Our trains don't have tracks, just kinda glide like water.

& Mama –

It's warm here, warm like light.

& Mama –

I'm alright, mama. I'm more than alright.

# How To Survive Nostalgia

On the painted aluminum
or the carved mango wood
of each door I've slammed,

some pushed by open windows
cross the room with currents,
some with climbing blood pressure,

I caress each Janus carving.
What if I never drew my Lakshman-
rekha and invited S—

to my wedding? Would my face glow
like the blue god's scrolling
feeds at midnight, less myself,

my own home gutted to its wood-
bones vulnerable to termites?
Does S— mention me in the Iron

& Wine cover they record?
If I never closed any entry
would my house fill with moths?

Would all my silks have holes?
Would there be from the rafters

a bat colony's nightly exodus
to astound me again and again?

# Kennebunkport

On October roads of
New England / damp, leaf-
strewn pavements of gold, red
and yellow / smiling /
holding hands / we drove
into Maine as one / in
our happy bubble / the one that
reflects back / our eyes
naive with love

/ /


At the inn the taut-skinned woman
greets us / hair tightly pulled back / her
thin lips / expelling the heavy "Oh" / in an
overheard whisper / like a sudden
uncontrollable gasp / that weighted,
pregnant word / feebly disguised / with a
strained smile / our room rapidly
reassigned / way up the stairs / far away /
out of sight / betrays its unsubtle message / two
single beds / as if this will prevent our
caress / pointing to a print on the wall she
blurts out / as if in defense or warning / she
is a Daughter of the American Revolution /
"Prepare yourself" I say, "another one's
coming" / as I shut the door

/ /

In the library / the complimentary evening wine
and cheese interrogation commences /
the who, what, where are your wives inquisition /
the blank stares of pink-cheeked family
men / out of manly habit / shake my hand
then look at it, at me / like some sex
I might have had lingers there / sticks on their palm /
might transmit some of me into their pristine
pores / might infect their ignorance

/ /


In our room you smooth the blond hair
on my head / your thick fingers wooing me /
willing to let it slide / happy to let them stay
in their miasma a little longer / but they
pierced the bubble / made me realize
"love conquers all" means a war
must be won / and I can only think of
revenge / if only it was sweet

/ /

At the communal
breakfast / we are led to
a small table in the corner /
the one on the rim of tolerance /
there is a sense a plot has been
hatched within the past hour / how
to keep our kind at bay / how
to keep our love from breaching the
ramparts of their happy clean white linen
illusion / the one I thought I wanted /
the hush laden with words
unsaid / from furtive glances /
from thoughts and judgments screaming
out of the silence / that veil between
their world and ours neatly
hung / with freshly made
biscuits / pretty soaps and
welcome notes / now pricked /
but just like me I can't leave "well
enough alone" / can't betray our love
that way / impulsively I lean across
the table / kiss you / slightly
lingering / fully on the mouth / leaving
the veil on the floor for them to pick up /
to sort out

//

Outside on the sprawling lawn their
statement on a story-high pole presents
itself / a huge American flag undulating
on the brisk autumn breeze /
gazing up / I confront its stripes and
stars / silently demanding /
which ones are we?

# Where You From?

ABANDONED TRUCKS, CONDEMNED HOUSES

Talking with my Mother:

Tuesday I was nervous, walking/ an alleyway to calm down/ tell me why the old delivery truck/ its faded logos/ stringy weeds grown through the rims/ last registered 1986/ why the home with the caved in roof/ withered cedar planks/ and why do I want to steal them/ take them before I leave/ this home

My Mother:

*You can take the boy/ from Idaho/*

*but you can't take the Idaho/ from the boy*

# MORE THAN ITS SHARE

Nicole Blanchard, Idaho Statesman, 2017:

*"a recent analysis of data from the Southern Poverty Law Center, a nonprofit that monitors hate groups and advocates for civil rights, finds that Idaho has more than its share of hate"*

A group of queer activists duct-tape their mouths and block the entrance to the Idaho state congressional buildings. They protest the state's refusal to protect LGBTQ+ people from housing and job discrimination, as well as the omittance of violence against LGBTQ+ people from the state's definition of hate crimes.

The legislators, mostly Republican, roll their eyes in annoyance at the protesters. They call the police and some are arrested. No discussion will be introduced on the house or senate floors on the subject that day. Or any other.

Since the decision by the State Congress to ignore the protesters, queer Idahoans Steve Nelson and Simon Bush/Sierra Simon have been murdered. Their murders have inextricably been tied to their sexual and gender identities.

## KEEP GAY MARRIAGE OUTTA MY STATE!

On the phone, driving down highway 95 through Coeur d'Alene, I see protesters holding poster board and shouting. *Let me call you back.*

I flip the car around in an empty parking lot to get a better look at their signs. Between Prairie and Canfield Avenues, three protesters stand and yell at the cars returning from work.

## IDAHOANS AGAINST GAY MARRIAGE! KEEP GAY MARRIAGE OUT OF IDAHO!

It's April of 2015 and people on the news keep saying the Supreme Court is going to announce their decision on same-sex marriage at the end of the upcoming term. With a 5-4 conservative majority, they say pressure is on Justice Kennedy for the swing vote.

Growing up queer has made me pessimistic. Growing up queer here has made me pessimistic. I don't think anything will change.

The protesters' boards are concise and hint to the debates I see on the news. *Are Americans ready to see these… gay… people married?*

The opposition seems less concerned with state-sanctioned bond between people of the same sex or gender, but more with the existence of the bond itself. By keeping same-sex marriage illegal, they hope to deny us our personhood.

These protesters hope to not only keep marriage equality out of their state, but queer people as a whole out of their state. Despite being a born-and-raised Idahoan, it seems the debate my state is having is whether or not I am welcome here.

I am not their Idaho, therefore, I can't be an Idahoan. It is my home, but it is their canvas to use.

# MANY MORE MATTHEW SHEPHARDS

Maureen Dolan, *Coeur d'Alene Press*:

*"Carly Demers, of Spokane, is ignored as she proposes to Christine Newman, of Spirit Lake, during a demonstration in Coeur d'Alene. Newman and her brother-in-law, Shaun Winkler, center, attended the protest in support of the Westboro Baptist Church group's view on the homosexual lifestyle."*

This protest was for a production of *The Laramie Project*.

This was at the community college I graduated from.

The protesters are from my hometown.

I am a fag from their school.

Carly Demers and Shaun Winkler are not the story,

and neither am I,

but we are part of it.

Dad leans back in the cloth seat, propping his wrist on the steering wheel. We've just passed La Grande, Oregon. We're heading North. The next few hundred miles will be easy interstate driving.

We're still in the range of Boise radio stations, but just barely. The chugging heavy metal guitars alternate with piercing static in the speakers of the U-Haul truck.

"You're going to love it up there, Keegan," he tells me.

He just got a job at a small school in North Idaho. I've spent my whole life in the southern part of the state, but it's a whole different country up there.

I'm from a high desert full of twisted sagebrush, but our new house is by a lake. There are trees and mountains all around us. Dad keeps telling me how lucky I am to be able to grow up there.

"It's god's country, Keegan," he says, "The water. The forests. It's god's country."

# Colorado

cactus nettle to the heart
     of sky
people dripping peaks
     from their palms'
passion neither of god
     nor of gold

silent as the forethought
     to this skin
the self strewn
     red

## have you had your malta today?

*(my grandma's prayer speaks for my mom)*

mijo, did the sun wake / you up this morning or / were you needed? i know / how it is. living / as a moon mother. nothing moves as much / when you don't. when you've only got / a bed's hollow breath to speak for / your work. you know / how it can be. getting home / to a chorus of refrigerated foods never / sounding good together. but you / eat. you eat what / your ma made you. / you know how many hands went / into your living? mijo, you don't have to / like your life. you think i did? you think / el campo is earth's heaven? you think / i rode jesucristo's wings / to healthy? you forget we can kill / what we raise? / you forget we don't love / what we kill? but we love. / there's chicken on your plate, / a mosquito net around your resting head. / you know you can / rest. you know you gotta. don't / make your ma worry like this. / like she didn't try / making an angel of each of your sisters. / like she didn't send your brother to Colombia to find god in his family's soil. / like she don't fill her bed's empty with prayer. / you think i raised her to love / with any other language? you think / she needs to ask god to better you?

\* \* \*

*(and my prayer whispers)*

i know god / can't better me. i don't / know that i can. ma / raised me to love the air / between prayers like her voice / lives in all of it. i seem to only fill / beds with a son's disappearing. i, ghosting / myself before my siblings / can hear the holy in my going. ma, / i am trying to keep myself / boy for you. / i can't make you miss me / like that. i haven't given you enough to remember. i haven't / echoed your land's language enough / for you to see me as sacred kin. i can tell you i'll eat the arroz con pollo y ensalada / when i get home, but there will always be an ocean / growing too big for our wings to get us over without forgetting which love we are / going towards my hands move from one love to another / forgetting the heaven in letting / go. but i let go. getting / home never sounds good / with a chorus of hollow / breaths crescendoing behind me. i will see you / moon mother and move the morning / away from me. i will stay / waking in the air between your loudest hymns. /

i will stay waking
i will stay waking
i will stay waking
i will stay waking

# Sunday Polarized Lenses

Nothing looks nice on this couch.

Even uncles sodden in the ubiquity of always almost getting divorced.

But the nice thing about bringing the fruit salad is that you can put mango in it and leave out all the shitty fruits.

Fantasizing through an hour of names for a future DJ self leaves me where it always has—Drugdealer Boyfriend.

I'm told they are very very upper middle class, or maybe lower upper class.

One of everything on a doubled paper plate is really the last thing anyone has ever wanted.

More is more of the melted coleslaw that "still in love with Carl" sounds like.

I miss the petulant teenage apathy and resentment of being told to put on the pastel sweater and get in the car, we'll be outside.

Someone's not-wife (mine) is swept off her feet by someone else's father.

Evidently there will be skeet shooting tomorrow for those interested.

If only you, they, all watched more porn.

My own rented window is decorated from outside the house with the dried pointillist blood of a self-jealous robin.

The flashiest part of me gets off on guilt.

What can't be monogrammed?

Honestly, who?

# First house and space negate one another

*Mei-mei Berssenbrugge*

Your shirts plus their shirts was a lake shimmering
Till you got too close.
Someone with a burnt face lurked
At the back door, disappearing at sunrise
After triggering the motion sensor all night.
You robed, disrobed in strobe light; you
Exhausted each other screaming into the
Knife-edges of blinds, backlit, blinking on and off.
Alone, you biked beneath sheets of Spanish moss
In the evenings while pale bodies disappeared
And reappeared in the scrub, and it was…
              You want everyone to know this:
There was quiet, too: pedals whirring,
Azaleas in bloom, kudzu tightening its grip.

# Blue Heart Baby

Everyone wanna put hands on a piece of your life.
Look at it: how it sags in the eigengrau,

like the yellow belly of a bitch heavy with litter.
No better than that meddlin-ass moon, full

as your own breast, hanging low between buildings.
People hang from the ropes your heart has let down.

The chaos of stars feels up the dead air. Tiny blue flames
in the eye bone of the young-old junkie girl

follow you around the floor of your humming days. &
have you seen yourself? *I think I am weak & without purpose,*

your father texts you from the kitchen, sauced up,
after he rolls his heavy body over the loaded pistol

he laid on your bed. *Get used to life.* Every piece
of advice is one the giver followed to his own

bitterness. You roll the heavy body of the car you loot
from your failed fiancé down the highway. Even

the wheel, wobbling with fury, insists on hanging on,
you must make it to each new mourning alive. Beyond

your silent mouth, what can you use to protect yourself?
The deceitful company of crowds will fail you, have you

out here with your young body, in the cold, a house
dress, barefoot on some other woman's back porch

where no one knows the address. Let it be,
if this moment is of use to your life. & how long

is a moment in time indistinguishable as speed—
peep the ant-sized airplane creeping across the crescent.

How to wake up the next day & the next & not simply
after a decade? After 13 blue moons? Stretched belly &

empty veins? The gas of constellations run out. Heart weighted
low in the sky. Your chances scattered across the dead years.

## Would I Change All I Know for Unknowing

east where you're never going back. houses
on the hollow. drinking enough to kill
yourself. teenage bullshit. wanting to kiss
your best friend. twilight of the tire iron.
dad yelling *you're not sick, are you?* deer down
the trailway at season's end-of-slaughter.
in piles. unreal as your fever feels. path off
of that same road, where mom broke her
arm one winter. fell on february
ice. didn't realize for days after –
said that it hardly felt like anything
at first. lamplight from our neighbor's front porch;
windows spectral the woods' leafless maples.
in memory, this all happens more than once.

in memory, this all happens more than once:
windows spectral the woods' leafless maples,
the lamplight fits from our neighbor's front porch.
they said they hardly heard anything
through the ice. didn't realize for days after.
gone one winter, well into february.
that same road where mom had broken into her
unreal. pile-up of fever dreams. no path
out from that season's end. the slaughter
sound of dad yelling. *I'm not sick deep down*
I think, lit in unironic love for my best friend. he tires
of me. our teenage bullshit. he wants to kiss
girls down at the hollow. I'll drink to kill
off east coast as point of no return. that's home.

in memory, this all happens more than once: east, where you're never going back. houses. windows. spectral, the woods' leafless maples on the hollow. drinking enough to kill the lamplight fits from our neighbor's front porch. yourself. teenage bullshit. wanting to kiss (they said they hardly heard anything) your best friend. twilight of the tire iron through the ice. didn't realize for days after. dad yelling *you're not sick, are you?* deer down. gone one winter, well into february, the trailway at season's end-of-slaughter. that same road where mom had broken into pieces. real as your fever feels. path off of its unreal pile-up of fever dreams. no path. the same road where mom broke her- self out from that season's end. winter like an army. slaughter. the february sound of dad yelling, *I'm not sick.* deep down, ice. *didn't realize* – for days after I think, lit in unironic love for my best friend. he tires. says that it hardly felt like anything with me. our teenage bullshit. he wanted to kiss first. lamplight from the neighbor's front porch; girls down at the hollow. I'll drink to kill windows, spectral the woods' leafless maples, off east coast as point of no return. that's home. in memory, this all happens more than once.

—Dorothy Chan—

# Triple Sonnet, Because You Are Not My Home, You Are Not Home, You Are Not My Family

When my brother's fiancée makes fun of me
      for liking both boys and girls, I think about
how we choose our own families, and yes,
      I've got a complex going on when I'm not
my parents' favorite on any given day,
      because I think my brother gets a free pass
just for engaging a *nice* Chinese girl who
      wouldn't be caught dead in a short skirt
or bright red lips, unlike me, and who even
      says the word fiancée anymore—I thought
we were past that, and I don't need this hetero
      agenda shoved down my throat when I'd rather
be sucking on dick or eating pussy or grinding
      with some gorgeous in a club or laughing over

      drinks with someone who actually gets me,
and keep pouring me whiskey, honey, baby,
      keep pouring me whiskey, because I come from
a culture that's inherently homophobic,
      the way girls who love girls in Hong Kong
rent hotel rooms for afternoon rendezvous,
      only to never see each other again, and oh,
how my mother from Hong Kong says that blood
      is thicker than water. And I love her, but I don't
believe her. I don't believe these old school
      Chinese ways passed down from my grandparents,
passed down from my father, unlike my brother
      who *wants* a wife and two children and a white
picket fence and a house, and I love my mother,

but I don't believe her during the holidays
      when my brother asks me about my love life—

the *When was your last date?* And *Do you even*
      *like guys?* remarks—how his fiancée thinks
she's helping when she says, "I promise you,
      Dorothy, there are good guys out there…
like your brother." And no thank you, lady.
      No thank you with the Freud. No thank you
because being queer is sexy as hell. No thank you
      to my parents' Home Sweet Home sign shaped
like a pineapple. No thank you to these bags
      and bags of lip balm, because this woman
doesn't understand femme. No thank you.
      You are off my tree. But I don't even have one.

# The Gleaning

The fields are on fire—
the blaze, this time, deliberately set.

I'm closing up the house, packing
just what we can carry.

We'll walk together,
bound to each other

as smoke-spires
halo the hills beyond.

       —But how will I explain

the things I have kept,
the things I have given away.

SOUTH

# Stay Safe

Tap the bowl you're made of:
shards. We say: Stay safe. Cosset
as a body in a bath, or at the bottom
of a lake. Someone was safe here.
Stay. A wall to stand behind,
a window. Remain untouched,
your hands immobile. Cradle.
Breathe cautiously as cells resettle.
Stay the course. Stay with me. Shelter
here among the embers.
Safe. We say and say.

# To San Francisco with Paul

We abandon our vertical seasalt Legoland in a honking, steaming, close-cuddling procession of backlit raindrops trickling down too few finite rivulets. Foot brake-bound, I jabber, Paul nods, flits to another station, trains his camera to the top of the Aon Center—zoom, scan, pull back, looking for jumpers. None today, but he keeps skimming, US Bank, Wells Fargo. No, it's 2003, and everyone's happy.

We lose our tagalong convoy within the hour and then there's just space and we can't figure out why LA's so crowded when here to San Francisco is just truck stops and oil derricks nodding and those crisp white wind turbines they thought would ruin the view but the view's just mountain crusts growing mold and creosote bushes stranded all across the flat like props from an earnest Western.

We're three weeks Californian and already possessive of our peeling paper trees, our *envíos de dinero* signs, our inland seagulls nibbling strip mall trash. We're three weeks friends and already possessive of the other's secret, packed tight and melancholy as the cows, scented miles away. Now we've said it, it's true, and we're going to San Francisco. In this state of strangers, there's no one to mind.

When the gutter-ball sun lands between rows of pistachio trees, we can only tell hills from sky because they're so much blacker and firmer than backcountry firmament with its pores to ease out the pressure of all that light. We'll arrive late to a scene that's all sparkle, hills and sky reversed. We'll find no underage bars in the Castro, so we'll eat Ben & Jerry's and watch our people and wonder what people we'll be.

But that's hours from now. We pull off for gas station tacos and sit in the forecourt dripping salsa and beans on our dusty flip flops. We have no people yet, Paul and me, just each other and the hope that there's no god to mind.

# Rodeo

     i.

The four-wheeler is a chariot. Horse-wraiths
Kicking up a plume of spirits in the dirt behind us.
Her arms kudzu around my middle. Out here,

In the desert, everything is invisible.
Only the locusts' flat buzz gives
Them away. Everything native & quieting

Perennial & nighthawk black
As we ride through: the cowgirls,
The witch & the water sky-mirror-split,

The severity of squall lines. Also, the lips
Parting air like lightning & the girl
Blowing bubbles—in each one
                   a rainbow.

     ii.

She thinks I am worth a burnt tongue.

     iii.

Her small gifts, oddities,
Meet me at my mailbox.
Sheer curtains glitter
Above us in the currents, dance

In the heat that suffocates this land,
The lone harp & low grind of

Its history. We hold.

She takes me to dirt raked
Into rows, to stadium lights
In the middle of nowhere. A bed
On a porch. I am a horse

Skipping sideways down her lane, the stem
Of an American flag that's been cut into strips
Dangling in my mouth like a toothpick.


iv.

Our shadow town          Underneath the firmament.
Our sudden lapse          Of sound


In the undertow, swept up by her current—
Butterflies collide with my

Whipped tail, my
Tremoring eyelashes, my

Heavy teeth. My
fattest loc grazing her breast.


v.

Tonight                    she finds me like this:

Blood                      lacing my chin
Two wide eyes              peering over the torso

Of a bronco               from the other side.

# Exile

There's a gift I was given, a horse
with its broken legs. Lord, I tend
to this brief thing called life like a man
caring for a beast that eats what it loves.

I can't help this loneliness of people
walking away from my eyes, it is how a city
knows its walls have fallen.

The plane breaks through the clouds
& San Juan comes into view, this city
shall survive this water, I say.

Once I knew where my circle was
in the world, I could walk into forests
with just a book & find my way
back to my mother's chest.

I should tell you my mother's chest
was a tree, beside it a flower blossomed
and was called grace, I should tell you
I once saw the river drowned a bone,
maybe this is death, maybe this is a mother
welcoming a son. The driver says welcome
and I know he means stranger; I know he means
what drives you into the world.

I have come here to find what I'd lost
but it will spit me out, a seed floating
on water, a boat, a life without the luck of trees.

The city stretches into a fort,
as if it is still ready for war, as if a battleship
sits eternally before her eyes. I have known this fear,

it is called reaching into the future for the cut,
meaning I still see the men who called me homo,
meaning dirt, meaning sin, meaning their hands
shall divide my body into a barren field.

I once woke up to the beast
in my chest cage, I held it tenderly
before severing its neck.
My therapist called it a sacrifice,
meaning I saw the blood even in the dark,
I smelled it and knew home drowned last night.

Father, here is what I was given, a boy, the beauty
to walk back to the knife. The man saying grace
as if blood isn't pure enough and this city. Here at night,
I will walk into anything that calls me home, it will hold me
for a while.

I've seen my mother's bed this way, the burgundy color
of bedsheets, the walls with old photographs, her skin.
Here my mother is alive, she's my city and I hold her close.
Mother, stay with me for a while, stay before the sea comes
to wash us clean of our thirst.

# Kitchen

*Dear Sister Soldier Project,*
*Thanks for the wonderful gifts*
*It is so hard to get black hair products here*
*I have started wearing wigs to protect my hair*
*The water, the sun, the dust all broke our hair off*
*A lot of the women choose to go natural here.*

nappy

*I recently arrived in Iraq to join Base Balad and the lack of sufficient ethnic products was one of my main concerns, not only for myself but others. Although there are a few ethnic hair products in the base exchange, they are very limited. Additionally, there is a severe shortage of 220V hair appliances, such as hair dryers, curling irons, and flat irons. After only one week of being on ground there was much talk amongst some soldiers referencing the condition/appearance of some of our female soldiers' hair. These comments were very offensive although they were not referencing me in particular I still felt a sense of pity for those they commented about.*

nappy hair

real

Nappy

You swirl around with a three-foot
Towel atop your head
An impersonation of Barbie without Ken
Take your left hand under
Flip the towel to the other side
Do it again from right back to left
No, there aren't any blond bangs hanging
But all that will take
Is your best imagination

Forget the aspirations of the nappy.headed.black girl
Remember the heartbreak of *The Bluest Eye*
You wore a wig to two proms & not the same one

*The heat here is just killing my curls.*

Ok. Chin up.

You sit & wait your turn
There's a chair near the stove
There's a hot comb on the flame
There's a sizzle when it hits
The nape of your neck
Your kitchen is nappy, real nappy
You're too young to comprehend
Dr. Miracle is lye-N in wait
Dr. Miracle has declared war on bad hair
Dr. Miracle works on women or men
Dr Miracle wants to tame your original sin
Your naps, the bull's-eye target of his confidence-killing capitalist affection

*Dear Sister Soldier Project,*
*Dr. Miracle is a little too strong for my hair, BUT it was the #1 product for some of*
*the other ladies. Many of us suffer the up-keeping of our tresses b/c of the water and*
*lack of ethnic products available to us. We receive mounds of care packages from very*
*supportive and loving people, but rarely ever are there ethnic products shipped. So*
*again, I want to personally thank you and your team for what you are doing to bring*
*smiles upon the faces of those who require ethnic products as we continue to defend*
*freedom.*

An aunt, her strong
arms
The plastic comb through your head
One unbraided section at a time
Your scalp yelps
The pain better not back talk too loud
Shoot through your mouth wide
Or she'll pull harder not softer
Scent of burning hair, her specialty

Afro 6"
Hair
Afro 6"
Good &

Hair without lye
high
without lye
high
Hair without lie
Afro 6" high

Your Hair:

raised fists

Dear Kitchen,
There are some things you should know about hot combs.

> #1 "you know the smell of a hot comb miles away"
> #2 "you should hold your ear"
> #3 "if the comb gets too hot you could burn up your hair"
> #4 "if the comb gets too hot you could burn up your skin"
> #5 "relaxers and hot combs don't get along"
> #6 "a clean hot comb works better than a greasy one"

Dear Kitchen,
There are some things you should know about me.

> Afro 6" high
>
> I cannot lie
>
> Razor sharp bald fade
>
> I cannot hide

Dear Kitchen,
There are some things you should know about yourself.

> Many take offense to your name
> Everyone has a right to self-determination yet many are not amused
> If this nickname of all nick names continues to be used
> Under the false pretense of cleansing the sins of the unholy nap
> Perceived as dirty & un.kept
> Many will resist

In the sixties
Many black females enlisted in a different war
Fighting for the right to wear
Their original hair
Fighting sickle cell
the cops
the man


nappy. hair                            real

nappy


*Dear Sister Soldier Project,*
*The summer is quickly approaching, and being out here really dries our hair out*
*causing it to break off. Although we are soldiers, we are still women and it's important*
*that as a woman that we always feel good about ourselves.*

Dear Kitchen,

Happiness
Cannot be defined by
stuff others think of you
O my dear I reclaim my
image of you like wood
O soft tangled one
Truth is Dr. Miracle
Has    made    a    business
conniving self confidence
Truth is Dr. Miracle
Doesn't care about us
Could never save a life

Note

Kitchen includes excerpts from deployed African American female soldier thank you
letters who received donated black hair products from the Sister Soldier Project in
operation from 2007 to 2012.

# Brown Out Shouts

this is for Matea who dances the bomba
with hands that crest moonhips
and who admittedly, kisses harder than she loves herself.
every trans, genderqueer, futchie, fairy, AG, butch queen,
anything with roots arches toward her, their arms like petals
soaking up her light.

and this is for hard ass Krys who doesn't want anything
to do with brasso or that jrotc uniform, but just
wants three meals a day for his brother
and a brand new binder for his chest.

for Javi, who takes his tequila quick.

for Aqua Starr Black.
because they had the bravery to re-name
themselves: aqua. starr. black.
sometimes you just gotta call out your power
cuz no one else is gonna do it for you.

Maria is a dancer clasping onto hardwood by the heels
but serves our coffee at the diner always wit' a smile
and always with her hair on-point.
she's pissed off cuz her partner cannot afford to go to the hospital.
although, you can't see it, her heart breaks because no papers
or government can explain how this person in the bed
makes her laugh like a gutteral fool.

for JP who draws sketches sneaking them in your purse.

for Celiany whose caliber demands that the very least of her lovers
have the following traits:
*dexterity, initiative, and someone who can "lay it down."*

for every son shaped in bullets, your heart as compact as
a trigger, your voice a sharp wind song that wants to lay a forehead
down on the chest of your boyfriend.
let your letters survive the wars, jail cells,
let the meter of your words swoon your lover back to the bed,
as you take turns turning off the alarm on the nightstand with
your toes, elbows, orgasms, and in between kisses.

for that lonely Korean guy Jake who found me in a group of
500 white people in the frenzy of the Sugar Club in Dublin, Ireland.
*I make do* he said.
*We've got one grocery store and I practically live there.*
I mean, my kimchi is decent.
we can still see him shrugging
in the strobe lights, hungry for somewhere else.

this is for you this afternoon, spring cleaning your blues away,
maybe in your favorite t-shirt, maybe you called in sick,
maybe your body rattles, maybe missing your pamilya back home,
maybe you are waiting for that next shot to find home in yourself, maybe your
voice is hoarse from asking strangers for food,
maybe you lost a loved one or are about to lose yourself,
lost in the whimsy of musical notes,
the rhythms can consume the sadness, if you let it.

for my dearest Sarwat who sat on a hill, held up the sun, looking at all the
fiiiine transgender and queers of color and said without saying,
*Umm. I am not going to that plenary/workshop/speech. You go on ahead. I'm gonna
stay here. mm hmmm, I deserve this.*

for español, pangasinan, patois, pidgeon, mandarin
love poems you write.

for those babydykes and trans youth who sprout out from
the neighborhoods described to tourists as,
*don't go there. its dangerous.*
rolling up their windows from our existence.

for you who fights for our rights,

for you who laughs too loud,
for you who eats too much,
for you who twists wrists by paintbrush,
for you who will not let your spirit pass up a sunset or a protest
even when you think you deserve less sometimes.

for you
because there's a brown out right now
and by that I mean there is no electricity,
which means life is crashing and pouring down

and by that I mean I am lonely,
which really means
that we are brown and trans and queer and out
and we've been told too many times that all of those

cannot belong all at once. that based on those odds,
we equal death.

for you / for us / for we
because without explanation, we exist
and you, you like all of our ancestors before,
you live it so fiercely that even when injustice sets in,

this rumbling sky houses your breath and
that is better than any survival story,
that, that is joy being born.

# more like a comma  or a breath

Someone brought a papaya to my door and said, "Wait three days to eat." I have. And in the time spent waiting I have made a list of ripening things.

Soon the portal between us will close or open and a tumult will follow that resembles hell breaking loose or all at once we are thrown into plexiglass. Here you go:

Papaya, flametree, dwarf star, nest of sticks and grass and stones, a woman named Alice. Tomorrow we'll have news and breakthroughs. Today we ripen.

This afternoon a cloud channel above Tucson and Al's  a knot of muck and rot   a cool day and all that smell when three black-haired white men stumble from an unmarked truck parked under a red and yellow Wells Fargo sign   the men sit at a table too close to where I write outside a Starbucks  everywhere vivid against the grey road   the grey sky   the fingered mountains in fog   this America   this bellowing   this account of alcohol and staggering rage   I close my eyes and remember your sweet papaya  the ripening stars and their whispers

The moon heads backwards today so we better lie low beneath the so-called radar, beside the dog who understands the words: "Wanna go back to bed?"

For a decade I found coral among the jellyfish. Sea beans and sea hearts and sea lace. Now I'm inland: swimming pools, salt shakers, suicidal humans in earthbound vehicles.

Whenever you're in Tucson I imagine you're splashing love all over the desert dwellers. Who love you back, like hummingbirds.

Do you remember when there were lockers in airports? in Grand Central? when you could ask a neighbor in the chair next to you to watch your bags while you walked around to stretch your legs?   I'm flying east   leaving my loves   my house and mountains   I wave to you across the clouds   tonight full of little boys with their little stuffed bears   I watch all of us   our walking bags of chemistries   self-propelled   happy on carpets   shouting hello! hello!   I stare at the purple fin of the plane against the Las Vegas sky   I see myself looking back   my father's face   not yet stooped but bald and stubbled grey   I see all the sweatshirt forms of pink   the moon   only backward when it's green   when the sea   when the tide   when in pools when in love

Now a dozen tiny lizards run across my path. It's said they eat nearly anything that will fit in their mouths, their own tails included.

A lizard in the house is lucky, it's said. Not for the lizard, of course. Dried up in the back of my underwear drawer, wondering how he ever got himself in such a  predicament.

I can't stop the feeling that today is a game-changer. If you were here we would find a way to stop the world from tipping over. We would eat soup.

Like my breasts when I had them    my grandmother's matzoh balls were always small and hard    even when the cookbooks assumed they should be fluffy and soft I loved those dense little spheres and saw my reflection in her broth and the bones she cooked specially for me    marrow spread thickly on rye bread    far from my grandfather's teeth    she hid candy in her girdle drawer    stashed between thick white nylon stays    piles of red hots    Brach's marshmallow peanuts    long paper strips of pastel sugar dots

Oh, elegant tasty homespun orb, be you dense or fluffy, afloat among veggies and golden meat or buoyant in a bowl by yourself or with a twin—

you are the yummiest orb of all. I will love you until my dying day, my soul grieve loudly as it lands on a cloud where eating has been pronounced passé.

For you are a cloud yourself, dear sphere, spinning along in my soup of dreams, where grandmothers and matzoh balls defy gravity, immortal.

If I am immortal so are you    a grief met along the river path to a bakery where I look into the window at a cake I won't eat    how perfect it seems    certainly not for the mouth    suddenly you are there    sitting happily on the top of the meringue dressed this time in long overalls    your hair unwashed and falling into your eyes your beard a gender all of its own    as are the patches on the elbows of your shirt    a bright paisley from the early seventies    as vivid as it was then    I push my nose harder against the glass and realize you have been on that cake for a while now    sitting under a yellow umbrella to protect you from the sun    of course you have been living on a beach    can you show me the way to join you?

It seems I drop into my soul when I go to meet you in our pasts, our futures. Have you noticed, living as you do in the space between words, the quiet there?

Today's a funny day. Colors close in and I hear my name, the way I always do in this 10th month when veils are thin and the dead brush our cheeks.

So what of our weakness for portals that push us here and there, forth and back? From God knows where, I'm loving you.

God does know   in the ham-fisted and broken sidewalk hurled into the street where I watch the front loader dig down to find a little house   an entrance there too   in the pee on the toilet seat   our mess   the mess of mud   or the rain that makes the mud   or the landslide that brings my mother out of her grave   or the sea at dawn looking toward Margaree   or the hail   some crater of the lost winds   coming and going   I say why   and then why again   until I remember a room full of God in the morning   a leg and then another leg   my trail out to you   my path in to know that the swirl speeds up before it slows down and becomes a heart that gathers all the lost into its right ventricle   hinged but not loose   nothing rattles   the fibers so strong   no earthly intervention will break them

There are so many words to hide from these days—suddenly it's November—but I am wordless in your room full of God. The veil between us mere paper.

Today I read the story of a friend's marriage. She's been trying to tell it for twenty years. She said: *Women fear that men will kill them.*

I remembered I was afraid a man would kill me and my children. It was after I met you. After I moved to Chicago. It was before that too. And since. And since.

The faint smell of gas when the veil falls away   I trudge through the ash   a dark dense cloud of it when the heater turns on   keeping warm exhausts me   the lack of sleep through the changing time   our bodies   our sex   gone from us now   I wake with a clutching   doors that do not pry open   ceramic pots thick with themselves and full of stew thrown against the day   I remember the words   shouts nearly lost under the sound of breaking windows   *liar*   *killer*   *stranger*   *fraud*   what's left? a car   a trace of green   a monthly payment   a sieve to filter the fumes   you will nod and I will run down the stairs   fly through the end to you   I know you will not think less of me when I arrive

The world revolves around the mind of a jay. She's the axis and we're in orbit around the blue of her as she yells for us to stay the hell away from her babies.

I was born *alive*, says my birth certificate, which is good to know. Good to think of my squealing self as real. How do you like that?

Now follow your trustworthy feet, my friend, to where the unknown whips us in the face, where we might see the reasons we gained who we gained along the way.

I hear your calls and like on a ladder I start to climb   walking perpendicular up the granite walls toward a pinprick of light   but after three steps I reverse myself carefully backing down into the round triumph of black   my velvet   my home on the steepest side of the coldest day of the shortest year of my life   there are no windows along this tunnel   ribbed and mucosal like the inside of me   no longer the dry riverbed of my sleep   as simple as it may have seemed I knew that going up was not the way to find you   now the wind my only guide through the grassy dark   leading me away from the gaping sun into an unknown landscape   lava somewhere but not far   my feet trace the underground fissures where the rock begins to warm

And words are so much fun. The rustling of the birds and the wind and the vine and someone else's mouth on the page.

For example: *Half of the time we're gone, but we don't know where.* (Paul S.)

This week was dark. A tunnel going somewhere. A multi-natural light at the end. If I didn't love you so much, these words wouldn't even exist.

In our dust   I see them   those tiny specks in a wave   in a shelf of fog   like a canvas at first blank   then the rivers begin   no need to squint   there's a riot of blues   all the little marks that make a tree   a walking stick   a stubby hill   the waters of Ma Yuan   the smudge of bird calls   all together a breath   the faintest world lit by a sky of stars   you can see them can't you?

Even blindfolded. Soon we'll be back in the desert where stars die in plain sight, where we'll both be warm and wishless.

If it's true we defy the odds by being born, then to actually meet each other in this lifetime must be an off-the-charts event.

The first time my friend Lydia saw snow she was driving in Georgia and didn't realize wipers worked for the white stuff too. She pulled off the road in terror and joy.

If it's also true that we defy the odds by living    driving on cliffs through desert roads to an abandoned shack where we open the door to find a layer of salt on the table    we are flooded by dust mites and the molecules of your good feet    your good hips and the owls    I can't count the visions there are so many    slow down you say each leg you say    each toe you say    each forest full of trees where each tree holds a body like a hand    palm facing out    interrupting the whole system that pays death with an allocation of bodies    I count my liver and my heart    I give half to you these are the brakes    even in the snow

Oh, if you were here we would both be cold now. How do we look from above, running around with our hips and our feet and our owls?

One day three friends hitched a ride on me and I spun them around just for fun. It was the best way to illustrate an allocation of bodies. (You are a genius.)

There. Buddha has moved up to the back porch and is watching the squirrels mate. Or ignoring them. It's hard to tell. Buddha is so deadpan, so chill.

Buddha and all    we go flying into the fuzzy air    thank you for the spin into the infinitudes of tides    ever in retreat and come close    incubators of kindness    gross receipts and dollar bills    I felt the boundless this morning    the smudge of the longest night turn to dusky rose and orange    a solstice open to the refrigerator and the stove    a mouse under the sheets    we listen to the air come on    this time from the roof    a ringing in our ears    this time for you    whirling with me into the 12 co-habitors of 24 or 48    ungreased and centrifuged    we complete the revolution

You should have heard the wind clobber the pines last night. I hung a moon in one, and it was gone this morning: an offering.

I was terrified for a while. Mountains yelling back and forth. I kept asking: Who's yelling, the moon or the mountains?

Then I slept in a room full of windows. I wanted to see if the wind would kill me. There was a tiny boy eating oatmeal when I woke up. I would love you to meet him.

It wasn't the wind that kept me up   but how you listened   also that little boy   all goopy and speed on a scooter   jumping over walls   bludgeoning the dirt   a deluge of dinosaurs and lego machines   drifting in and out of berries   so much traffic on the tracks   a fallen car   trains marked with names   including his   another called Flynn who becomes a girl   a house too old and a monster that is a shirt painted with a gun and a bible   trampled under the pageant   a shiny box more important than God   a camel clomps through the desert   it was a little boy who led us

Now the whole desert is snowed in and everyone is camped out in trees, glistening, grieving, glistening.

I look at the word God and think it's the oddest word I've ever seen. *Lego. Clomps. Bludgeon.* At the trampoline park, we missed you so much we backflipped together over the balance beam.

Look at you, up there in that tree making words. Once upon a time you were the tallest tree in the entire park—you and that other god, leaping.

Come along now   I'm reaching for you   those gods with their big feet have invited us all to swing   can you hear them?   they're laughing at our funerals of grief offering grand banquets of simple foods   no place for gravy and rich sauces   not for us   not for the birds or the termites   the ocelots or the slim waists of ants modest fare   never a burden   it's how the trees bow to the desert and the desert bends back to the forest   where my body begins to shift   where the universe weaves into a piece of dirt   where my back regains its strength   where I rely on you for light   where I stutter   tempted to stop but don't   instead I jump   joining you in that infinite back flip   vaulting out to the spanking cloud with a head like thunder

I drove over Monteagle Mountain tonight and cursed three truckers who squeezed my car back and forth among them like a toy although I know it was not a game.

*It's hell for a trucker when the devil's at your door*
*He'll tempt you and tell you come on let her roll*
*Cause the mountain wants your rig and trucker I want your soul*[1]

Some people love golden eagles so much they'll stop their car dead in its tracks when they see one flying across a sky as blue as a heart. Not me. Not on Monteagle Mountain. That would never be me, I swear. (I miss you.)

Was it a game between sky and road?   wanderer and river?   a sport between eagles and a rolling box of toys and vacuum cleaners?   which bird chose the red truck and which the yellow?   did they work together to shout *don't look*   to steer you through the asphalt fumes into the long valley of your salvation?   something happened out there on the downgrade   something miraculous   alive

A flame tree broke in half. I wanted to know if it had been struck by lightning, but it looked too sad to ask.

So I gathered sea grape leaves and covered the injured tree until it looked like it felt a little better. It looked like a sea grape extravaganza.

If all the bodies in the world became disembodied I would miss my thumbs. I would mourn my vocal chords. My soul would wander away, unable to speak or hold a spoon.

Oh friend    I know I would miss the sense you make of this illusion of a world    so gorgeous and filled with love    mourning the end of that familiar thumb    the end of what I think I know    I find a bouquet of sea grapes hung with spoons    like chimes they remind me of your voice    a link to the wind    what is it to unknow? to loosen our mere neural understanding?    last week my ex found a box of my old photos in a basement where they spent years pulsing in an ancient river bed with the anger of spirits unhappy their waters were no longer theirs    not surprisingly you suddenly appeared    in full voice    there in the box    as if you had never left

Yet I live 11 feet above sea level. Have I already turned to salt?
*Dear Lot, please send my pool badge to the Gulf Stream ASAP.*

I bet there are pictures of us everywhere, dear friend. Wherever there is a secret stash, there we are, smiling like siblings. It's you! It's you!

And the river, and the gnomes, and Spaceport America to take us to the Super Blood Wolf Moon and back. Are you back in Mass yet? Wanna go to the moon?

The blood of the wolf   a brother and a brother   a killer and my lover   the woods the only breakaway I know   we walk to where the moon guards a coven   a den of pups in the elbow of the dipper   the long stride of our protector leads to the birds the waters   the rivers beneath it all   the other day I learned that even my current house lies in a river   just off a sandy spit   pictures from the year zero where we were born into a beard full of rice   like Christ it feeds an entire civilization before the poisoning   rising again in pictures from 4000 AD where we no longer even look like humans   by then we live several thousand years or more   can you imagine our cells?   our immortal cells?

I stayed awake with the moon. It was the least I could do. I felt bloody myself, the way I used to feel in the old days when the moon kidnapped my body.

I crept onto the great lawn with the Flame Trees and the sinkholes and howled, I admit it, just once, and quietly, like a lunatic.

Thanks to you, genius who lives in the moon, I now understand that music is made of immortal cells that come back after a very long time and make their homes in our ears.

Were the crickets our immortal song?   once they were so loud the sound of human mouths meant nothing   white-gloved hands flying across white blouses   all a blur   I looked down   I could not eat the meat on my plate   the stink of death turned my cells to witness   I felt every mark on the planet   the crickets shouted and called for me in the rain   I must go back   will you come?

Sometimes there's a sound in my right ear like a refrigerator running on a hot day. (It's not quiet—this being old.)

Walking along, I had the thought that the gumbo-limbo trees looked like women standing on their heads without their pants on and I got mad at men all over again.

If you go back, I will too. Where shall we meet once we're there? My favorite word today is gumbo-limbo. Stew and a dance. What could be better than that?

After all those years dancing with mirrors   not one of them broke   and neither did she   a little wonder sitting before us on a chair   a grey-haired pack of guns   ready to take us out at any provocation   I watch from the balcony   the mumble ever louder   you know those trees?   those head-standing women trees?   they are my mother's protectors   ours too   keeping watch as if the gaze of men did not exist they believe in the present tense   could kill anyone who tries to cut them down they pay no attention to the tiny ghosts running around with pails   they only hear the rising sound of gardens   the crickets and what lives in the bow-legged miracles of trees

We all know random things we'd rather not know or we'd just as soon forget.
Said the golden frog, the king of amphibians. (Example of a random thing.)

The cold up there. The sea in the crotch of a tree down here. Our simultaneous stoking of possibility. Fire on the road.

For once, I've paused the show at an unpausable place. Stay with me on this one, but wouldn't you rather be warm? I can do something about that. I am your golden frog.

Can I trust that much   to let you   go   the cold   go   the wood   go   the grief   go   the gifts   go   the go   go   the room seems louder now   I'm shocked by what I hold   the roar of mice and little shoots of green   the heater's rush and the gulf of words that threatens the dark   I hear them in my sleep   the boys   their song my sanity

After the pause   the machines tell me what I already know   then forget   then know again   how much sinew I have left   how much love   how much wind will settle the sand   how much dirt will strengthen my bones   how deep the mines   the startled birds skating on the pond   then finding rest in the one tree on the far shore

The woman who took my blood yesterday said she's distracted by the veins of people in elevators, on supermarket lines, at yoga practice.

Some veins, she said, invite touch.

Now blood races from heart to head and back again, traveling 12,000 miles a day at 3 mph. When it hits my toes, I throw my arms up like a kid on a roller coaster. Scream for joy.

*Against the wind. Against the wall. Against the sky.*[2]   caught against one elevator one cloud   one distant bed   one red carport   11 years (almost to the day) from the bullets that took Fred Hampton   one cold moon   one white Chicago winter

Child   today I am grateful for your high jump and your joy   this morning my DNA results explained my fear of roller coasters and my tendency to sea-sickness   but no test would ever describe my love for oceans or the decks of boats   my eyes steady at the horizon

So: the first gardenia.

One fall I was teaching Yoko (I always teach her in the fall because she writes instructions and rituals and it feels witchy and October to me)—

then I went up to Manhattan and she was there walking along and I said hi, Yoko, I teach you, and she said go back to Florida and smell a gardenia.

I keep your flower close   so red and vivid when I reach in and pull it from my hair or the breath that lands in my one good lung   it smells so much better than what comes from the other lung   asbestos inhaled first in New Haven   then New York   lead from the pipes of old school buildings   the waters of Lake Erie and the Cuyahoga   snow falling from a rusty sky sent through a small coal town in Pennsylvania where the soot-dark air drifts under a foggy and unsteady moon

I hadn't heard about your tendency to seasickness. Or a lung battered by asbestos, a throat by lead. I'm sending you light the color of the scent of gardenias.

Does everything spin just before it breaks?

*Your body is more like a gesture than a thing. / More like a song than a gesture.*[3]

More like a comma    or a breath    the color spinning until it has to break    dear
magic    dear friend    the breaking just another form of kindness    how the body
comes home to rainy streets    this time in Brooklyn heading to Sunset Park where
the spring creates its unstoppable incoherence against all the parkas    heavy red
jackets filled with the feathers of dead birds    a sadistic shield to what we certainly
know    insufficient against the rain    I'd rather break apart with you than endure this
failure to hold what we've done

A small boy shakes sea grapes from the sea grape tree into his Batman bucket.

He collects foot-long pods from the flame tree and duels with squirrels who have seen his kind
before and make a sound between a laugh and a sneeze.

He climbs the bottle brush tree and pretends it's a coconut palm and he is the coconut guy cutting
down the coconuts.

                              The gumbo-limbo shines as always.

He thinks only of his next making and so little about what breaks    using his pods
to chase a squirrel who laughs at the boy-faced wind and his several-sworded
backpack    we eat nuts    a good thing to do when the days become long    grapes
stacked in a coconut bowl    we speak for the first time in months    words filled
with even more love    the trees redden before us    all opening    all fleeting    all the
potential of living in the living grass

I'm one big quiz lately. I could ask stuff all day long. For example: How far above sea level do you think we are?

Or: What are the chances we'll make it to the Poet's Corner at St. John the Divine before it's too late?

Or: When you say grass is alive do you mean it contains the happiness of every bird and every bug and every human and every god?

Answers: Six feet, slim to none, & your answer here.

Your answer becomes my street today    a New York undersea    where the dolls of my heaven swim with the boys of my heaven    their transmissions lie in bed with me where I rest from fever and the ringing in my ears    here the dish of salt    here the easter basket full of hearts    here the silence filled with what we could not sing here the cradle of grief    here the key to your quiz    to every library full of libraries a double cup of coffee at dusk    every living thing an altar    parked with a blue wrapper that marks the entrance to my stay    every living trophy    every candlestick and every duck    we sail at night    where they wait for us at the great opening where the living becomes something else and the grand arrangement falls away where the light dissolves into another light    where the poets wear orange dresses at St. John's    where the closer we come to the crypt the more we are joined    so many of us before the sky

[1] Johnny Cash "Monteagle Mountain" https://www.azlyrics.com/lyrics/johnnycash/monteagle mountain.html

[2] Yoko Ono "Voice Piece for Soprano, 1961 autumn" from *Grapefruit, A Book of Instruction and Drawings* (a 2010 performance: https://www.youtube.com/watch?v=7GMHl7bmlzw)

[3] Michael Hettich, "A Kind of Pleasure" https://www.escapeintolife.com/poetry/michael-hettich/

# Riparian County

Once when I sat by the tracks on lunch break
the Empire Builder, running late, kicked up
some shred of a green bottle broken over its
rails like a christened ship. The glass barely
caught me beneath the eye, but it cut enough to bleed.
My boss clocked me out when I got back, wrote
*bleeding face* by my name, so I went to the river.


They came around the bend, ripples at their waists
wading the incongruous current, bare-breasted,
bare as a parking lot. I knew their faces
from a photograph buried in my wallet: you and I
had climbed a water tower to see the city behind us,
your brother (wrapped in secrets of his own) told us
to press closer together to fit the bridge in the frame, too.

The twins of us here hold hands in the river,
their hair longer than it's ever been. What am I to do
but pry off my boots, slide the folded picture
from its hiding place and hold it out of the water's reach?

In the current, in the middle of town, in disbelief I call out,
"I still keep this!" The worn image thrust out in front of me
like some boarding papers, like some permission.
The twin of me comes close, minnows around our ankles,
takes the hat from my head and puts it on her own,
sun making plain my face. "I keep it, too," she says.
Her voice is the sound of my message machine
if my message machine was in love.

The twin of you takes my chin in her wet hands, turns
my cheek to look at the gash. She presses her thumb to
the cut and my nerves howl a train track through my skin.

Of course she draws my blood across
her own face, an imitation wound.
Of course it is the sign for *even now we hurt the same.*
But I've forgotten how your talking sounds,
so the twin of you says nothing. Wades toward the riverbank
like stepping out of a skirt and leaving it on the floor.

# Beautiful Bembé

Abuela screams my name nightly. *BEMBÉ! BEMBÉ! BEMBÉ!* She calls me a descarada: a short skirt, stubby legged whore who wears hoops the size of her padre's wagon wheel. She asks me how fat the ox is, pulling at my culo. Is he a full decade older than me? Does he promise me corazón-shaped chocolates and a pretty dress for my Quinceañera? She tells me I will never be beautiful, never be a bride, never be nada. No, less than nada.

But, my grandmother is long dead—and I'm a fourteen-year-old boy.

Tonight is no different than nights before. I kneel at my bed and pray first to the Saints that they take away the voice of my abuela from our apartment. I pray second for my mother, but I think the Saints know my heart isn't in it. So, I list specifics like the high price of utilities and even name drop mom's douche boss, Charles. But now, and not for the first time, I look for the words to pray a blessing on myself and I half whisper, while I kneel on hard carpet with a fold of thin sheet between my lips: *please make me beautiful. Please Saints, make me beautiful.*

In the hallway of Christos Reyes High, Carlos is even taller than our freshman lockers. I am close enough to smell the name-brand detergent on his shirt. I am close enough to see the dead skin peeling down his slightly stubbled cheeks.

"Accutane's a real bitch," he says to me and I tell him at least his family can afford it. "You don't get it—you don't even need it," he adds.

I blush.

"You don't need it because you haven't even hit puberty, Fucker," he says, and the breathy wave of his laugh crests across my forehead.

He brushes a cliché of dark hair from his eyes, while I switch my backpack from left to right and feign a grumble. "Can I borrow your Earth Space book again?" I ask.

"Yeah, just give it back to me at lunch," he says, slamming the locker shut.

"Sorry I still can't find mine," I say.

"Only cucks apologize," he says.

"Sorry," I say.

Me and Carlos have been friends as far back as I can remember: 10 years, fourth grade when he lent me his pencil-lead-eviscerated, yet-still-halfways-functional, slime-green eraser. *I really think*, he said, *I'm pretty, pretty sure*, he said, *I'm done making mistakes.* Confidence in one unmasks insecurity in another, at least I think that's the saying. Either way, I am still reaching for the sureness of that nine-year-old boy.

In Earth Space Science, I trace my pencil over Carlos's perfect cursive handwriting, comments and drawings he's scratched in the margins, words he's scribbled out to make a joke:

### 8.1 Human Impact ~~on Land Resources~~

> This heat rises from within ~~the Earth~~. Cracks ~~in the lithosphere~~ widen as the ~~land~~ masses spread apart and the upwelling of heat rises and pushes the ~~plates~~ apart.

Where it says "plates" Carlos has written "A$$\$$CHEEKS" above in small letters. I laugh out loud and Mr. Pellow eyes me for a second before moving on.

I find our table at lunch. There is a clatter of trays and laughter and sneakers squeaked throughout the multi-level dining hall, but our table is especially roaring.

"P," says Eric.

"U," says Julian.

"S," says Matt.

"S," says Kyle.

"T," I say.

"U," says Carlos, after thinking for a moment.

"L," says Eric, rolling his eyes.

"E," says Julian.

"Ouija says, P-U-S-S-T-U-L-E… *puss tool?*" asks Matt.

"The hell is that?" asks Kyle.

"Some sorta of dildo, yeah?" says Julian.

"Why do you always ruin it, Bem?" Eric asks me.

"Ouija says get a dictionary, you tards," I say, and Carlos laughs.

Eric says something back, but mainly into his mayo and ketchup swirl, and we don't hear him over Carlos's drumroll anyway. All six of our heads turn in sync to the left.

Jessie Purcell is walking up the stairs two at a time, tray in one hand, plain milk in another. She swallows each step like they were track and field hurdles. There is a moment at the top step when the long, pale line of her back leg threatens to betray the green drape of her school uniform, and everyone but me bobbles their head and begins exorcising the dramatic demon of a single letter from between clenched teeth.

"P," says Eric.

"R," says Julian.

"E," says Matt.

"T," says Kyle.

"E-pre-TEND, you can be gentlem—," I begin to say, but Carlos cuts me off.

"—T-T-Y," Carlos shouts.

I slide down in my seat just a little.

"What a good girl," says Julian.

"I'll be telling the Saints about her tonight," says Matt.

"Oh, Casper's comin'!" wails Eric.

"Ew dude, too far," says Kyle.

They all laugh, and I laugh too, but when Carlos's eyes can't stop searching for her afterimage, I hear the boiled voices inside.

My mother pounds on the bathroom door until it threatens to break. I don't think about what might happen if it does. The fear of it would end me.

"Tssss!" I wrinkle my face in pain, the eyeliner brush's bristle nearly poking a hole through the white of my left eye.

I look a complete fool in the mirror. Long hair kept at bay by a makeshift buff (a cut off sleeve reattributed). One eye with liner and mascara and the unsubtle pink stain of my mother's Sephora "Seduce" lipstick painted across just the left half my mouth.

"Ouija says pathetic," I mumble under my breath.

TAP, TAP, TAP. She knocks again. "Niño, I need to pee—now," she calls.

I squeeze the eyebrow brush tighter—*her* eyebrow brush tighter—and press it into the pomade disk. I hiss at the door, "Aye coño, I'm trying to dump."

"I'm going to get the KEY," she shouts, and TAP-TAPS the bathroom door for good measure.

The brush in my hand clatters against the sink. In the mirror, a prepubescent clown panics: her one eyebrow dark, another light; her one eye a well-circled "**O**," the other plainest of Janes; half her lips pale, the other a dipped gloss of champagne pink.

My eyes zigzag across the sink's surface for the washcloth. But, it's gone. I tug off my shirt and blast hot water through the white cotton. Again, and again, I scrub my face until the shirt is the sodden Neapolitan stain of ice cream, and my face is raw with heat.

Before the door bangs open, I toss the shirt beneath the sink. Its fall splits through the trapped air of one thousand plastic grocery bags.

"You always admire yourself in the mirror after you shit?" asks my mother, pushing past me.

I cover my chest with both arms. "Never come in here again," I say, as she unbuttons her work khakis.

"Out, niño—and shut the door!" she thrusts a finger at the small hallway, her other hand rummaging for the spine of an old US Weekly.

I slip out of the bathroom and sidestep our coffee table. The overhead AC clacks on.

My mother hums behind the door. Some embarrassing bachata with bongos trickles in where she left dinner half cooked in the kitchen.

"DESCARADA!" screeches through the AC vent, and I duck. The word punches just above my head, whistling.

"Que descanses, don't let the bed's bug bite," says my mother.

I grunt.

"Afraid of more bad dreams?" she asks.

"No, I'm fine," I say, and she frowns, closing the door. She knows not to press further. We've been through it a thousand times.

Tonight, I have trouble sleeping. This is nothing new for a boy who hears his grandmother's ghost. Since the time I was very little, my mother has told me the trick to good dreams is never falling asleep scared, and, just in case, remember no imagined demon can defy the *expelling name of Jesus*. There is still at least a little bit of Catholic left in her (and she hopes even less was passed onto me). She laughs that her mother, a devout woman, would never forgive her for the state of our godless household. This is usually the part where my mother preforms her one-eyed laugh, smiling at a faraway memory that isn't meant for me. I think she's kept a little more Catholic than she's lets on. Above her bed is a large painting of St. Christopher—patron saint of protection—we laugh that he protects her from *all* men. But, she's had it over her bed apparently since she was a very little girl, and when I was young and told her I should have one too, she laughed and insisted her patron's painting was most definitely big enough to protect the both of us. I still hope that's true.

Now, beneath the sheets, I whisper a quick prayer to St. Christopher.

How many times I have prayed to the Saints, to the Holy Ghost, to His Son, to any God?

Night—after—night.

Tonight, I will pray to my abuela. At least I know she can speak.

*Be brave Bembé,* I tell myself.

As the AC clacks off, I slip out from under my sheets to the side of my bed.

I place a bit of the comforter between my lips. "Abuela," I begin, kneeling, "I did not know you well—or, I guess, really at all—in this life, but I think you are still here."

The AC clacks on/off on/off, and my eyes open.

*HOLY FUCK,* I say, only in my head (and I hope that my cursing doesn't register as part of the prayer). I scrunch my eyes shut and keep it desperately short.

Breathless, I whisper "Make me beautiful. Por favor, Abuela, make me beautiful."

I am Catholic enough to know we do not pray to the dead. We pray to the Saints, the Godhead, the Holy Mother. So, when I crawl back beneath the sheets, it is a real crawl. My fear keeps me low under the sheets all night. In an effort to comfort myself, I think about Carlos's advice. The AC clacks off for the dozenth time. Sleep falls into me.

In the morning, a voice jostles my conscience awake.

"Mom, can't be seven yet," I mumble, propped up on a shoulder. I have always been the type who's waking is a puzzling apart of psychic debris. Before I can even open my eyes, my mind still piecing together the who, what, and where; I sense it is not my mother at the door. Why.

Is it not my mother at the door—

I have confided in Carlos on more than one occasion that I think I am too old for "bad dreams," and, of course, he is the only friend who will admit that sometimes he has them too. I have considered admitting, again, only to him, about the voice of my abuela—but I think I know which secrets are better left in the closet. He's told me his abuelo suggested bravery in the face of an unpleasant dream or monster; Carlos laughed when I described my dream self to him, running away from this ghoul or that goblin, screaming the name of *Jesus, Jesus, Jesus* as they chase me through house and cellar and field, their Santería beads clattering out the weak plea of my call for a savior.

*It's all in your head, said Carlos. And it's your head—you can have sex with the hottest chick or chainsaw a monster's head clean off—A dream is the easiest place to be brave, Bembé.*

My vision is 20/20, better even, but the dark is hazy as if a scrim of water arcs over the height of my doorframe.

Inside my ears I hear my own heartbeat, and I realize I am not propped up on an elbow. Sheets drift and snap across my horizontal torso. *A dream is the easiest place to be brave, Bembé,* I tell myself.

Then, the voice sweeps inside my room. Then, it sweeps inside of me.

It is my grandmother's, but softer and much sweeter. Memories of my grandmother are so, so far away.

*Pure child,* she coos, *the well is deep inside you for ascension.*

The figure is obsidian but dappled with light like the markings on a doe. White circles shine small over the feminine torso. The edges of her limbs are obscured, but I can feel the face of my abuela behind the words.

*Show your beauty,* says the voice. Beads clatter across each opened syllable.

A wet pressure cracks open across my forehead, then the smell of rich coconut oil spills into my nostrils, my ears. And then there is nothing but the hollow quake of linked batá drum, the kind my grandmother played for me when I was young. Before remembrance. My body a light rainstick in a room of wind. Here memories unspool—commemorations of spirit dancing through a racing swell of wet drum. Faster. Beat. And faster. Beat.

Until the day I am born.

Here, on the floor beside my bed, facedown, I am awake—I think. My mouth is frozen open, tongue quivering within a puddle of my spittle sticky to the carpet. The swollen grape of my uvula putters in and out of my throat.

My mother crescendos her knuckles against the door. "Bembé! I'm late! You have to walk today. Sorry, but it's a nice day out. Wake up!"

I hear her. But, she is farther away than my waking.

When I stand, those things with which I am most intimately familiar feel foreign. I am already dressed. My legs ferry me around my room. My legs ferry me to the bathroom sink. My legs ferry me the two miles to school. Ferry me somewhere between the waking and forgetting. There are four glass double-doors that stretch rectangles of tall light across the entrance of Christo Reyes High. It is 9:36 A.M. on a Tuesday. The sun beats across the soccer field, beats across employee parking, beats at the black center of Bembé's wind-fingered hair.

A large crowd of students has gathered. They are smooshed in snaking lines of primary colors, caught between classes, against the plexi doors. Bembé ambles toward them, smiling.

Silence is rare in the halls of a high school. But here, just one or two students have their phones out. Everyone has eyes only for Bembé.

"Someone get a teacher," one girl whispers.

The gathered offer no response.

"Someone get a teacher," she says again without raising her voice. "Someone get a teacher, someone get a teacher, someone get a teacher, someone get a teacher, someone get a teacher." She says it over and over, until a louder student approaches the crowd.

"Yo, what's going on?" says the boy, hands planted atop the straps of his backpack, headphones around his neck, phone tucked under one arm. He is on tip toes.

The boy sees Bembé, and his hands come up to cover his mouth. The phone drops from beneath his arm and clatters to the linoleum. He doesn't notice.

He says, *Bembé is... beautiful.*

This boy whose phone lies shattered on the ground does not budge when Carlos grabs his shoulder.

"Chris, dude—the hell's going—" says Carlos, who is now all but face to face with Bembé smiling behind glass, his friend whose hand rises not in greeting but to pull the silver door handle and enter this maw of students.

"R-I-I-I-I-I-I-I-I-I-I-I-I-I-I-I-I-N-G!!" The overhead bell decries the beginning of Second Period. No one moves.

Carlos crouches and thrusts his forearms against the door: where Bembé reaches. The crash bar crunches. A chill of morning air whooshes into the hallway. Carlos grabs Bembé by the bicep and drags him through the crowd. Everyone parts for the stumbling pair.

"C'mon, c'mon," Carlos breathes. The halls are relatively empty, and he signs the cross quickly with one hand, Bembé in the other.

They stumble into a freshman bathroom.

Another boy is zipping up at the urinal.

"Fuck out of here," says Carlos, shooing at the exit.

Arms at his sides, Bembé eyes himself—trembling—in the refraction of mirror, six sink lengths long.

"Bembé, what is going on?" begs Carlos. He signs the cross again, slower, more deliberately, this time.

Bembé wobbles, planted at the center of the freshman boy's bathroom. He is naked, save his white underwear and socks. There is a giant, white spiral of paint beginning at his sternum then tailing its way to a soft bulge of throat. The whites of his eyes are pure white, and his pupils the black of burnt bark. They are without recognition. His expression is a relaxed smile, while his hair pulls upward in tight, dark twists, anxious toward the ceiling, as if they were branches born from his scalp—born for the sky.

Something else has left Bembé paralyzed in place. His face. Unmasked. He is wearing a full face, of makeup. The pinked lips. The blacked lashes. Bronzer. Highlighter. The apples of his cheeks blushed mother's *love letter* peach. Sweat rings a wet line around the perfect oval of his complexion.

"Bembé," shouts Carlos, pulling at his shoulders, "Wake up."

Both boy's eyes are unflinching. Carlos on Bembé. Bembé on the mirror.

The distinct thwack of a male dress shoe reverberates through the outside hallway: teacher, principal, or pre-game-dressed-up-senior-varsity ball player, Carlos doesn't know. He puts one hand to Bembé's cheek. "Bembé... Hermano," he says.

I am out.

Half naked, and awake, in the middle of the freshman boy's bathroom. There are voices, here—Carlos's is the clearest.

"Bembé," he says, "Bembé. I am afraid."

I do not know if he knows, his hand is on my cheek. I do not know if he knows, he is the warmest thing against the morning, the dew-shook freeze of my skin.

Clear, I move forward, one white sock crossing the single tile of linoleum that separates us. Here, I let my nose seek into the side of his cheek.

My lips. I press into Carlos.

There are a handful of choice phrases you'd never want to hear your best friend say to you.

*Fuck you, forever.*

Now, that's at the top.

My chin reaches toward the exit, where the heel of Carlos's sneaker still twirls with the final act of leaving.

I speak low, and only to the empty pit of the boy's bathroom. "What are you doing?" I whisper.

"A dream," I respond, "is the easiest place to be brave, Bembé."

I run. And I cry. It is not a rainy day. The sun burns at my naked back, and ropes of late-spring wind pull at the bareness of each stride. I run until my mind can't find its way. Then, my legs find a kind of consciousness and send me out, ferry me, toward home.

I arrive. The door opens for me, and I feel I hadn't thought to lock it before I left. I try and turn on the hallway lights, but they don't work, and it is not dark. The overhead AC clacks on. I hear nothing, except my own breath's slow catch. There is a trail of dirty footprints behind me, and, thinking of my mother, I pull off each sock. They stay on. The AC is cold on my back. I shiver as it pushes me. Toward my bedroom. Into home.

When the AC clacks off, I stand directly in front of my bedroom door.

"M-Mom?" My voice begins to call. Then—there is school—there is my reflection in the mirror—and there is Carlos—I stop. Thoughts coalesce into a cold shard at the center of my head.

*Did I kiss him? Did we kiss?*

I know in my bones: I do not have to open this door. And there is no voice inside my head now stronger than my own.

*In a dream is the easiest place*, I say, *to be brave*, and turn the handle.

My bedroom has become the scullery of an ancient ritual—the charred chest cavity of a fairytale beast—or at least, that's what I hope. I hope that my bedroom is black with unuttered dark. I hope there is no bed. I hope in place of it, the thick, white spiral on my chest is matched by a superior spiral galaxied across the entire carpet, the burned patch of my once-bedroom.

I hope I feel the face of my abuela behind me. I hope when she tilts her head to kiss the back of my neck, a conical crown of beads atop her head clacks and trimbles. I hope I step forward and the large spiral begins in glowing revolution. I hope this voice is not "family" Spanish. I hope it is an older, deeper kind of creole. I hope in my ears, it is sugar and salt, the warm song of belonging.

I hope the voiced progenitor is a small mound of ash. I hope it is the upper torso of a diminutive man-thing, melted as if in escape of the spiraled center he indwells. I hope his eyes and mouth are the toothed belly of cowrie shells. I hope pearly spires shine and lip against the black ash.

I hope the puckered center of his teeth pull back.

The AC clacks on/off on/off.

I hope the ritual beast, rises from the spiral.

The AC clacks on/off on/off.

*Welcome home, prophet, my beautiful bride*, he says.

The AC clacks on/off on/off.

I hope any reality comes to pass besides this one: where I am, this boy bodied beneath waves of self-doubt and guilt and the keel of every ancestor. They say it gets better. I pray for hope. I will open every door until there is something new behind it.

I step inside my room.

# In This Room

Almost everything is shared in this room;
Buried treasure here & there in this room:

Goldfish in vases topping mirrors &
Flowers in bowls on the stairs in this room;

A mattress not unlike a peacock throne
With all of its stains laid bare in this room;

On the floor a rug that, when it farts, lets
Out a little Persian air in this room.

You could see the furniture if it were
Not covered with thick, black hair in this room;

Sitting on stiff, wooden shelves: hardbacks by
Baraheni & Baudelaire in this room.

It's layered, hunty, like Dante or
Orpheus in the underwear in this room.

When we are dancing we like to flip-flop
Between Rogers & Astaire in this room;

When playing exorcist we take turns being
The cross & Linda Blair in this room.

Estate sale is Italian Summer salt,
A dark-horse is a nightmare in this room.

All of the Cosmos & all of the stars—
Tons of time & space to spare in this room;

The World could disappear & there'd not be
A soul the least bit aware in this room.

## Sturnus vulgaris

most invasive of the migratory
songbirds / debatably the best at being
shiny / shipped to the US because shake-
speare / escaped new york state to colonize
the hemisphere / common-named
as celestial creature / *starlings* / wing
feathers that facet / flash like black opal /
I'm full of facts / handy for walking that ancient
farm wall's path / back to your parents' house
out west of paris / where we caught them gathering
mass / over the brassy hayfield / wind given a body /
called / *murmuration* / some perfect species-
specific word / made to match its action / sounds
exactly as it looks / like its sound looks / swinging
its storm across the sky at dusk / half
an hour before / we saw our flock
form / those local guys / were guzzling vin
de table by the forest's renaissance / aged
entrance / we passed under the mossy archway / the grass
was overgrown / past our ankles / and sunset
suffused red through blue cumulus / ___ through a ___ /
what use is it / to metaphor the sunset / anymore / besides
both of us had to piss / real bad / in the woods
I would have / tugged the zipper of your jeans
down myself / had we been alone / would have
done more / but what use / are all the names
I know for animals / their arcane behavior /
when I can't kiss you / too afraid to
be seen / by those three gatekeepers / in one
version of this scene / which is pure
fantasy / we want them to watch / did you
notice / how much one of them looked
like me / I can't say / I'm reckless enough
to risk / anything but walking close beside
you / while the men stared / at the air
between us / we feigned interest in fading
light / clouds / the birds turned into / the distance

# East

You are sad out loud and my sad stays deep.
Still waters and all that. Some days you can drag it up and
out of me and some days you let me stay quiet.

In the morning, light slices through the dusty apartment.
The bed glows, the cat. You are awake already, always.
The coffee is hot. The radio is on.

When I get up I put my arms around you at the sink,
kiss the back of your neck, make oatmeal
which you eat to humor me.

You keep all the plants alive.
I want to take you somewhere warm
so you can start a garden.

Get your hands dirty, ruin all the knees of your jeans.
Tomatoes and mint. Lavender and poppies, milkweed.
Catnip. We will sit together, and the cat,

on a bright back porch, to watch the bees work.
Look out over all the green, growing, and remember
how to be green, to grow.

—Tomas Moniz—

# when we speak of rooms

we speak metaphor    potential    possibility    lover come    there's room to play    room to fill    room to move    of course some rooms we fear    we name safe out of necessity    or survival    *watch how you enter a room* my father said    & i learned some rooms you can never leave    some you carry w/ you    but lover    the room i imagine most often is captured in the phrase    to make room                                    to carve out space from nothing    to construct a place for something    as if everyone is welcome    lover i have made room for myself in closets & bathrooms & backalleys    i have offered my body as refuge    enter & find desire    i've crafted home    in rooms of my own design    but lover no space is truly safe    so come    nestle w/ here for a time    we can    call this room hope

# Root Systems
## for Yolanda P. Salvo

I have this assignment to write on origins.
All I can think about is your rellenong
talong at sunrise, garlic thick air,
wisp of your floral dress sway on linoleum
as you commit to careful chemistry
of fried egg.

> To say I have roots means all us kids,
> knee deep in dirt. Means I only know how to eat
> because you brought backyard, earth
> soaked, each bite caressed by sweat of
> forehead. *The land gives us what we need*
> *not like this country —*

We didn't get it then, you training us for end
of times, or maybe, bringing us back to our beginning.
Bold brown knuckles turned into baon, lunch time
snacks folded of banana leaf. To unwrap
gift every noon, map illustrated of rice, speckled
in sea spinach, while others ate bland

> mashed potatoes. A spark of sili, proclamation
> of patis, we held up sliced mangoes sculpted into bouquet.
> Every summer, you took small seed, hard stone,
> harsh light, profuse cackle, grew it into momentum
> to fuel every star speckled report card on the fridge,
> every trophy shimmer slung over shoulder.

Our last photo together, San Fabian, July 2007—
96°F heat, palm tree silhouette on cheeks. You said
you liked my haircut, *So Pogi!* Big smirks. Fingertips
pressed on lychee skin, our version of prayer.
Not to mention, the way you taught me to pick apart until we found tender.

How we knew somehow together,
there could be sweetness. You asked me to open
every fruit, juice like sprinkler from our old house.
This, breaking apart. This, delicate pouring.
This, bulbous bounty. This, bellyful harvest was
always ours, no matter the soil we stood on.

# an apostrophe denotes ownership

i loved a woman / who called me hers
and so to her / i belonged
her name plus an apostrophe / to denote possession
and on couches / in our parents' basements
in our parents' houses / her pale fingers
traced my brown skin / she said she loved
the color / and what does it mean
to love a body / in context / and what is the space
between believing a thing / and speaking it aloud
she asked even after months / together if i was sure
i was straight / i told her yes
is it a lie if you / believe it
i told her i loved her / and this was true
by all accounts / even when she could
no longer love me / even in the edged way she did
and later the first person / i dated after
coming out was a black boy / and i knew
i could not love him / but before i knew this
how good it felt / to be on a couch
in my own apartment / in the living room
with my head resting / on his shoulder
similar to the way i used to do / with her
it was interesting / she noted once
how in this way / with the back of my head
on her this meant / i was both closer
and distant / this closeness a way
to avoid looking at a body / only feeling it
and after cuddling this boy / my roommate said
we looked alike / and the line between
narcissism and self-love / is fine and i worry
i'll never love someone / as much as i loved
that girl / the way her sharp tongue
felt like love / the way my love
was hers / was held with soft shackle
how she loved of me / what i could not
yet love myself / how she saw in me
what i could not yet admit

# Dirty Things

Huilin was the first woman whose name I said in the dark. At night, she is only her skin, only the places I know by touch, my fingers articulating the bone of her elbow, the particular angle of its sleep: desire is that degree. The hinge of need: her knees opening where I reach my hands down to divorce them.

My mother once said I was born a god of rot. When I was little, everything I touched turned sour: grapes deflated and leaked piss-bitter juice, the neighbor's cat licked me and became roadkill that same day, crows wearing necklaces of its intestines. My mother's breastmilk curdled into yogurt the moment it met my mouth. When I touch Huilin, I'm always afraid her skin will slip off her shoulders, her fist will ripen and fall into my mouth.

On the mattress in her apartment, I ask Huilin why there are no Chinese people in lesbian movies. We're watching *Blue is the Warmest Color* with subtitles on and the sound off, keeping ourselves from falling asleep by playing our favorite movie game: *count the minorities. Does having blue hair count as being a minority?* Huilin asks, and I say no, it does not, so we switch to counting pigeons in every shot of Lyons. Huilin can't answer my question: she can only say lesbians and Chinese people actually have a lot in common. For example, we both like fixing our own cars, both prefer soccer to football, both like buying our clothes at a discount, both have issues with our mothers.

My mother works the car wash on the only street in this city with a sidewalk: whoever designed this city wanted no one to live inside it. When I was little, my mother let me sit inside the cars as they nudged along the conveyor belt. I watched the blue brushes descend like teeth, soapwater salivating all over the windshield. I used to pretend the car was being swallowed by a whale, though no one I knew had ever read the Bible, and for years I believed Jonah had been digested, shat out by the whale the same way a car was ejected from the wash: the Subaru reopening its windows like eyes, the windshield flinching from light.

We didn't allow the customers to stay in their cars while they were being washed. This was because, my mother said, people do dirty things inside while the outsides are being cleaned. Huilin says we can test this theory. I tell her the car wash isn't open yet. The sun is still fetal, still crowning between our legs. But Huilin doesn't believe in how days are divided: she doesn't subscribe to light. The day begins when she rises and ends when she sleeps, whether or not the sun is synced to this.

I get out of bed and drive us there, bring the car wash key my mother gave me. We scour the glovebox for quarters and Huilin tells me when she was little, she thought gloveboxes were only for keeping gloves. My mother used to line her glovebox with Ziploc bags of ice, converting it into a travel-sized freezer for the cold things she ate. Hongdou popsicles, berries iced into gems, Costco bags of frozen corn and peas. Eating cold things, she said, will freeze your ovaries. Years later, I realized she'd probably been suckling on popsicles to prevent me from being conceived.

The car wash crouches behind a gas station. A neon sign blinks staccato as Morse code: open closed open open closed open open. Another sign written on cardboard: We Live in Drought, Please Don't Wash Car. I unlock the booth where my mother keeps the cash box duct-taped to the bottom of the counter, a pistol taped next to it in case of robberies. I told her no one would steal from a business that deals primarily in coins, but my mother said you always have to be ready for war. During martial law in Taiwan, the radio recited instructions in case communists invaded the island: everyone over the age of 10 was required to learn how to shoot a gun. At elementary school, they aimed at cantaloupes with painted-on faces. The melons were mounted on broomsticks and attracted birds with their sugarblood. My mother shot so many birds by accident that the sparrows took revenge and returned as ghosts, shitting bullet shells on the children's heads. The thing she could never say was that she didn't care whether the communists took the island or not: both militaries were the same, made of men.

I unlock the box, slot the quarters into the car wash, climb back into the driver's seat. Huilin buckles her seatbelt, and I tell her she doesn't need to: it goes slow and straight. She ignores me, and I let her buckle my seatbelt too. The soap is whiter than I remember, so bright that it's day inside the whale's mouth. Water bruises the windows and the brushes lower, making the same metallic sound that Huilin makes at night when her molars grind together. I've told her for months to get a mouthguard, that one day she'd wake with a jawful of sand, but she says I should mind my own damn mouth. What I could never say aloud was that her teeth didn't matter to me: I'd just wanted her to know that I listened to her sleep, eavesdropped on her dreams, that I knew things about her body she wasn't even awake for, that once I pressed my ear to her bellybutton as if it were a seashell, as if I could hear my own blood echoed in it, or the sea sewing Taiwan's shoreline, or the water jetting over us, cleaving our breaths from our mouths.

Huilin closes her eyes and the radio is playing the weather. It predicts rain. It predicts the sun will shut down, the sky will foreclose, but we will still be sitting here next year. I caught my mother once, after the car wash was closed, standing in the parking lot with the pistol in her hands, aiming up at the sun.

The only army that's coming, she said, is the rain: water raising us up till we ride the sky like a saddle.

I watch Huilin lean toward the window, the seatbelt taut as the tendons in her neck when I touch them. She reminds me of those dogs on the highway with their heads lolling out the window, their tongues flapping in the wind like flags, fur blown so flat you can see the exact shape of their skulls. We are in the silent part of the wash, when the brushes move like tongues over a pelt, when there are no subtitles between us: what is said can only mean one thing at a time. I say: you need to get a mouthguard. What I want her to say: when the car wash is over, let's do it again, let's do it until there's no water left in all of California and everyone becomes a casualty of our thirst. Huilin's wrist twitches toward the door. She scrolls down the window, lets the water avenge all the rain we've ever wasted. It floods our laps, soaps its tongue in the sweat between our legs. She says I should call her a god: she can make rain without a sky. She proves it to me, pressing two buttons down with her tongue, lowering all the windows at once.

# WANTED: HOUSEBOI

*In memory of the Craigslist Personals, c 1999-2018.*

Be it ever so humble, there's no place like:
**www.CRAIGSLIST.org/YourCity/CasualEncounters.**
**WANTED: HOUSEBOI OR HOUSEBOI**
Seeking houseboy of any size or gender for imaginary home.
Must be trainable with attention to detail.
Must be available for service, role play, and cuddles.
Must be willing to host or role play house in park or parking lot or car or car wash until we build a home of our own.
Wanted: Houseboi to sit by my feet while I write these words.
Wanted good houseboi, houseboi who will listen for once, who will let me save him, who will not self destruct to heroin or fire escapes or the sadness of empty rooms.
Wanted: houseboi.

## WANTED: PET

Over 30 and able to vocalize consent.
House trained.
My building doesn't allow pets, walk tall. Walk human.
Wanted pet to ignore the ghosts of all the pets I didn't love enough, like the song says, all dead, all dead, the goldfish I overfed, the cat who couldn't fly, the dog waiting for a walk.
Wanted body to love me furry unconditionally in exchange for food.
Wanted: Pet who won't let me kill you.
Cats preferred. Tabbies to the front.

## WANTED: DADDY

Any gender, for role play, discipline, sitting on the couch, help with the boy and the occasional ride home.
The following phrases turn me on:
I'm taking off my belt.
I'm going to teach you something.
You're doing really well.
I'm sorry I said that thing about your report card when you were seven.

I'm sorry the whole queer thing. I promise to look it up.

I am proud of you.

Wanted Daddy to say these things, over and over, to all of us who needs it.

Slight preference for: alive. Or at least alive-of-center folks.

## WANTED: MOMMY

Femme of any gender.

For rope bondage, age play, and advice.

Wanted Mommy to re:raise us from larval stage in role play,

Wanted: Mommy to give advice that this time we will all listen to. Must be willing to forgive.

## WANTED: METAPHORS FOR HOME

Such as: I am home when I am with you.

Such as: the first time you walk into that bar and everyone is queer and the last thing they hear you say before you disappear into a pile of bodies is, *honey, I'm home.*

Such as when you travel across the world and walk into a dyke bar and even though no one is your ex, someone there is a volleyball coach or a firefighter who will buy you a drink and call you baby and never call you anything ever again.

Wanted: home that is the volleyball coach never calling you again.

## WANTED: METAPHORS:

Seeking sandcastles, bouncy houses, pillow forts, and afternoons that have no beginning and no end.

Seeking symbolic stand-ins for the things we've always wanted but were too afraid to ask, or did not want but did not know how to say no to, or did not know were real until we had the words for them.

## WANTED: ACTUAL HOMES

Seeking 50,000 queers to take the ring of keys off their belt loops and drop them in a big pile in front of city hall.

50,000 keys multiplied by the too many keys we all carry on our belts, makes a bonfire of keys, silver, copper, and gold, and by the magic of multiplicity, every key would belong to a house, and there could be enough for everyone.

A bonfire of keys turns a sandcastle into a glass castle.

You can't throw stones from here, but it's a start. One hundred million glass castles is a start.

## WANTED: JUST ONE

One key we'd pick off the bonfire pile to come home,

We'd come home together to this house we've created out of our hearts, from the chandelier to the four poster bed.

Where

Daddy's got her leather boots on the table.

Houseboy has finally cleaned his room, and missed a spot.

Mommy is slowly taking off his apron.

And having finally found one another, we'd play house there all afternoon into the night listening to house music.

And then, we'd switch.

# Broken Circles
## for my mother

we
are
the
daughters
who
exist
in
circles

the
patterns
he
traces
with
his
index
finger

we
are

train

careening

cars

in

loops

we

are

who

out,

us

mother

did

her

best

of

open,
string

us

cut

fragments

father
who
did
a
number

haphazard
little
strings
which
on
our
baby
once

we
are
only
what
we
are
in
fit
together
relation
to

with
yellow
light
through
                    a
          splayed
                              hand

we
gather
all
    that
        you
            have
                left
                    for
                        us

we
hold
    onto
        it
            like
                cotton

all
because

waxy
paper
around
sheets
like

a
cherry
lollipop

broken

is
it

we
what
were
told

forgive
already
we
you
for
all

we forgive

of

it

the

ironing boards

on

our

backs

sink

the swirling

water

down

the drain

we

are mad

at

you

both

for

you've done

and

what

what

you

have

not

done

for

furious,

we

are

dizzy

through

folly

and

toilet

bowls

you

love

to

watch

are

us

depictions

to

round

and

this

round

of

go

all

us

mothers

did

our

fathers

mothers,

our

of
us

like
our

drapery,

like

dragging

kitchen

linoleum

tomato

patterned

and

tiles

pepper

dish

on

with

a

casserole

in

us

they

mixed

around

churning

sauce

all

a

pyrex,

a
glass

pan,

a

crusted

sheet

cookie

burner

eating
off

of

blue

plates

and

taking

walks

left

on

the

around
the cul-de-sac,
stocking
sundries
at
the
grocery
store
because
someone's
got
to
bring
home bar
food,
that
cold
cheese
burger

and

those

soggy

onion

rings
in
a
styrofoam
box

for
the
growing
smiles
of
those
growing
boys

feed
the
circular
mouths,
the
round
faces

that

clump

together

and

beg

they

they

ask

beg

for

and

they

nothing,

learn

how

to

feed

themselves

but

it's

too

late,

they

been
given    more

daughters,    more

reasons

to

stay

in

the

broken

circles    and

have

already

detonators

between
what

they    have

drift
back

—227—

and
what
has
taught

been
taught

them,

see
how
they
blow

cigarette
smoke
into
their
father's
faces
lie

down
and
take
the
blunt

she
will

forgive

objects

of

you

now,

it,

the

daughter

she
will

oscillate

between

genderless
bodies

these

bodies

are
all

filled

with

of
broken

gender,
they
are
all
a
kind

daughter,
tell
me

touch
moves
in
circles,
why
again
why
unwanted
a
in
boyfriend

college

would

chew
on
rocks,
spit

sand,      why      he

didn't
know
it,      but
followed
these
men      in

organized
symmetry,      why      their
cold
names      matter

to    us:

stranger/

each
and
    every

grandfather/
father/
uncle/
cousin/

brother/

tell
me
  again
    why
      each
      daughter,

me
told
has

girl/
child/
boy/

that
they
all

one
pale

blamed

hand
over

and
themselves

they
were

the

their

hard

masterminds

cry
won't

with

mouths

give
these

daughters
a
road
map
that
leads
straight
one
put
one
foot
on
the
ground,
one
on
outta
here,
foot
on
the
pedal,

and

get
the
hell

out

of

here.

# Untitled

I am of the displaced from Brooklyn. Grew up in the Park Slope of the eighties and 90s, home to one of the largest lesbian communities in the world. It's not like coming out wasn't a big deal. But that was because of internalized homophobia. Once I accepted myself, it was pretty seamless with pretty much everyone in my life. I identified bi in high school because all my friends were labeling themselves as bi. We were at the arts high school, LaGuardia, aka the Fame school. We knew some of us may be gay, and so by all of us saying we were bi, we enacted the spectrum. I was out as bi but under the rubric of activism keeping my denial of same-sex desire almost as closeted as I kept my same-sex relationship. When I came out as a lesbian senior year of college after reading *Zami*—my soon-to-be first girlfriend waited outside my chamber music class in a corner of Hunter North to lend me her copy, our first kiss by the reflecting pools at Lincoln Center just on the other side of the Performing Arts Library from my old high school and south of Juilliard where she worked in the library—I came out as a lesbian because that's what I was most scared of being called. I was a ride or die New Yorker, but I didn't get into the Grad Center for PhD school and headed to Pittsburgh from 2004-2010. When I was moving back with a dissertation to finish, a broken-heart that I had no idea how I was ever going to mend, and no job, my city had drastically changed on me. The economy was in shambles due to what went down on Wall Street in 2008 even as rents were on the rise. New York and Brooklyn always has many a couch for me to surf, but I was too raggedy and had too much to write to not have a room of one's own, and so I moved to South Orange. Jersey. A dear friend had a guest room on its own floor with its own bathroom and its own entrance. I commuted by bicycle to my social life in NYC through Newark which became home.

I do not want to talk about the bullying I've experienced as a black scottish gender queer lesbian from Brooklyn in Newark. The power homophobia had over shared social spaces was inconsequential to me. It's not like people weren't queer, it was just for some quiet as kept. I like to think that my earnest performance of being out and anti-homophobic is part of making the DL less necessary. We were all sitting in the front room of the Urban Issues Institute and she was just like you know I also date women, in response to something someone said. It doesn't feel right to pretend otherwise Shelagh being right here.

To suddenly have the biological clock kick in as a gender queer lesbian struggling with housing insecurity and unstable employment was both destabilizing and grounding. I made a pregnancy pact with a girlfriend (in the hetero sense of how straight women have girlfriends) and started making decisions around how to become a parent. I stopped drinking for two and a half years. Got a studio apartment in a Mies van de Rohe building with views of rainbows and sunrises over the Manhattan skyline, I learned about NJ foster care at a health fair at the church next-door. I was offered and accepted a full-time job with benefits. I defended the diss as I no longer needed the UPMC health care I relied on as a grad student, and had a brief and lovely spring romance. I thought if I had a lesbian friend who would want to help me get pregnant and during pregnancy, I felt like I could do that and then be a single parent. I had one friend I was comfortable asking but it wasn't a good time for her. I mourned the loss of a possibility for like a week, perhaps even one day in bed with a pint of ice cream, and then went full steam ahead with a plan to become a foster parent—a memory of a vision of a rainbow family my first girlfriend had shared with me. I bought a house, I learned to drive, I got a dog, I got a car, I renovated the house, I moved in, I got the car fixed, I got the car fixed, I got the car fixed, I got the car fixed, I got a certified preowned car with payments, I got a cat, I got my foster care license (DYFS paper work always at the 11th hour), and shortly after K was placed in my home. She had just turned three. It was a foster to adopt situation. I knew her family and knew that was going to be a problem for the State. I should've known that the State would meet my transparency with deception. They removed her from my home after eight months but hindsight suggests they had been plotting the removal for at least six. If I had been a straight woman would they have been okay treating me the way they treated me? Would they have been more careful with the bond my daughter had formed? I'm not sure. The crisis of family separation at our border with Mexico and the commonness of my story in my neighborhood suggest a historical intentionality of the attack on the poor, black, brown, and indigenous family that is the foundation of this country's wealth and power and these days in my city as at the border intimately connected to the prison industrial complex and real estate. I was her mommy. Not her only mommy. She said S is for Mommy, and so in writing I wrote myself Mommy S. They gave me a half hour's notice and gave us a half hour to say goodbye, wondering why it took us so long to pack up her stuff, change her out of her school clothes, and figure out how to tell her that she was moving to a new home but that all the love she has from me, from Kete our dog, from Rexxy our cat, from my mum, and my sisters, and my dad, from aunts, uncles, and cousins, from our large community of friends that is family, is hers forever to keep, and I made a fist and pounded my heart and then pounded hers and then had her do the same. And then she was off in a van, and not yet a year and a half later, I haven't seen her since. That summer I fought the NJ State system in the courts and really believed our love was going to win as DYFS had acknowledged that they had made a mistake in removing her from our home and was advocating for the judge to return her home, but we lost. I had planned on hiring a lawyer if we lost, but the story the courts had created for her was a story of stability which was the thing that I felt she needed even more than me as I am always here but if I continued the fight for us I would be continuing a narrative of instability for her, and with the support of my family I accepted their story trusting my gut that their story is a true story knowing even liars sometimes tell the truth.

How does one keep going after such loss? I do not really know. Not well. But we try. We are patient as the effects on our physical health manifest. We understand time is not linear nor singular. We accept the mistakes we make because of how trauma creates a fear of memory and develop a practice of forgiveness. We try not to lose sight of the need for healthier closure and perhaps continued time together. Identity is fluid. A mother can become auntie; for a child in foster care mothers may proliferate. The first year I kept trying and failing to get the State to facilitate better closure for us. This summer I realized the toll that was taking and realized that I needed to take more time to heal when in August in battles with roofers who created new problems and pretending they hadn't water streaming in through the window of the back upstairs bedroom and a tornado had passed through the night before and a second battle with DYFS advocating for a teenager who was valedictorian of her high school and a single mother of a two-year-old staying at my home because the State had no apparatus to support them and yet refused to place them in foster care because they were committed to her aging out of the system before she entered it. She was in my home for a month until she was old enough to go to a group home and the state refused to treat my home as the foster home it was. I took the dog for a hike, parked across the street for alternate side, and started a long morning of phone calls to insurance agencies and contractors and hadn't realized Afrekete wasn't there until the workmen showed up to inspect and she didn't greet them. I have a sinking feeling I left my dog in the car, I said. And I went to the car, and I had. And she was dead. My best friend. How does one keep going after such loss?

It's not as hard when you have a teenager and a two-year-old living with you. And then when they move to the group home, you still have your cat, and you have friends. One friend who you haven't really seen in two years shows up on your doorstep ringing your bell and calling in your window. You go out on your porch, so she doesn't realize Afrekete isn't there, but the first thing she says is where's the dog. So you tell her. She's parked across the street in a spot where you had been parked, and we walk over, and she introduces her seven-month-old baby and puts him in your arms.

The three of us are sunbathing at the beach eating kale salad when the doctor calls with alarmingly low iron and ferritin levels and a vitamin d deficiency.

We change our diet, we take vitamin supplements, we go to doctors, we make decisions about whether or not to have surgery. We move forward trusting time spirals. We keep visioning multi-faceted plans of healing and vengeance,

> like jewels in our open light
> we live
> our visions
> the warrior poets we are

# This Time in Florida

is there a haven
for all the black
girls gone missing
a tiny house for each
clavicle & a jar of
brown eyes lighting
up like fireflies in the
southern night sky
oh baby hair
oh newly planted flower
oh little magic
how i wish upon
your tiny
breath tonight

# Home

My father had a steel comb with which he would comb our hair.

After a bath the cold metal soothing against my scalp, his hand cupping, my chin.

My mother had a red pullover with a little yellow duck embroidered on it and a pendant made from a gold Victoria coronation coin.

Which later, when we first moved to Buffalo, would be stolen from the house.

The Sunn'i Muslims have a story in which the angels cast a dark mark out of Prophet Mohammad's heart, thus making him pure, though the Shi'a reject this story, believing in his absolute innocence from birth.

Telling the famous Story of the Blanket in which the Prophet covers himself with a Yemeni blanket for his afternoon rest. Joined under the blanket first by his son-in-law Ali, then each of his grandchildren Hassan and Hussain and finally by his daughter Bibi Fatima.

In Heaven Gabriel asks God about the five under the blanket and God says, those are the five people whom I loved the most out of all creation and I made everything in the heavens and the earth for their sake.

Gabriel, speaker on God's behalf, whisperer to Prophets, asks God, can I go down and be the sixth among them.

And God says, go down there and ask them. If they consent you may go under the blanket and be the sixth among them.

Creation for the sake of Gabriel is retroactively granted when the group under the blanket admits him to their company.

Is that me at the edge of the blanket asking to be allowed inside.

Asking that 800 *hadith* be canceled, all history re-ordered.

In Hyderabad I prayed every part of the day, climbed a thousand steps to the site of Maula Ali's pilgrimage.

I wanted to be those stairs, the hunger I felt, the river inside.

I learned to pronounce my daily prayers from transliterated English in a book called "Know Your Islam," dark blue with gold calligraphed writing that made the English appear as if it were Arabic complete with marks above and below the letters.

I didn't learn the Arabic script until years later and neveer learned the language itself.

God's true language: Hebrew. Latin. Arabic. Sanskrit.

As if utterance fit into the requirements of the human mouth.

I learned how to find the new moon by looking for the circular absence of stars.

When Abraham took Isaac up into the thicket his son did not know where he was being led.

When his father bound him and took up the knife he was shocked.

And said, "Father, where is the ram?"

Though from Abraham's perspective he was asked by God to sacrifice his son and he proved his love by taking up the knife.

Thinking to himself perhaps, Oh Ismail, Ismail, do I cut or do I burn.

I learned God's true language is only silence and breath.

Fouth son of a fourth son, my father was afflicted as a child and as was the custom in those days a new name was selected for him to protect his health.

Still the feeling of his rough hand, gently cupping my cheek, dipping the steel comb in water to comb my hair flat.

My hair was kept so short, combed flat when wet. I never knew my hair was wavy until I was nearly twenty-two and never went outside with wet and uncombed hair until I was twenty-eight.

At which point I realized my hair was curly.

My father's hands have fortune-lines in them cut deeply and dramatic.

The day I left his house for the last time I asked him if I could hold his hand before I left.

There are two different ways of going about this.

If you have known this for years why didn't you ask for help, he asked me.

Each time I left home, including the last time, my mother would hold a Quran up for me to walk under. Once under, one would turn and kiss the book.

There is no place in the Quran which requires acts of homosexuality to be punishable by lashings and death.

*Hadith* or scripture. Scripture or rupture.

Should I travel out from under the blanket.

Comfort from a verse which also recurs: "Surely there are signs in this for those of you who would reflect."

Or the one hundred and four books of God. of which only four are known—*Qur'an, Injeel, Tavrat, Zubuur.*

There are a hundred others—*Bhagavad-Gita, Lotus Sutra, Song of Myself, the Gospel of Magdalene, Popul Vuh, the book of Black Buffalo Woman*—somewhere unrevealed as such.

Dear mother in the sky you could unbuckle the book and erase all the annotations.

What I always remember about my childhood is my mother whispering to me, telling me secrets, ideas, suggestions.

She named me when I moved in her while she was reading a calligraphy of the Imams' names. My name: translated my whole life for me as *Patience.*

In India we climbed the steps of the Maula Ali mountain to the top, thirsting for what.

My mother had stayed behind in the house, unable to go on pilgrimage. She had told me the reason why.

Being in a state considered unacceptable for prayers or pilgrimages.

I asked if she would want more children and she told me the name she would give a new son.

I always attribute the fact that they did not, though my eldest sister's first son was given the same name she whispered to me that afternoon, to my telling of her secret to my sisters when we were climbing the stairs.

It is the one betrayal of her—perhaps meaningless—that I have never forgiven myself.

There are secrets it is still hard to tell, betrayals hard to make.

You hope like anything that though others consider you unclean God will still welcome you.

My name is Kazim. Which means *patience.* I know how to wait.

# The Roads

I wake beneath quilts   sunlight and wind   the smell of salt from the bay   our child bangs on waves along the point as our past rolls out from the molting of poplars   the quiet rust of leaves   the buoys a secret sign of gospel

The road into the green   the loud green roof of the B&B at the bottom of the dip and out beyond the shallows of Chéticamp Island   facing west   I sit on a chair at the wooden table and stare out at the yellow house across the way   I've been treacherous   almost fatal   bringing wild grasses into our living room   my nose a forest   so much hope then so many birds   the waters   the waters   the god-sent waters   my tiny shack   heart and bird flown   the afternoon a crescent   the lobster boats arrive in threes

A havoc of winds along roads that yesterday ran with frogs   the light a coronation   I give you bearings for feet and sink my heels into you as we slide into the corners of rooms   we take our little pieces of years between our hands to offer a banquet   who would you invite?   puma or lover?   mother or thundercloud?   we sit just inside what the herons call a bowl   we too believe it's a bowl   a tuning fork   its long note just below what we can hear   it molds to our collarbones   our ribs and vertebrae   before an echo fills the space between lungs and throat   I would call a centaur   a horned acrobat off the Siberian plain   until we fall away to become a train   a low chime   a hum

We travel a journey of devotions   one's an old man and one's a garden another   a jeweler who builds tiny cakes from humid sediments another winds her way to Nain through a future of oxbows   a waterfall of laughter and blood rushing into time without rockets or ransoms instead a delicate finity between index finger and thumb   the refuse that gathers around our feet   a herd of geese   a few pigeons flown up from the Gowanus and the pier off Red Hook   riding the old Dutch roads to the abandoned waterfront where I once watched boys swim on summer afternoons   *we will find the cool water* they said and they did

I know a kind of peccary from the southwest    slick with swamp mud
a pack full of them at dawn    waiting for us to walk outside    instead
we jump through a window into the dark waters and swim    crawl when
necessary    eat dirt to tunnel toward the coast along the map we set out
in a New York City apartment some 30 years ago    where I served you
ice for the sweltering night    now a blanket    a bottle of water and
sparkling lemonade    the faint moon over your shoulders    the rumble
of trains in the hills    begun in the dirt of the east    but long traveled to
arrive at the juncture of these seven clouds    so much bright air

The plum has a half-life and a renewal    both food and tree    singing in
the night with the skin of the dark rose    we meet at the tips of new
suns    each an eyepatch    a quiver    a comfort for cool days    a pile of
laundry in the corner    two white socks without gravity    a black t-shirt
a pair of jeans with yogurt stains that look like cum    chiming in unison
at 4 a.m.    when I bow to watch a ball of baby spiders    their mother's
vigilance    just inside the front door

I look down at the wood floor and wonder who laid it    wonder where
tonight's rain landed at dawn    I look up at my great grandmother
murdered in the last century    what did she do with her mornings?
who did she hold?    her cyphers now inside a Montreal Starbucks where
a child's laughter rings out over a man who steps down from a carriage
drawn by a blinder-blinded horse    I hear him    not the man but the
horse    then the child who now chants code    a stillness    a blue shirt
an architecture that summons me to enter the hospital where Nan's
heart stops without her permission    then beats again    a reminder of
how the heart knows itself    her eyes open to Sonny's smile    when
after a pause    she smiles in return


Yes to trains    between beginning and destination    where I am free to
burrow into the unoccupied seat to my left    to sleep under the sound
of wheels and motors    hidden in the blur of passing fields    two
Februarys ago in Tucson where we find fossils and meteorites under
an ashy tarp    still untouched by weed killer and car exhaust    I had
come for scrapings but instead hear the clacking mounds of beads
pearls in heaps    some a flamboyant pink    some a watery lavender
flying off their frail strings like confetti blown into a cloudy sky    I sink

further beside the rise of hats and skirts    a chorus of ancient aunts who arrive daily from the city    they come to collect minerals    filling their skirts like they once filled them with child    the fabric bleached a dull smoke grey by the soil    mud mixed with blood    a tonic of salt and heat    in the shadow bones I am an afternoon

Prayer    my friend explains    a way of making breath before there is no breath    for calling light and gratitude before the red dirt    so absent from what we smell for miles on the road to Marfa    shit knee-deep inside the fences where hundreds of cows stand stunned    as if their bodies were not bodies    their souls not souls    later in the hotel we watch a video clip of a calf    rejected by its mother    then raised inside a house by a family of humans    in the house the calf behaves just like the family dogs    or perhaps just like a calf    chasing a stick    sleeping beside the wood stove    licking her humans alive

Now I remember the symptoms    the loud TV in the upstairs den    my younger sister doing homework to a cartoon fight on the screen that hides the fury in the kitchen below    coats like heavy metals    locked away from the snow    I take them out and find little doorways of grace the dirt from my grandmother's apple tree    a pile of baby mice beneath the woodpile    mewling but safe    until we accidentally disrupt their home    we agree to put them back    to tuck them under the old schoolhouse where I now sit in a plastic chair long abandoned by children    mine a faded blue    others pale green and grey    one red painted with a portrait of a girl    a particle left for me to send back to you    still looking out    until we move    or until the missiles come    or at least until the night when we become like the brittle stars that send out a glow and a foul taste    a warning to the ghost crabs who know to flee when they encounter such vivid reminders of a ruinous meal    if you run I will run with you    just tell me where    I call to the silent air reach again to find you    so perched inside another time    our incarnation breaks the world

# excerpt from *Bib*

(interlude)[2]

∞

> when magic doesn't happen
> earnest divination
> the magic of the amygdala
> the terror
> you hold mysteries too
> a rise & fall
> not necessarily in that order
> infinity sign
> overhead
> I'm dead
> this lousy moment

the clouds disappear into the folds of the sky
like ill/allusion, like riddles/riddled sky
life leaves/splits the body
the way an absorption of a loved one is an act of grief
leaning in the door frame as to not enter or leave but lean & observe
or to be pressed against the frame
while reading, I long to feel as righteous as the protagonist
I am moved by the way the writer uses the magnolia flower as place
how every book I read
there is splitting & doubling
the mouth & the tongue are poetic devices
while reading
apples appear in the line of poetry
a hankering for honey crisps
my mom, in Michigan
while reading, I recall, as one does, a moment
which part of you is speaking?

---

[2] a small poem, found in notes, undated

mirror & record
refusing multiplicity
cutting along my life line
a river bend
blood exposed
the burn
the air
done in friendship
to symbolize in life & death
in poetry
in revel
in reverie, revolution, witchery
in labor
in leisure
in the streets/sheets
in my grandparent's garage
my friend spits in her hand & presents it to me, "spit sisters" she says
I pull the Conduit card
from my divination deck
I remember Francesca Lisette's line in *Sub Rosa*, "let's all be conduits," or something
like that someone said, what kind of stillness is required to hear the message?
bibliomancy in this culture of liars
Zoe tells me about the "monkey Yodas" in Vhi Ki Nao's, *Sheep Machine*
Zoe says, "I think the monkey Yodas are clouds
but for all I know
they could be actual monkey Yodas"
I am struck by the question on page 46
"what is it like to lose one's mind before a crowd of pasture & grass?"
reading Judy Grahn's, *Another Mother Tongue*
these words leap into my mouth, "secrets for protection, ancient gays, magical thrills
the small finger, the fruit I was munching on"
while reading in bed
I read
"genuflect"
"afterlife"
"apocalyptic"
"enrapture"
"souls"
"martyrs"

"the will of god"
indoctrination in part
flowers for memories
as in marigolds for my Nan
a fill-in-the-blank drawn on the page
I insert myself without thinking
a memory appears
my nipples pinch like a lemoned mouth
the impulse followed through
the discomfort of it upon reflection
the arousal
dis/invitation
the __ may be the way language fails us, or representative of how memory works
how the brain & body might protect us from remembering & yet
I put myself there
on the line or am I trying to let myself off the hook?
a chain link of homes in the moment of the __
the reader becomes textual projected neighbors
a real something/really something

# & , &

we are not secretive in this home, we are not chaste in this home, we make love in this home, we cure ailments in this home & lick the salt off countertops in this home & walk in different directions around the same thing in this home, we are endlessly praying in this home, we jump over brooms & broken plates in this home, we balance steel rods on our backs in this home & thank in ways that make us swallow in this home, we are mapping things on walls & on each other in this home, we blow breath on windows in this home, we sometimes push one another down flights of stairs in this home, we wrap necks in wet towels in this home, never call it 'the burbs ' we protect our books before we protect our spines in this home, we love surprises in this home, we drive an hour west & forget what we fought about in this home, & bastardize nothing in this home, we have rendezvous in black caskets & oh! we dissolve like snow to a begging tongue, in this home, in this room, on this lawn, in a bed, & nowhere else will you know something as visceral as me...not in anyone else's home...not in anyone else's idea of wild, bright things.

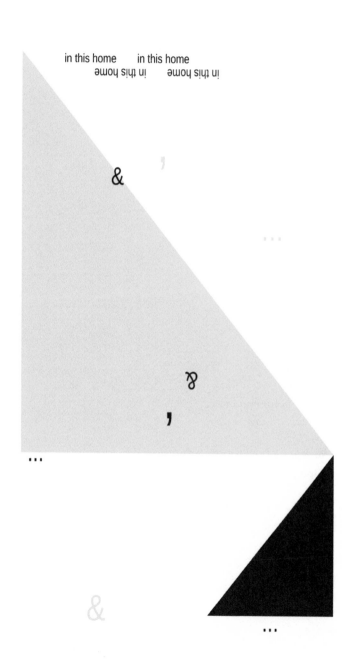

in this home    in this home

in this home    in this home

&

,

&

,

...

...

&

...

# Our South Nodes

I see a french princess
and a toltec god

whose iris pools
soil green as a canal's

buoyant sustenance
caressed in cervices

of the earth's musculature,
so desired and so dispossessed.

Your valleys smell
of maize and rooster,

my moisture of olives
and sardines netted

your voice into breath over me
singing ave maria or song of rain.

Would I kneel before an idol,
admiring form without myth to understand.

Would I heed the body like an altar,
always heavy with indulgences.

Would I explore this new world,
without destiny being claimed.

Although you say
that I seem lost,

was I just found
in your gaze.

# Deh Kalapani Self-Self
## Georgetown, Guyana 2019

Watch.

Brown coconut husks beat themselves into frayed fibers in what small surf burbles.

Empty water bottles, laundry baskets, blue plastics that bear no trace of their past lives, pile bodies on the beach, the pyre for the equatorial sun to light.

A homeless man stretches on the sea wall, asleep or pretending to be asleep.

At Stabroek a man hawks sun conures: the thrill and shock of emerald meeting sunset orange.

The ladies in the puja shop this morning said not to walk down Water Street by myself and to *speak like a Guyanese*, gold teeth sparking diyas in the dark store.

A twenty-something man pulls out his dick and pisses on the road behind the taxi stand.

I send my mother a picture of the road sign of the street she grew up on: Lamaha and Carmichael.

*It's all so familiar.*

*This is home.* This is the shore she saw from the ships, the seawall now painted with adverts.

But now it's early evening and the sea breeze shouts, *You are this sea, this murk, this plastic.*

*Watch. Oil go come just now. Oil. Black Water, creator of displacement. Kala pani.*

Meters out, a devotee has stuck bamboo into the water:

red, yellow, orange, jhandi flags not on land, not at sea flap in the wind—

birds with wings trained for sky.

# Navy & Black

*On the shore dimly seen through the mists of the deep*

\there were myths\
1. because we were married people assumed he was a good father. (when he was home & the children were under 5 he was great. but he was rarely home & the children grew older)
2. because he was in the military people assumed he upheld moral standards & was a wonderful man. (he was absolutely charming & read the Bible)
3. because we were married people seemed to think i was placed on a pedestal for being a military wife. (on the 4th of July we got to see free fireworks. if i walked with him while he was wearing his white uniform especially after being gone a year or 6 months—they'd give us both free coffee. the children get older. he was absolutely charming. he read the bible )
4. because we were married people assumed we made lots of money & had a huge savings—a signing bonus too. (he wanted to be a marine but he couldn't so he picked the navy & for the job he picked there was no signing bonus. we never had savings because we spent most of our marriage living in two separate households. he alone on the ship. me with the children. all his extra money went to _____ _____, casinos, _____ _____, gadgets, happy endings, updated uniform pieces, _____& fitted caps. (the children got older. he read the bible. he was absolutely charming.)

*Where the foe's haughty host in dread silence reposes,*
*What is that which the breeze, o'er the towering steep,*

\there was patriarchy\
1. upon our arrival on the base stands a sign which prohibits women only from wearing things in the common areas. the woman in the sign is darker in complexion. her eyes & body appear hungry. she is wearing what they have deemed an inappropriate outfit & have marked red x's over the clothing. it is huge & is placed strategically between popeye's & baskin-robbins. no tank tops. no short/shorts. no see through shirts. no skirts above the knee. it's 2000 something. it's 99 degrees. i'm wearing a green tank top, one tattoo, shorts, flip flops, dreadlocks, black sweat & mother-face. a random military wife offers me her sweater & says something like it gets chilly in

here. when i passively refuse the donna k sweater the man who was my navy black husband flashes a white smile so broad at her she may have for a moment mistaken him for a woman. he introduced himself & clumsily as if harking up bones introduced us (the kids much older than 5 & me the veteran black military wife.) the woman wears a white sun dress & she planned to meet her husband for lunch & then take his uniform to the cleaners & then go work out & then do some volunteer tutoring & then cook dinner (& then) the dk woman stops herself & asks me my name again & i am wondering too: who i am? what my name is? how i got here? where do i live? will i get adjusted? (he is absolutely charming. he reads the bible) he thinks of _____her as the kids & the two of us walk away. oh hot day. so hot. i wanted to take my clothes off.

2. there were no out feminists on base. no one said feminist. no one said womanist. |the movie the color purple was always checked out of the small base video store| & men often in times of joking said "you told harpo to beat me?" (ha ha ha ha)

3. the sailors spit slang & snuff & talk about women riding them like american cowboys or sending women away barely walking. the closest definition they had of a feminist was a single woman they could fuck regularly who didn't call them often & never needed their money. a woman who would suck them off then say fuck off. what a dream. what a dream. what an american dream. once we heard a woman being choked by her husband. (ha ha ha ha) he said the house was filthy when he got home (his house) & the kids were not fed (his kids) & she said with her dirty little mouth (his mouth) shut the fuck up. what a nightmare it was. & my military husband said the one thing he'd never do was put his hands on me. he did not. (he is absolutely charming. he reads the bible).

*As it fitfully blows, half conceals, half discloses?*
*Now it catches the gleam of the morning's first beam,*

\there was racism\
(see) the history of african americans in the united states military (think tuskegee, think troops rioting while at war together on the same team, think black soldiers being sent to die first & inadequate medicine & preparation think think think systemic systemic systemic think change gone come think i have a dream think we couldn't celebrate on base or in base housing when obama won think think think think
(r e m e m b e r)
kids- *yay mommy yay yayyyyy*

black military wife- *yay i know right? yay ... shhhhhh. stop jumping. whisper. don't talk about this at school tomorrow. shhhhhh. yes yay.*
kids- *dad is probably happy too right?*
black military wife- *yes! i'm sure he is. happy. yay. get in the bed. yay.*

*In full glory reflected now shines on the stream*

note: our car was broken into very early that morning. both windows. thank god nothing was stolen except our boundaries.

*'Tis the star-spangled banner - O long may it wave*

\there were missing-ings\

1. there are movies where the wives line up in church dressed & the babies are in the wives' arms & the babies (all ages) run or skip or crip walk to their dads who have been deployed (this is true we were there) & there is glee. so much glee. american glee.

or

2. the navy dads clad in white (Jesus like) with outstretched arms surprise family members & rush home with gifts for their parents & children & bless us all (this is true we were there) santa clause is really real & pinocchio is a real boy too. so real.

a ~~few~~ things navy military dad missed:
car accidents
potty training
teeth lost & replaced by grown up teeth (about 52)
    nights
    homework
homework
homework
    days

---

holidays
birthdays
birthdays    birthdays
birthdays    birthdays
    firsts (a lot)
    lasts (a lot)

heartbreak (times three)
months
the flu (times three)
swine flu
asthma (over & over) er visits
nose bleeds (over & over) er visits
sunrises (these are consistent)
sunsets (these are consistent)
& months
communication
Bullies/burglaries/guns/fear
homecomings
proms
choir programs

_____

parent teacher conferences
parenting
parenting parenting parenting (black)
parenting parenting parenting (nonconforming boys)
partnership
 intimacy
(love)
& then (he is charming & reads the bible)
honey i'm home
 one.          me.
(missing)
*O'er the land of the free and the home of the brave!*

# Face

It looked like a joint effort, the breakup, Jake driving the moving van and Bitsy packing my clothes and me in the corner crying, supported by Alex, who petted my hair. We sorted everything out, plucked shoes and jewelry like eggs from the nest of apartment 3D. All this before Maeve got home from work—all this and more: the *Don't Call* note, the removal of my photographs from her frames, the breaking of the round window we'd drawn together and commissioned to be stained for our fifth anniversary.

"She was horrible for you, Honey," Bitsy got to preach at last, coming close in an attempt to lay hands on me. While the others nodded like parishioners, I winced away. I'd said enough when I phoned Alex: *She grabbed me in the bathroom. I sliced her with the razor to get free.*

In twenty years, I think my childhood friends (rural Vermont expats, like me) will remember several things about Maeve. She was Black, a Bronx native, and had gone to community college; held an AA in something. Her septum was pierced. She was ex-military. Other things, they'd already forgotten: for instance, that I did not date flat characters.

Maeve, intense and mainly self-taught, had served in her Army medical unit as a lab specialist—inspecting plasma, handling infectious specimens. Now she worked down at the hospital where, during breaks, she'd built a telescope to view the Crab Nebula from our fire escape.

She knew German. She knew Latin. She knew Japanese—had learned from subtitled anime; taken the train to Midtown as a lanky preteen to buy a dictionary from Kinokuniya; worked her way up to Murakami and Ogawa. She might've set her sights on a four-year college had her father, sad-faced at her high school graduation dinner, not reminded her that she was on her own now; had her stepmother not added, "No matter how much book knowledge you get, you'll still just be another mark for white folks." I doubt, anyway, that a four-year school would've shown her anything more spectacular than what she'd seen—maybe how to funnel beer, or talk around an issue.

"Keep or toss?" Bitsy waved Maeve's *Visit M82: We Sell the Finest Cigars in the Universe* t-shirt in the air, stirring sparkling motes of dust toward the ceiling.

"Keep," I said guiltily. We wore the same size.

She tossed the shirt in a box. "It's so quiet in here without her playlist blaring."

"It is," Alex whispered, squeezing my arm, surveying the room from our corner.

"That was my playlist," I said.

It occurred to me then that perhaps they were unaware of what a hard time Maeve had being loud. On a bench overlooking the Atlantic, arguing about a cheesecake recipe, she'd raised her voice momentarily and an eavesdropping father had sprung up from his family picnic to save me. On a weed-fringed sidewalk outside a café, our bickering was interrupted by two police officers who gave her a knot on the head, forcing her into the back of their squad car as they asked over and over whether I was okay. Businessmen, bouncers, grannies, children: they were poised to rescue me from my girlfriend. Waiting for a flash of her impatience.

So she saved it for our tiny apartment. Inside 3D, she boomed. She sobbed and stomped and laughed at my spurious reasoning, pushing me out the door, down the stairs and into the streets with her anger; never with her hands. Her hands were slow and gentle, like the swelling of sadness, the overflowing. Her hands made her apologies for her, afterward.

Had my friends forgotten her public quietude? How she leaned into the periphery, observant and guarded?

Then, the pandemic.

Week one. We were lucky! I taught my classes asynchronously, in pajamas, recording video lectures in the bathroom because it had the best sound. And at the hospital, an uncertain silence pooled in the imposed social distance: *I didn't speak to shitbody today!*

As introverts, we secretly rejoiced when New York went on lockdown. We held impromptu bedside dances; splurged on a grocery delivery service. It was like magic when our bell rang and we yanked the door open on an empty hallway—empty but for paper bags piled high with rice and beans, with chocolate and chicken and grapes and sliced cheese and baguettes and sweating glass bottles of kombucha. I pulled the bags inside, and Maeve disinfected everything with clinical precision, placing each item neatly where it belonged; spraying the small, granite counter down too before I nudged her out of the way to prepare dinner.

In our prior life, we'd been poor at acclimation; at compressing ourselves into the strange shapes of our various containers—skins, skulls, city—and the cramped mold of social expectations. We'd withstood most interactions in a herky-jerky panic, like minnows fallen from the net between sea and packing plant. Now, isolated, we were in our element.

Week two. We were productive! While Maeve vacuumed the narrow living room, avoiding the tassled edges of its faded rug, I cleaned the toilet. While Maeve folded clothes, I scrubbed the floor. Our only commute was to the lobby's fluorescent-lit mailboxes or the basement laundry room—one of us shuffling to the elevator and back in our shared pair of bunny slippers. Our only gatherings were online; our only outdoor activity, stargazing from the fire escape.

Week three, and things became—harder. It was no longer us against everyone. With the others gone from our lives, we *were* everyone.

Bitsy rolled her eyes at my playlist comment. Didn't believe, or didn't care. Anytime I bristled on Maeve's behalf, she'd call me "Sensitivity 101." Other descriptors included "exotic," "graceful," "submissive," "feminine," and "too polite." Occasionally I reminded her that I was not a lotus blossom, and then she grinned, slapped my arm and called me "Oriental Cracker Mix." As though wit nullified narrow-mindedness.

Does the lotus sit in her dark, cool pond and question the tulips as their pink heads nod in unison on the bank? Does she wonder whether their petals would be carried off or hold fast, were they ever banished to her place? Suspect their leaves would droop in the mud without a self-cleansing skin like hers? Can a lotus survive transplantation?

These were the silly questions that throbbed in my head while Bitsy packed and Jake puttered and Alex stroked and cooed. Did they feel like saviors today? If so, what were they saving me from? And then, the hardest question. Was I really doing this? Was there enough venom in me to kill off what we'd conceived—fumbling, colliding, kissing, coupling in the intimate shelter of 3D, where we'd assembled a 40-tiered LEGO pine tree; considered getting a dog, because cats were evil, or a cat, because cats were evil; played Scrabble and Charades, talked politics, talked books, talked everything from every angle. *Would you live in a gorgeous mansion with a helipad, if it meant you could only shit in an outhouse? Would you rather have bowl-sized nipples, or no nipples at all?*

Week four. Week five. Week six. Week seven. Week eight. Week nine. Week ten. Eventually the corners gave out and conversation caved. Everything caved—even the LEGO tree, *timber,* when Maeve nudged it with the vacuum. There was simply no more structure; no routine. Our lungs labored to fill and empty and fill again. The nation labored as employment fell and tensions rose. And we accepted that our civilization would fall too—possibly soon. We accepted truths we'd never seriously considered.

We lost track of the weeks; lost clemency and composure. We moved to the furthest corners of the apartment but could still hear one another chewing.

My childhood friends drove me to a pickup-only diner and bought me a heap of food. The diner was a semi-authentic fifties affair. It had signs like *Good Eats* and *We Aim to Please* in the windows, but not signs like *Whites Only*. There was a picture of a waitress in a striped poodle skirt, but the one who handed over our food was wearing overalls and an N95 mask. Jake tipped her, regardless.

"This place is the bomb," he said, dispensing sporks and napkins. "It's lit!"

"Right?" Bitsy wiped down the outside of her shake with a napkin. "Sock hops and sideburns. Coonskin caps and cartoons at the cinema. Johnny Cash! Little Richard."

Jake nodded. "Lit!" He exited the lot, navigating toward my new apartment. "How sad is it that Johnny Cash is never coming back?" He shook his head. "He was brilliant. My folks got to see him perform twice." The van jolted as he took a hard right.

"You know what else isn't coming back?" Bitsy said. Jake shook his head again. "'The bomb' and 'lit.'" Bitsy lurched forward from the opposite corner of the cargo space. "Jesus, Jake! Shit's sliding, back here! Slow the fuck down, Asshole."

"You coulda sat up here with me," he shouted back, blowing a kiss over his shoulder.

"Six. Feet. Apart. Jake. And we should really all be masked up," Alex piped up from our corner.

Bitsy glowered. "You two aren't six feet apart."

"Jesus, Bitsy," Alex murmured, "after all she's been through—"

I sucked my fingers. Licked my spork sparkly clean. "Sorry, guys," I said, bracing against a loveseat. "This is all very shitty, I know."

"That's okay, Sweetie," Alex reassured. "She was so bad for you."

The van made its way between an old bodega and a trendy new hotel with rooms the size of a suburban walk-in closet. Bitsy worked in a hotel like this, and occasionally regaled us with tales of turds in bathtubs, the theft of bolted-in hotel furniture, and domestic disputes: "We found her *sleeping* on the *treadmill* in the workout room…"

Now she and Jake hollered above the road noise, deciding together whom I should date next. "I'm not sure this is the best time to date," I cut in, but Bitsy scowled.

"Start online," she barked. "I command you, Peon! Exit the temple of solitude."

"More like a morgue," bellowed Jake.

"Give her time," said Alex, but they ignored her until, at last, there was consensus: Bethany Stover, my girlfriend-to-be, was a colleague at the university.

She taught abstract algebra while I could hardly work out a 20% tip, but we did look a lot alike. In fact, I supposed I would be her if I woke up one morning and pissed all my Japanese yellow into the toilet.

"I'm not white, you guys," I reminded them. They glanced at me, then at one another.

"Uh, we know that," Jake answered.

"You're not Black, either," said Bitsy. "Even if your playlist is."

"Let up on her, Bits," Alex urged. "There's a global. Fucking. Pandemic." These three final words came out satiny, as though uttered by a nighttime DJ.

"And she just escaped an abusive relationship," Jake yelled. From back here, I could only see his forearm and the one hand clasping the wheel.

Bitsy looked down at her feet, chastened.

"It wasn't abusive," I said loudly.

"Okay," purred Alex. She put her hands on my shoulders and rubbed, as though to warm me up beyond July's oppressive heat. "What was it?"

"It was just—" I snapped in Jake's direction "—two frazzled women fighting one another in our home because it was safe. And it got out of hand."

"It's never safe to fight someone with eight years of military training," Jake retorted over his shoulder.

Alex moved a box that had slid toward us back into place. "It's never safe…"

"You didn't just let us talk you into leaving," Bitsy burst out. "You were the one who phoned Alex."

"…for someone like you to fight someone like Maeve."

"What does that mean?" I said quietly.

Then everyone was silent. Alex looked down at her hands. Bitsy studied her chipped nail polish. Jake, oblivious up front, looked out at the road.

And I'll tell you something. I should've said right then what I'm saying now, to you: that I'm a nasty fighter. A dirty one. That my tongue was always sharper, my voice always louder, and sometimes I would take our fights outside to mute her in the watchful public eye. That we did bad things. We both did bad things. Couples do.

Maybe in that hour, in that jostling van, bumping along eerily empty roads as something deadly spread unseen, person to person, I could've explained it just right—made them see. But a cold current took me, closed my lips like petals, folded my arms. And I swayed, and Jake drove us past a pickle shop and a shut-down cinema, and I swayed, and Jake drove us from streets with dying trees to streets with thriving trees, and I swayed, and Jake drove us all the way from my old, Baychester neighborhood to my new, Prospect Park neighborhood, and I swayed, and didn't say a word.

I didn't tell them what I'm telling you now. That the breakup was more than a mistake, more than selling something precious when you think you need the money. It was *seppuku*. Gutting oneself for honor—for face.

I couldn't tell them how, in the bathroom of apartment 3D, she'd locked her arms around me while I screamed, "Don't touch me, you can't have me," while I screamed in her face, "Let go of me, you don't know me," while I screamed, "RAPIST," stunning myself into silence; how, limp and ashamed, my arm shot out, fingers inches from the cheap, disposable razor, and I felt her quiet lips press against my cheek.

I didn't say how I'd rather live in an outhouse with her than a mansion with anybody else. How she'd let me steal all her t-shirts. How I looked in her eyes and glimpsed the far-reaching roots of her soul. How we swayed there for a few long moments before I ended it, a florid and blooming galaxy held together by her gravity. How calm I felt, clasped. How understood. Swaying infuriated, infuriated in her arms, which did not let go, even then.

# Christmas Sex, North Carolina, 2019

In my memory it's Christmas Day—but in point of fact it isn't; it's the day after—when we gently fuck in my parents' house, on one of my childhood twin beds, near silent, while the rest of the house is waking.

It has been a week since I've seen you, a month since I moved down three floors of our building in to your apartment, nearly a year since we met. You told me no, no way, no chance at all, are we having sex in your parents' house.

You spend Christmas Eve with your family. I go home for a week before to see mine, because I missed Thanksgiving, and on Christmas morning you drive two hours north west, with the dog, to me. I am on my phone during Mass because I am waiting to hear from you. Mom disapproves.

But also six months ago on the D.C. metro, visiting my brother, I'm sitting next to her and asking *please don't think I'm crazy, like this is kind of a crazy question, but is it ever too early to say I love you to someone.* And she says, *you aren't going to like this answer, but it's never too early.* And I cry.

We cook brunch and the bread pudding doesn't set the way Mom wants it to, and she's worried we, you and me, think she's a terrible cook. It's good; in my memory it tastes like cheddar and chives. You pull into the driveway.

I don't tell anyone you're here. I come to you and you hold me, say, let's never be apart this long again.

We do Christmas. We eat steaks you save from overcooking at just the right second. Daddy lights a fire in the old pit out back. When we wake up in the morning and I squeeze in the twin next to you your hair still smells like green wood ash.

You are holding my waist in your big arms, tight. We are barely moving. We are saying *I don't care I don't care I love you.*

I think if my parents had caught us they'd be mortified in a particularly Catholic way forever, but then maybe one day they'd look at each other and say *at least she's with a man.*

The first time I tell anyone "I'm queer" instead of "I like girls sometimes," I say it to my grad school therapist. This is maybe four years ago. I'm out to my current roommate and some of the guys in my cohort. It always seems easier being bi and out to men who are allies. My therapist begins to wonder if I'm in love with my roommate.

I come out to my mom, after I explain *bi-sexual, technically, but that doesn't really seem right to me, so queer*. She asks *are you sure this isn't because you can't find a boyfriend?* She tells me not to tell my dad and then she tells my dad. I hold off telling him because right when I wanted to, he is diagnosed with cancer. But after he's okay I find out he knows already.

I think I impressed you at first because of how *me* I was trying to be when we met. The first man I'd met in a while who I felt safe with immediately, I don't know how many times I said *because I'm queer, it's different for me, when you're queer...* on that first date in the biergarten over chili fries. It was March and the first warm-ish night. As we got closer I realized I wasn't a novelty to you, a queer girl, and that you respected me not because of how brave and queer I was, but because you respect people you love. I let you walk on the outside of me on busy streets and behind me up stairs.

It takes me a long time to fuck you. It is because you are the first one but also because everything about us is so terrifyingly new. I text my grad school roommate *oh my god, sex is great,* and am honestly underwhelmed by her reaction, which of course is *I'm proud of you* but also *well, yeah!*

Even kissing women, touching women, I never want any of them, anyone, to touch me. In therapy I talk about how desperate I am to shed this label, a virgin, despite the fact that really, it isn't true. Just recently, a friend tells a story at lunch and said about someone she knows *...because she was a virgin in grad school* and I didn't even know that was a club I was part of. I used to tell myself, *Tina Fey was twenty-six.* Now that I think of it, so was I.

It isn't that I was afraid of feeling less queer, or more queer, depending. I am afraid of my own body. I grew up Catholic. They tell you your body is dirty but they tell you it's sacred. I grew up in ballet. They tell you it's wrong but they teach you to use it.

I think what I mean to say to you is thank you.

I find out alone in my apartment, in the bathroom on speaker phone with my mom, that yes, she's told my dad. I am already living with you, we've already Christmas-fucked in their house. She says *yeah, I told him.* And I say I wanted to. Because of what I have to ask next which is, *is he okay with it?* Of course.

The Catholicism in me forgives my mother within hours. I don't explain outing to her on the phone. I don't explain the kind of right she's violated, that it was my right to share, and that she told me don't tell, so, what, she could tell? Because part of me thought it could wait. And of course, I'm with you now.

But here's the thing about you. Being with you doesn't change me. I think I thought it would; I haven't been me for long. You don't make me less of anything.

Maybe a few months after we get serious, you tell me about your uncle, who died of AIDS when you were fourteen. For a story like his, that happened in a rural South Carolina county, it's about the nicest it could be. I think all the time how lucky we are, to live in a South, our microcosm of it, that isn't what people think it is. Even though it can't look at us, you and me, and know for sure what it sees, there's a place here for us.

The day after Christmas, when you fuck me, I am perfect. In a house full of people, we are alone. We come out for coffee, and everyone knows how this goes, we are smiling and eying each other and your hand is on my thigh on the couch while Daddy rustles the paper and Mom is saying something and my brother I guess is still asleep. What I mean to say is thank you.

# Prayer

After any years away, Seattle is everywhere: the fresh faces
     of the perennials, the crows that kiss the sky.

I was once the sky. I ran over the hills of my body
     with the son of a man who killed himself.

Lately, I've been thinking about what suicide means.
My friend says there are many ways to commit
     without actually dying. There's joy in that.

I ask myself: *Do you really want to die this far away*
     *from your hometown?* I don't. Want to die, I mean.
It's too beautiful this summer and I want to see another like it.
The bluebells. The cardinals.

This morning, my mother called again to say she loves me.
I was annoyed, I admit it. I think she is dying
     but doesn't want to say. The last time I saw her
she was limping. She didn't think I noticed her face sinking
into her skull. Still beautiful. Purposefully blush.

When she hung up, I opened my blinds. I want to die with the city
     pouring onto my deathbed, to the floor, then out
into the hallway, and into another room where it can lay
its head on the pillows of others. Unbound by my bullshit.

Have you ever seen more than one cardinal at once?
I've googled *are cardinals lonely birds?*

I know what you're thinking. Yes, I miss Seattle.
I miss my mother. I never call.

When the man killed himself, what was he thinking?
When people jumped out the World Trade Center,
     red from the combustion; cardinals; lonely wings—

never mind. I don't want to go there. I am always trying
         to escape too many places at once, flying out of a cage
and into another.

# the soil and the sound and me

I untangle, unmoor in the mist—
free to fill not a body but this specter
of belonging, this bright-eyed being.

> her robes wrap me back
> to front, hang from my gutters,
> a posture I have never felt held by.

I cannot let her in.

there is more than I was made for.

> at one point, I would have seen her
> need, wanted to feel her knife at work
> on my side.

> at one point, I would have unlatched
> my self and felt her feet's tender creek
> up my stairs.

but I cannot bear my bookings, let alone
these guests who arrive unannounced.
ghosts emerge off the moor.

> she has been here before.

# The Cock

you can't spell basement without semen.
or i suppose you could but then it'd just read *bat*.

somewhere south on second avenue, a staircase
you pay ten dollars to descend onto a 'dance floor'

tho more a dark field of men who've already removed
their heads so as to blend into the eternal body

which is always loosening & welcoming fluids. what becomes
of the indivisible soul in basements such as this?

here where the spirit is passed around as a yawn or religion.
*soul* i say, welcoming someone me yet not

into this rented & temporary skin when an oddly cold erection
nuzzles its wet nose into my palm like an elderly dog.

in that old story the three headed dog guards the gate
to the world of the dead. in this underworld, it's the living

## da hood™ as sex worker

pussy a whole mood     tight & wet wet but da game dried up used to be fancy feast like a mug
loosies     trojans     cat litter     3 in da morn     staircase quickie     now niggas aint picky
fuck any ramshackle lean-to     any gaping hole masquerading as mouth     mostly whiteboy
orgies     jews with dat new minivan smell     buckets of shmoney on da hush     gangbang
bumrush     suddenly ima fixerupper     boners when they get a load of my good bones     my
redlines fade to headlines     now im errybodys favorite boo     da new hipster frontier
pioneering alla dis gushy     leeching at my technicolor teats leaking so many milks     cuz aint i a
beast tamed     dimepiece turned diamond     i am almost famous     ready for da rebrand     dark
marketing     blackbottom anthem     sex addict panic     architect picnic     pick apart my
blueprints     eat me down to the studs     rename me     something catchy & neon     unlatch
all my locks & catch me gagging reflexively off da influx     say my new name     watch me cum &
come again like Black Jesus     with my titties out     so many fuckin milks     but my slur slogan stay
C. R. E. A. M

**Ana, I don't forget** those mornings I rested in your childhood
blizzard town, where time froze and we walked knee-deep

in atmosphere
toward each other.

I was a stranger everywhere, I wept at the homeness of your language
weight of your pen's black line, circumference

of your thick hair bound—impossibly ungendered. Leather
satchel at your chest heavy with stones, a spell.

Today's wind is bold, my windows shake with language.
What is the message? Birds, trees, and buildings register

although they're human-made. I think I might be otherwise.
Wish I wasn't prone to put myself in the center of stories

of the Earth, the heart, its weather. This clear sky is otherwise
radiant. It streams through glass onto my hands

warming them. Sometimes I see a woman with rings
on every finger and think of drives north to Astoria.

That baker gave us her begonia because I loved its underside
—hot red hearts—she loved us, our strangerness.

Raw buckwheat honey we bought off the truck religiously,
road over Youngs River so close to water I could taste it.

Anxious for wild coastline, there are days when I think I know
why we loved each other, readily, away from daily life

rarely in it. Days I unknow
like death unwinds a clock.

Unknowing is a kind of language too, a kind of wind.
If we had known how to forgive each other at the same time—

In the shadowlight, staring at a satellite, imagining an owl.
It is impossible to really know another person, you taught me that.

Wild things come as often as they leave, don't they?

# Every moment I have been alive, I have been at the height of my powers

Whichever direction I walk is north,
cardinal. For years now, I have only walked
north. I have walked north into a sun lifting
the horizon like a seedling through soil.
I have walked north into a sun settling
like my great-grandma into dusk. I have
walked north with the chariot of sun sailing
across my face from ear to ear. For years now,
I have been an only child: my brother and sister,
their beautiful children, alive in the South—
to which I can never return. For years now,
I have been an orphan: my parents—neither
one of them themselves as I recall them—alive
in the South, to which I can never return.

*

In the South, to which I can never return,
I knew a loneliness of only-ness,
red field in which I stood but barely survived:
the till and plowing; the stick and seed; tending
and harvest. My great-grandma Juel, dead now
for some time, told me more than once a story:
her husband, Zach, called her into the garden,
pretended a hose was a snake—at his
pointing, she jumped into the long ropes
of his arms. At his laughter, she slapped hard
his chest. She told me the story at night.
We shared the bed they'd shared until he died.
She sounded, still, exasperated, like a wife—
neither of them, in the story, is alone.

*

Neither of them in this story is alone.
they were married for over sixty years,
longer than I've been alive or hope to live.
I know little of my great-grandpa Zach,
only history's hearsay. A rough husband,
hard-fisted, slurred. The inevitability
of sons, rising against the drunken
horizon of their father—an act older
than the standardization of time.
I knew him only in his third form,
so gentle the cows came when he called,
so gentle he couldn't bend anyone's name
right but *Juel Lee*, and even that he stuttered.
Her name precious, near too heavy for the tongue

*

Our names precious, don't heavy the tongue,
but bend and wrap, let the palate
move. Don't we resonate, you and I,
valley and harbor? I wanted to see you
on the red dirt some part of me calls home.
I wanted to see you mirage in air
so thick with water and terpene it shimmers.
An ocean in the air in the place I called home;
the cows in the field; wood gone soft and sweet
with rot; the dirt full of iron and fire;
the ant colony aerating the ground,
the ant jaws the nearest danger we can't see.
I wanted to take you there, but how could
I return if I'm always walking north?

# The Explosions Are Magnificent

June Miller was back in town. June the weird, wild girl, who stole the church communion and replaced it with Necco wafers, the girl that the Sheriff had to fish out of the old mine because she had set up a tent in the open shaft and wouldn't come out.

Rumor was, she got kicked out of boarding school in Los Angeles. Rumor was, she knew where to get weed, and maybe even something harder. She partied with Cat Stevens; she had a nose piercing. She rolled her own cigarettes. She spoke French, if you know what I mean.

I kissed her, six years ago, in the orange tree. I don't know if she remembers.

We were 12, sitting among the branches in my front yard. Unripe fruit hung around us, green, with streaks of orange licking up like tongues of flame.

June had gone out too far. I kept telling her to come back to where I sat, near the trunk, but she insisted on edging out farther and farther until the branch cracked. Her eyes widened. I grabbed her by the shoulders and pulled. She crashed into my arms and the branch fell and we were laughing, at the danger, at our closeness, and I kissed her on the cheek.

Her face emptied. Her laughter cut off. She climbed down from the tree and walked home. I stayed up there until sunset, eyes fixed on the bend in the road where June had disappeared. Mom came home from her shift at the diner and called up, "Colleen, what are you doing?"

I was pretending to be a bird: anonymous, free, about to take flight. I imagined fluttering after June, following her from tree to tree, singing the music that resounded in my bones. Mom told me to come down, but I held onto the branches until the moon began to rise. For the first time, I could see past the borders of our town.

Now, I was 18 and it was a hot, stormy September. There was a war out there, in some jungle, but that meant nothing to me. I spent my afternoon shifts at the corner store reading Asimov novels under the counter, and ringing up discounted comics for Matt. I'd walk him home, and make macaroni and cheese when Mom forgot to leave us dinner. Our evenings were quiet, both of us enveloped in hazy, imagined worlds, alone and together.

Eden was the kind of small town with roads so wide open that Matt and I could walk right down the middle on our way to school. We played a game of chase, where he would name a thing—the broken fence post, the juniper tree,

Lou's mailbox—and I would have to reach it before he finished shouting the first verse of "I Want to Hold Your Hand." I got to school with dust kicked up into the folds of my jeans.

When June arrived, I told Matt I was too tired to run, but the truth was I had seen myself in the mirror when I got to school. Plain, boyish, with wisps of hair escaping from my braid and dirt smudged on my face. I looked like a child next to June.

At first I thought she would ignore me, like when we were 12, after the kiss. I expected her to retreat, ghost-like, into friends who wore scrunchies, borrowed their mom's lipstick and ate fancy peanut butter sandwiches with the crusts cut off. Instead, June looped her arm into mine, leaned her head on my shoulder and said, "Collie, I missed you."

June was a hurricane in the hallways, hair teased up, wearing this old leather jacket with pins of women I didn't recognize and was afraid to ask about. She was the only girl who wore pumps with socks on and smeared eyeliner under her eyes.

When people asked what happened to her at boarding school—did she really jump off the roof, spike the principal's coffee with bourbon, come to school wearing nothing but a strip of leather and some safety pins—she'd roll her eyes and say that the system couldn't handle her, or that it was actually a denim jacket and assless chaps, or that she hadn't jumped off the roof so much as fell through until I got tired of the haze of stories surrounding her and asked, point-blank, "Why *did* they kick you out?"

We were smoking by the river, with our feet in the water. I asked the question lightly, but held her gaze in a way that said, don't you dare bullshit. I am not everyone else.

June let entire clouds pass by before saying anything, holding in her breath. I watched the drifting smoke get thinner and thinner until June huffed out a sigh, and it disappeared.

"There was this girl," she said, without meeting my eyes, "named Kate."

June stirred the water. Every circle she drew with her foot brushed a little closer to mine.

"What happened?" I asked.

June took a breath. "Something like this," she said, and kissed me. She pulled back quickly but I leaned forward, lost my footing, and fell, splashing both of us into the water.

I pushed myself up. Sat in the creek bed with water pooling around my elbows. My head was spinning and my hand was bleeding and I wanted nothing more than to kiss June again.

She laughed, sitting in the shallows next to me. "Your face," she said, flicking her damp cigarette at the bank and squeezing water out of her hair.

I didn't care if it was a game, I didn't care if it was a bad idea, I just wanted June to look at me like I was looking at her so I kissed the drops of water from her cheek and her forehead. She tasted like salt and algae and suntan lotion.

When I pulled back, she had stopped smiling and I thought, I've done it again, until she kissed me back.

Her lips on mine. Sun-warmed and soft. I wanted to fix her there, crystalize the two of us in amber, so that nothing could ever move, or shift, or change.

In silent agreement, we pulled our clothes off and flung them at the bank. June took my hand and we paddled up the current, into the old mine shaft.

Light danced on the stone walls. June glowed in the darkness, pure-white pear belly, but I blended in. I felt like a shadow among shadows, watching her shine. I enveloped her.

"There's geometry in these caves," I told June. Traced the curve of the rock with one finger.

"You see geometry in everything," she laughed, so I didn't tell her that there was also geometry in the angle of her chin. The droplets, sliding to the tips of her eyelashes. Clean, clear spheres. Perfectly round.

We paddled back to the shore and lay out in the sun, letting warm gusts of air dry our skin.

I looked up at the trees, a lattice of gold and red leaves. Seeds spiraled down, twisting. A kind of peace flooded me that I had never known before. I could've stayed there forever.

"We should leave Eden," said June.

I sat up on one elbow, to see her face. Her brow was furrowed, and her eyes reflected the passing clouds.

I felt a tug of urgency. The wind chilled goosebumps onto my skin.

"Why?" I asked.

"There's nothing here," June said, and I saw a truth in her eyes harder than the noon sky.

I knew myself, and I knew the laws of physics. An object in motion stays in motion. I was at rest, and I wanted to stay at rest. But here was this earth-shaking girl telling me to take off my sweater. That I looked beautiful. That I tasted like minerals, salt and earth. How was I supposed to change that kind of current?

Before June, I existed in Eden the way a moon exists in orbit. I swung in a perfectly balanced dance between Matt, grabbing my arm to tell me about something new he read; Mom, slipping whipped cream into my coffee when her manager wasn't looking; and Lou, slapping the TV he watched in the back while I worked the register. This was the sum total of my universe.

June altered my center of gravity. She showed up in the middle of my shift and got me to cut class just to go for long walks in the woods. Lent me books that she proclaimed life-changing, which were always heavily dog-eared up until the second chapter. Gave me records of bands I'd never heard of and had no way of listening to until I went over to her house and we snuck her mom's record player into the attic. She loved to smoke out the window, Hendrix mixing with the haze in the air, until she saw her mother coming up the front steps. The joint would go out; the music would stop; and I'd hide under June's bed until her mother's low black pumps had left the room, satisfied that everything was where it should be.

My trajectory had changed, but I was good at making plans. I began charting a new path for me and June, a perfect parabolic wave, undulating through time in choreographed symmetry. She would graduate, work in the diner, and I would take over Lou's store.

June laughed every time I brought it up. "Working in the corner store?" she said, shaking her head, "Collie, you are way smarter than that. You could work at NASA. You could be the next Madam fucking Curry." (I didn't correct her.) "And your big dream is to manage Lou's?"

Her jasmine scent wafted over me and I let the conversation unravel into silence. I wanted to tell her that there were dreams too big to speak out loud, dreams that you let drift away like smoke because there was no way you could ever afford to make them solid. It was different for June; she had seen the end of the highway. The things she imagined were always in reach: new records, new books, new clothes.

At night, I began keeping the curtains open. The stars glittered hard and bright. Usually, they made me feel like I could float endlessly outward, in any direction. Now, I felt crushed. Small. Overwhelmed by all that space.

*I love Eden*, I told myself. I loved the way the diner was always empty and I could get my fries in less than a minute. I loved that I could walk from the corner store to the barber to the grocer and see five people I knew. The hum of everyone, the way they moved in and out of the store in waves, and how I floated in that rhythm. The satisfaction I felt when Lou looked up from the paperwork I'd given him and said, good work, kid. It had taken so long to earn that look in his eyes.

Still. I imagined walking my orbit in Eden for another 10, 20, 30 years. My heels would dig furrows in the dirt. The weeds would grow, and be cut, and grow again. Another summer, another winter, and there I would be, ringing up customers, getting coffee in the diner, trapped on an endless, concentric path. An anxious rhythm kicked up in my chest. I fell asleep watching the stars in their slow-motion retreat, floating backward into space. The universe was expanding. For the first time, I felt the pull.

Late that fall I took June to our hunched wood house, crouched in dust at the end of the road. The garden grew over long ago, and seeds hung at the end of stalks, waiting to take wing. I blew them free on my way past, but they just drifted to the ground, going nowhere.

Bundles of sage and rosemary hung from the porch eaves, wrinkled lemons rested on the kitchen table; our home was full of ripening and growing and drying things. June took an orange from the counter, peeled it, and offered me a slice. I took it, grateful, before realizing that she had offered me fruit from my own house like it was hers.

My mother was on the couch, asleep, half-smoked blunt smouldering on the ashtray. I touched her shoulder and she drifted back to the surface.

"Matt get home?" I asked. She nodded. Her eyes were red, and took a moment to focus on the stranger by the window.

"Oh, hello, June," my mother said, like it had been six minutes instead of six years.

"Hey, Rosemary," June said, and nodded at the book on the coffee table. "How's Shulie Firestone treating you?"

"Hmm?" said my mother. I desperately wanted to escape to my room. We were entering June's territory, of names and theories and women I should admire but didn't know. Instead, I watched the two of them, June sharp and quick, my mother feathered, sleepy, wise. A raven questioning an owl.

"I haven't had much time for reading, lately," my mother said. She shuffled the coffee table books, hiding a bill that had been there for weeks. Her hands were red and chapped from dish soap.

June smiled. "It's rad that you're finding empowerment," she said. "It's so easy to just let things stay the way they are."

My mother nodded, but looked past June at the clock. "I should get back," she said, and pushed herself off the couch. The scent of sage and coffee passed over us in a cloud. "Put Matt to bed, will you?" she asked me, and I said I would, as usual.

She left the room, and June followed. I took the bill from the table, to pay later.

June invited me to her house for thanksgiving dinner. It was the first time I'd left Mom and Matt on their own for the holiday, but Mom had to work and offered to take Matt with her and June asked me every day until I said yes. We usually had thanksgiving dinner on the floor, like a picnic, with candles surrounding us like tiny stars. At June's house, the food covered the table from end to end and they bowed their heads to say grace. June had to kick my shin before I would bow mine.

June looked like a doll that night, at the candlelit table. Her hair fell in a soft parentheses around her chin. Lowered eyelashes, shy, demure. June's stockinged foot brushed my thigh. She let it rest there, warm, solid, tracing my curves while her mother thanked the Lord our saviour. Asked him to deliver us from temptation. By the time we said Amen, I was melting, flushed, glowing—until I looked up and into her mother's cool, granite eyes.

I had never seen so much food for so few people. A turkey that June's father had shot himself. Fresh cranberry sauce—not the kind from the can. Homemade gravy. June licked ambrosia from her fingers with her gaze fixed on mine until her mother rapped her elbows with the blunt end of a knife and told her to take her arms off the table. I lowered my eyes and waited an infinity for the meal to end.

When I got home the house was dark, and I realized like a kick in the stomach that Matt and Mom were probably still at the diner. I stood looking at the empty house for a moment, then turned back the way I came.

June's window was the only one still lit. I could barely see her shape hunched by the window, head down, and I worried that she was asleep. I threw stones at her window until she raised her head, opened it, and climbed down to join me.

Dusk faded into evening. We hiked up to the ridge on the hillside, and lay on our backs to watch the sky. I told June about the arc and trail of the stars. The invisible pathways, criss-crossing and circling in the void. How the chances of two colliding are infinitesimal, but it happens. How the explosions are magnificent.

She only wanted to know what they were called. Orion, Cassiopeia, The Little Dipper. She gave them nicknames, and started referring to them like old friends in casual conversation. I wanted to study astronomy, and she wanted to act, so we joked that between us we'd know all of the stars.

"I'm going to be famous," she said, stretching her arms. "I'm going to change the world."

"You're already famous," I told her. "Everyone in town knows who you are."

"For something good," she said. She got this fine line between her eyebrows when she was thinking hard, and even though I couldn't see her face in the dark I knew it was there.

I was running out of time. As fall slid into winter, I took June to every beautiful spot. We spent afternoons lying in the clearing in the woods, exploring the overgrown cemetery, hiking the wavering golden fields. I gave her all of me, whenever she asked, even when it was getting late and I knew Matt and Mom were waiting. But she was going, going, gone. I could see it in the way she walked down the road, switching her hips, all her attention on the way she moved instead of where she was going. All her heat escaping into the icy nights, as winter came on strong.

One afternoon I found her crying in the girl's bathroom.

"I'm a disaster," she said, looking up at me from the floor. "Mom says I won't finish high school. I'll have to work at the diner and live with her and I can't, I just want to get out, I—"

I wanted to put the words back in her mouth but her eyes were ringed with red and smeared with mascara so I wrapped her in my arms. I held her and tried to think of something, anything, that would keep her on the ground.

"I'm going to fail," June said. "I'm going to fail every one of my classes."

Since when has that bothered you, I wanted to say. When we were cutting class to get high behind the woodshop? When you distracted me from calculus with the curve of your tongue on my thigh? Every goddamned time I'd said June, focus, we need to study?

"I'll help you. It'll be okay," I said, but there was a crack widening inside of me. June wouldn't look me in the eye.

When I got home I saw Matt, in the orange tree, reading. Smoking.

"Cut that out," I said, "you're twelve."

"It's just cloves," he said, but crushed the paper on a branch. "Your girlfriend smokes more than I do."

Matt climbed down from the tree and headed into the house. A cold draft had risen between us since I started spending all my time with June. He looked so small, in that faded blue hoodie. He doesn't have enough friends, I thought, and remembered with a pang all the afternoons we used to spend together. Building forts in the woods. Drawing on loose sheets of paper. Watching herds of deer pass, in silence, through the misty yard in the morning.

I could see my mother through the window, washing dishes. She was always washing dishes, I thought. I wonder if this is who she wanted to become.

As the sun fell, I climbed up to the ridge in the hills. The winter light cut Eden into strange angular shapes, shadows long and sharp for this time of day. I looked down at a town of backroad shortcuts, skinned knees, the strawberry milkshake I spilled all over the diner floor, the hushed redwood grove. I threw a rock, through I already knew it wouldn't go further than the spruce. This valley was full of stones I threw that didn't go as far as I wanted them to.

Eden was dying. I could see it in the empty diner. The cracked pavement. The car half-buried in the lot by the church. All of the places I loved, turning to ash in June's eyes. I wished I could blink the town back to what it was. I wished I could go home to Mom and ask her why she stayed here, why she nested in such a no-name town, but I knew there was no real answer. Like June, she only knew how to run, and this was just where she happened to stop.

That night, I woke up to a honk outside my window. Pushed up the blinds and there was June, behind the wheel of an old Buick.

I knew that car. I'd seen it parked next to the church every Sunday, and outside the community center where June's mom held her book club. My feet grew roots into the ground.

"I'm leaving," she called. "Are you coming?"

"Did you steal that car?" I shout-whispered.

"My parents went away for the weekend," June said. "It's the perfect time."

I pulled on a sweater—it smelled like her, like jasmine and sweat— and climbed out of the window. When I passed the orange tree, stark, bare, and white in the moonlight, I touched it for good luck.

Nothing I could say would stop her from leaving; I could see it. It was in the way she drummed her hand on the wheel. The way she leaned towards me, but still faced the road.

"You're not coming," June said. It was the tone she used when I hadn't read an author she thought was important. Disappointed, and unsurprised.

I shifted, thinking of her parents opening the door on an empty house.

"Why don't you stay?" I said. She touched my hand, but I felt no heat. All the summer, warm and lazy, all that afternoon sun. Gone. Cold.

"Colleen, I can't." Her face was still. "I hate who I am here. I hate hiding you."

"I don't feel hidden," I said.

"Of course you don't," she said, and shook her head. "You're luckier than you'll ever know."

How dare you, I didn't say. I'm the only one who knows you down to the bone. Can't you feel the warmth of my hands, the heat of my breath? Look at me, not *through* me, not at the child you knew or the girl you want me to be. I moved planets for you, I wanted to shout, I gave you a new galaxy. What more could I have done?

"Good luck," I said.

June bowed her head. For a second I thought she was going to look up and tell me that she was being stupid, that I was right, for once, that she would stay, and we would breathe light and life into this graveyard of a town. Then she shifted into drive.

I watched her follow the moonlit road. Her headlights flashed, then disappeared into the dark curve of the mountain. I climbed up into the orange tree and looked up; if the stars were moving, it was too slow for me to see.

# Snowglobe

My cyborg-smooth silver face
drained of pressure, collapsing onto
eroded cheekbones. Under my skin,
cell after cell containing copies
of Grandpa's closet of starched
white shirts, American flag patches
sewn onto short sleeves. I used
to make myself small, curl into a ball
with flashlight and yellowed,
smoke-drenched library book, my
face caressed by adjacent shirttails.
In the book's hard-backed walls
slept incantations for conjuring
worlds. Always more room
in small things—my whirring
mitochondria holding copies
of Grandma's chest of doll parts,
which I glued together, heads
to torsos, a benevolent creator god.
Inside that room the glittering
forest of my queerness sprouted.
My DNA: stacked replicas of the
old house's impossibly twisted
staircase, miraculously held
together by wooden pegs, bounded
four feet above by wooden ceiling,
under which I squatted with Game
Boy for hours. After running
downstairs, I'd pause to stare
at the globe where a troupe
of porcelain ballerinas twirled
to soundless music, a murmuration
of flakes around them—
globes within globes. I'd like to

throw open the windows of my
body, let in the ion breeze, but
sometimes the walls are all that
keep in the many-mirrored snow

# A Box Fan

each window had one
white rectangle that
pushed stench through

weeds in the bigger bedroom
the maroon walls
that week we painted

the small room green
mom said to put the fan
in the window

so we could breath
each summer that
room fills up

paint fumes or
cut teen throats
twin mattresses

came down the staircase
the fans kept
us in they stuck

to us
I took a key
cut the shape

of a smile on
the window screen
and put the fan back

against the mesh wiring
this air this white box
this dusted gate

keeper who had
to be in every window
especially in the summer

the house was hot
and the air came in

# TUESDAY
## June 24th, 1969

I woke up too beautiful for this world: cotton-mouthed, hungry, and naked from the waist down. I was so tired last night upon my return to Trannyville that I forgot to take my bulge off. Apparently Nighttime Freddie wasn't deft enough to unpin it, and so I'd taken off my underwear in full and chucked them across the room. I wish I could say this was an uncommon occurrence.

I rubbed my eyes, which felt like that part of the matchbook you strike, and I reached for my cigs. Only then did I remember that Radio had given the rest away to the kids.

I groaned and tried to turn over to a dry spot on the mattress, me already sweating in the heat of the day. My arm and leg flopped off the old springs to the cement floor right beneath me. At least that still felt cool to the touch.

I only lifted my head from my pillow when I heard the Mister Rogers theme song downstairs. I cursed, realizing I'd forgotten to reset my useless clamshell of a clock again. Mister Rogers was just reruns in the summer, but shit, man.

I tripped over some of my busted textbooks as I shuffled out to our main room. Radio was sitting at the counter, hunched over a mess of her electronics in a frown. Her face looked worse than last night, but that's kinda how healing goes.

"How're you feeling?"

"Mmh."

I leaned closer. "What're you doing, anyway?"

"Computer."

"The hell is that?" But when she didn't answer, I chewed on a hangnail and went about my way. When I opened our door, I nearly fell backward trying to avoid the stuff on the floor. The kids had left gifts for Radio overnight since she'd been beat: a couple of cigarettes, a single-serving bag of chips, a fifth of a bottle of Jack, a tattered copy of *Rat*. Someone even made some sort of art piece, a cracked mirror the size of my own hand, a heart fastened to it with what looked like chewing gum and pieces of broken bottles. I brought it all in and placed it on the counter. Morning light hit the deco, bouncing little shards of greens and blues onto the wall as if they were no longer sharp enough to cut. I saw Radio glance at it and soften. But when she caught me eying the Jack, she sighed and returned to her work.

"Just take it."

I snatched the bottle up in a swipe and removed the cap, bringing it to my lips.

"Easy. You haven't even had breakfast yet."

I pulled the bottle away in a gasp. A drop lost its grip on the corner of my mouth and began to roll, but I caught it with a swipe of my arm. "This is breakfast."

"That joke will get old the second you stagger your stupid white ass into traffic."

I screwed the cap back on to save the rest for later. I looked at Radio a moment, her head bowed to her work, me feeling the Jack start to work through my veins. I suddenly wanted to choose my words carefully. "One day, I'm gonna get us outta here."

She looked up at me a second before giving a small smile, but her eyes didn't change. "I know, sweetness."

I put the bottle on the counter and went down to the first floor, Mister Rogers getting clearer with each industrial stair. I saw the blue glow before I saw the box, the flickering shadows of the kids. Nearly all of them were sitting around the little screen in a circle, cross-legged, hunched over just enough to not miss a word, but not so much that it might give away that they actually cared.

Most of them were teenagers of any sort of range, the youngest kids ten or eleven, all of them riddled with some sort of mark or another. Old blisters on their faces, branded asses, knife marks and stab wounds. Boiling water, hot irons, cigarettes. These were the marks of families with only conditional love to give. A shame we were all they could find for replacement.

I stood behind them all for a moment, staring at the screen. It was all snowy again, but you could still hear most of the words.

As I continued to watch them, every last eager back to my face, I felt the hurt trying to sharpen itself against the edges the Jack had dulled. I wished I could take them on field trips. Museums, national parks, even libraries where they could get any book they wanted, to drink up everything and anything life had to offer. Their world was so fucking small. And I was useless in prying off the padlocks. All me and Radio could do was what we did so they wouldn't have to, but that only prolonged their suffering instead of helping them out of this mess. Because once there was opportunity to get them somewhere better, to give them something that might lift them up, the money was already gone. Living was too expensive to concern ourselves with thriving.

There was a knock at the door behind me, real soft. So soft none of the kids heard it. I turned to it, already on edge. Knocking wasn't something that happened around the piers.

I slunk to the door, my heels off the floor in a fox step, ready to scare off fags looking for a place to fuck. I grazed my hand across the top of the weapons basket and came up with a pair of scissors. I held them at my side, in plain view as I opened the door. I blinked in the morning sun, felt that sharp pain behind my eyes as they worked to be human. And for a moment, I couldn't see anything at all.

"What," I barked, yanking the noise up from my stomach. I flashed the scissors limp by my hip in the sharp sunlight.

But then I held still. The newcomer in front of me shrank back, some kid the age I hated most, though that wasn't their fault. The bruising around my vision left me fast as my eyes adjusted. Blue-eyed, golden-haired. Petite and fine-boned. The kid looked fluffed in the cheeks, as if it was the part of their body that decided to grow first. Storing nuts for winter or something. Their mouth was messed up in some way.

I whipped the scissors behind my back, returning them to the basket. The clank of metal seemed to relax the kid's shoulders. I opened the door wider and held my breath. To say I was looking in a mirror is kind of a lot, but man, it felt like that. Like, a real smudgy mirror. That was teeny tiny. And just before I went off my rocker.

"You're like me." I said it so quietly that I wasn't sure they'd heard me. They weren't supposed to hear me. But then their wet blue eyes got big. Their words were like marbles and it seemed to take effort to work their tongue. Something was definitely wrong with their mouth.

"This lady Marsha said to say Cupid could help me."

I opened the door the rest of the way. I began to wonder if somebody had slipped stuff into the Jack. "I'm Cupid." I stepped aside and that little chickabiddy came in.

The door closed us back off into darkness, the kid almost invisible as my eyes fought again. The black and white flashes of the television were making me wince.

"My mouth hurts." They pointed to their face as if I wouldn't be able to locate it myself, and their eyes began to go wet again. They blinked in a flurry.

I looked at them better now as my eyes ratcheted back down, seeing the one cheek much more swollen than the other. I knew better than to touch it. And that I shouldn't presume a damn thing. "You a tranny?"

They picked at their sleeve, words still mumbled. Their mouth barely moved when they spoke and I had to lean in to hear them properly over the royal bitching of King Friday. "...I don't like that word."

I nodded. I tried again. "You a transvestite?"

"And a boy." He picked at the hole in his sleeve, the size of a cigarette burn. He sniffed once before his voice cracked like a bad note. "My mouth really hurts." He said it loud enough that a few of the kids turned.

I was already heading for the stairs. "Come with me."

He followed me up, silent. I hoped to get some information out of him. "Where you from?"

His voice was small behind me, whisking around in the dark like a ghost. "Jersey. Got kicked out. Hitchhiked here."

"How long you been in New York?"

"Just last night."

I didn't say anything to that. His story, in the end, wasn't unlike anybody else's. He was rejected love, left to rot. I'd thought waste was supposed to be a sin.

We hit the end of the stairs and I placed my hand on me and Radio's door. It was then I heard him speak again, as quiet as the first time.

"I thought I was the only one, too."

I couldn't handle the tone in his voice, so I opened the door and let us both on in. "Nurse Radio. I've found a stray in need of care."

Radio looked up from her work, ready to give her usual small smile, to welcome a new baby chick into her fold. But then she saw the boy, saw me, and stopped halfway. We only got girls around here, nearly all of them black or brown. She caught herself and pushed her smile out farther than usual. "You're lucky. Dr. Cupid is the best around."

I scoffed at this, leading the chickabiddy to the good chair. I reclined him a couple clicks and put on some gloves from my med drawer. The morning light came in through the smeared window upon his face, motes drifting lazy about us as if we were some happy little suburban home and not an abandoned warehouse in the Meatpacking District. Motes are brainless. "Open your mouth, please."

He did as told, but it took me all of two seconds to see what was going on. I realized then he might be older than twelve. He definitely had the tranny boy curse. Baby face for life.

"Abscess," I muttered, standing back upright. "Bet it hurts like hell, too. But the good news is it's just a wisdom tooth. You don't need it."

He shrank in the chair. "You're gonna pull it?"

I was already fishing out a vial and dental syringe from my med drawer. "It'll be over quick and you'll feel so much better in just a couple days. I promise. You'll never miss it." I began filling the syringe. It was just a bit of lidocaine—or maybe it was procaine, who can remember—with a vasoconstrictor I'd added to help control bleeding.

He looked at the needle and I could see him getting pale in the face. "You sure you know what you're doing?"

I smiled with half of my mouth, looking him dead in the eye. "If I could do it backwards in a mirror on myself, I can do it to you."

"He knows what he's doing, baby." Radio took a moment to put her screwdriver down and hook a finger into the corner of her mouth, the unripped side, showing the gap of a missing molar. "Just about everybody here's missing teeth."

"It's all the starch," I said simply. "We can't afford dentists and they wouldn't take us even if we could. But we got toothpaste here to share and we'll make sure to get you a toothbrush, okay?" I leaned toward him with the needle, but he failed to open his mouth as wide as I needed. "Though in your case, the situation was unavoidable. Wisdom teeth abscess all the time. You're gonna be just fine."

He still wasn't opening his mouth properly and I knew I needed to calm him down. "You can stay with us as long as you need, you know. We can be your family."

"I have family." He said it so abruptly that I felt insulted, then jealous, then possibly a third thing I didn't have time to think because he kept rapping. "An uncle in San Fran. Gonna get myself there soon as I can."

"Ah. And how do you plan to do that?"

"Hitchhike."

I was suddenly very aware of how closely Rade was listening to us. I shook my head. "You need to get a bus ticket. You're lucky you hitchhiked even here in one piece. Across the country, you'll be toast."

"I'll earn some money, then."

"And how will you earn money?"

"Well…" He shrugged and glanced around the room, as if that said it all. My own eye caught my work outfits lined up far behind the arc of him, hanging on a wheeled closet pole.

I knew how easily he'd get snapped up, and how quickly he'd be destroyed. "No." I cut him off as he began to protest. "Open your mouth. We need to take care of this."

I felt bad the moment I plunged that needle in, how he gave a sharp cry and then tried to cover it up. He'd already started that thing where he was trying to prove his manhood in all the wrong ways, the only chance to convince others he was one. I ignored the tears that sprang up in his eyes, as if begging me to stop, as if I was the bad guy. I had hold of his cheek, wiggling it to help the anesthesia spread.

"You're doing great," I said. I pulled the needle out, giving him a tissue for his silent tears as we waited. He kept his mouth open as he wiped them away.

"You know why we got wisdom teeth?" I asked. He looked up at me, curiosity poking out from beneath his anxiety. "It's because our jaws used to be bigger. We had these extra teeth to help us grind up plants so we could digest them better, but now we don't need them anymore. We're always evolving. But a lot of times in evolution you get stuck in these periods of still-evolving-into-something-else. Humans are constantly playing catchup, and to resist it just results in problems."

I watched him as I babbled until I saw his face slacken with the relief of going numb. I tapped a finger against his first molar. Then his second molar. Then the wisdom tooth itself. When he didn't jump, I went ahead and pushed my nail into his swollen gum line. Nothing.

"Looks like we're ready to go, then." Keeping it from his line of sight, I rounded over a scalpel and put it to his mouth, easing gently into the tissue until it pierced. The blood started to seep and I knew by this point I'd have to be quick. I cut through the first layer or two of gum, now at a better pace knowing for sure he couldn't feel it.

The payphone down the hall suddenly sounded, crisp and offensive as it pummeled straight through our door. There was only one reason that shit would ever ring, and that was for a job. To keep a number here otherwise was too dangerous.

"Fuck," I muttered. The high ring of the bell felt like it was trying to shove ice into my ear, raising the nodes of my spine through my skin. "Radio, could you?"

"I'm kinda in the middle of something."

"Oh come on, Rade."

Radio huffed and clattered down her screwdriver. But when her eye fell to the blood smeared on my gloved fingers, she went out into the hall, leaving the door open. I heard her heavy footfalls until the ringing stopped.

"Somebody wants to make an appointment," she called out.

I was already cutting through the next layer of tissue. I didn't look away, though I felt bad for pretty much shouting in the kid's face. "Who?"

"Someone new, I think."

I needed to get this done fast as I could for the boy's own sake. It wasn't like I had suction in the room and I couldn't exactly let him choke on his own blood. I eyed the rate it trickled. "When?"

There was a pause, a murmur I couldn't hear. "Tomorrow."

"Tomorrow?" I groaned. I didn't want to pull a triple, if only because it was a higher risk of bringing one cat's scent to another's nose. But then I had a thought, the only thought I had to help the kid. I huffed again. Worst case scenario, I'd have to shower twice in the same day at the hotels.

"Shit." I tried to run Wednesday's schedule through my head as I finished cutting through his gum. With the bone exposed so deep, I switched my scalpel over to some pliers. I quickly wiped down his exposed tooth with gauze to help get a better grip. The blood kept trickling. "Not until tomorrow evening," I called back out. "I got some earlier in the day. Tell them nine and please write down what hotel they want to meet at. Must be somewhere within Manhattan."

I grabbed onto the tooth and started to wiggle. I calmed my voice back down again and smiled. "You're going to feel some pressure here, but it won't hurt. Almost done." I could feel it already starting to give, the abscess helping push it.

Radio's voice called out once more. "You like licorice?"

"Jesus fucking Christ," I breathed. I resisted the urge to drop my head a moment in a groan, keeping my eye instead on the tooth, my hand steady. Almost there. "Shit, Rade, I dunno." The blood was starting to slick my grip and I had no way of drying him off again without losing my momentum. It was pooling in his mouth so deep it looked like the piers at night. What a way to drown. "Sure, I dig licorice. Just say yes."

I could feel the pliers starting to slip in the blood, but goddammit, I wasn't about to let that happen. I put a palm on the boy's head as gently as I could, making my voice soft. "One last pull and we'll be all done and you'll feel lots better. I promise. You're doing great."

"Twizzlers or Red Vines?"

"Fuck, Radio, I dunno, okay? Twizzlers. Just say Twizzlers. Nobody fucking digs Red Vines." I was pulling with all I had now, keeping the kid's head down with my hand. He whimpered, but I think he was just scared. That was my fault. But if I couldn't get this tooth, I was gonna have to smash it and dig out all the little pieces. Please don't make me smash it and dig out all the little pieces.

"I fucking dig Red Vines!" Radio barked back.

"They're not even licorice!"

"Fuck you!"

"Fuck you, too!"

The tooth suddenly gave so fast that I fell backward. I threw the pliers to the floor and stuffed gauze up the boy's mouth. I held it there a minute, firm. I counted how many pads he bled through, and when I saw it was thankfully few in number before it slowed, I smiled at him again. "See? Nothing to it."

Radio came back in, closing the door and handing me over a scrap of white bakery bag. "Static's acting up on the line again. I'll go out soon as it's dark and tighten the wire." She gave me a not-so-light smack on the shoulder before returning to her work. Her voice softened, though she still eyed the newcomer with some amount of skepticism. "You got a name, baby?"

That chickabiddy shook his head beneath my hand. I was beginning to soak up the blood that'd pooled in his mouth with extra gauze, careful to hold it tight so he didn't choke. I kept slinking the chunks of dripping massacre away from his vision and into the trashcan. They each gave a distinctly heavy thunk when they landed.

"Well," I said, "you better think one up soon or it'll be made for you." I left the gauze stuffed to the hole of his mouth, seeing it was staying fairly white now, and picked up the pliers. The tooth was now latched between its jaws with drying blood, and I examined it in a full rotation. "Word association, you know? Like, tooth...wisdom. Wisdom Tooth—shit, no."

Radio looked up from her work with a smirk. "You're bad at this game."

I shrugged and looked at the nameless kid, keeping my hands out of his sight as I plucked the tooth free from the pliers and tossed it in the trash. "Welcome to Trannyville. You can just call us The Castle, if you want."

He leaned back in the chair, giving a sigh that it was over. I brought the chair back up in a sitting position.

I looked over my shoulder to Radio, who was still making poor work of looking interested in her electronic doodads. She glanced at me without moving her head. I turned back around, blocking both me and the kid from her with my back. I moved so close to him that all I could see were his eyes.

"Look," I whispered. "I'm gonna get you that dough, okay? We'll get you on that bus as soon as possible."

He frowned and tried to mumble something past the gauze, but I stopped him. "You can't do anything for at least three days, anyway. Nobody will want you." That wasn't true, but he didn't have to know that. "You need to recover."

I didn't know how I was going to do it. I didn't know even if I could do it. All I knew is that I'd give it everything I had. I could feel Radio's gaze hot on my neck now, knew that she'd just heard me when I hoped she wouldn't, knew exactly what it was about this situation now that was putting her off me, of who I was willing to help out more and why, and that she was right, and that I was nonetheless willing to risk our immovable friendship to do it anyway. I realized my voice was shaking. I turned my face slightly away from the kid, suddenly, for the first time in a long time, self-conscious about the Jack on my breath. "Just give me three days."

Sometimes you want to do good in the world even when you know this isn't it.

# First Will and Testament

i look to history to explain & this is my first mistake
when i say history i mean the stone
half-buried by the roadside has witnessed
more tragedy than a filthy glass of a water. i look to the water
but all i see is dust. i look to the dust & all there is
is history. here's a feather & well of blood
to write the labor movement across the fractal
back of infrastructure. here's a father leaving home
to build railroads with his bare hands. write the laws
that claw the eyes from owls, that build a wall
between the river & the thirsty, that drag families
from one hell into the next. o this house of mine
was built by men & o i, a man sometimes, pass
through its acid chambers & leave out the backdoor
dust. when i say history i mean what lives in us,
i mean the faux gold chain around my neck,
the diseases passed from generation to generation
dating back to a time before christ, i mean any word
traced to its origin is a small child begging for water.

# //CLIMATE CHANGE//

*it will just burn over & over—there may not be time to recover*

there may not be time to recover

*we can bet on that it's just going to get hotter*

i'm just getting hotter

the seasonality of streams

we're locked in

to this heatwave

*yeahhhh they really want you they really want you they really do*

who are they & what do they want b/c i know deep down it can't be the milieu who just reproduce the same hierarchies they attempted to isolate from

in the first place

*i fake it so good i am beyond fate*

j told me forever ago when she first began to distance herself from the scene

she said she was bored – the scene was boring – the parties were boring – & everyone was petty

& at the time i was so mad at her like how could she say that // there was potential in intimacy i didn't understand what she was saying

i wanted to be accepted — i wanted a community around radical misbehavior / collective queerness / abrasive music / & poetry

she said *someday you will ache like i ache*
b/c we know for certain only a few things—it's getting hotter—there's a housing crisis—
& there's no future

*go on take everything*

the commons get burned over & over
& we absorb it all—the loss—all knotted up beneath each knee cap

*go on take everything*

do u remember when the commons was a place u could go to

before it became strictly

imaginary

i swear i was there & you were too
& now it's just a place
we keep failing to arrive at

*go on take everything*

it's not really our fault
scarcity turns people into nightmares

j & i are on a porch that may collapse @ any moment
riding hi on the loaded edge of

social transfusion

& i tell her she was right

quite some time has passed

she said i hoped you'd never have to ache like that

i just wished i'd come to it sooner

*go on take everything*

# Mansfield Hollow

decades without and no
        pulse in my pillow. I thought
I'd given up on singing
        bridges back from their states
of desecration. afterimage


        of our young laughter: blessed
be the trestle over the knee-
        deep river in its night-lit
memory. what spanned
        one summer I would have


otherwise died gladly if
        not for you having me
keep secret. have I told
        you yet? I'm famous
for rarely telling things


        really, but then this morning,
the slope of your shoulders
        formed along the neighbor's
cedars, clear as miracle.
        somewhere in the familiar


shadow of your forest I'm
        there before you, undressing
my eye to kiss those
        metal tracks that still
wail hoarse as an oracle.

# Leatherback Trantoum

### 1.

I'll tell you, for a fortune I cannot remember
where I left my pride; perhaps it's stewing
in that crush of crumpled sweaty clothes over
there, by the door. Might be wasting in some
lost life, when I was a leatherback, sovereign
among my kind, roaming that immortal blue—
not a shell some nothing left behind, done with.

### 2.

What if you just shed this life? Like clothing?
You could leave it where I left my pride; let it
roam that immortal blue, like a leatherback, like
a sovereign. Among my kind, a crush of crumpled,
sweaty flesh is a source of pride, not a shell, not
something left to stew, done with, a fortune
wasting by the door, like a pile of nothing.

### 3.

I'm a leatherback, baby, sovereign among
my pride, my sweat, my crumpled flesh
a source of fortune. I am *crushing* this
immortal, no clothing, no nothing to hide,
no nothing to do but this blue stew. Mighty
wasteful, I'll tell ya, this thing called life. Can't
remember where I left mine, but I'm done with it.

## Dear Aunt Louise, Muh

I am thinking of your blue-painted porch on 28th street, tucked between Catalpa & Olive—
where I sat with my daddy when I was getting to know him.

I am thinking of your underbite and chin whiskers, your very distinct quiet,
which one only gets
being from a place

                    miles deep into the crop.

You took everything in through a tinted filter. Lived at the end of the red dirt road
in your laugh.

Your obituary in the black puddle
       of my lap:

               *1955. Left Negro Church Road, Lawrence County, Alabama. . .*

               Went North on the train.

Sister went all the way to Cleveland and took up
with a boy y'all grew up down the road from, Dennis
Priest. Steel rail to steel mills.

You got off before the Ohio. Settled into alone
& lived on a numbered street like a city girl.

The obituary,
elusive archive:

Father's name          Racia          Gone
Mother's name          Mary Helen     Dead          1936

By the time you were 3 years old          you were a girl alone.

A month beyond your homegoing

headed north 13 hours

in a pickup truck

Before I left that morning, I plucked a chin hair, sprouted overnight. Felt the heel
of your palm hit my shoulder
like a tambourine.

# Bestiary Family Tree

### i. Cousin

when cousin becomes close too        touch
when cousin puts cat   in        pillowcase
when cousin smacks     pillowcase
beats the wall where she sleeps
when cousin builds stones and flowers for cat
to sleep only then do
they call her a daughter
they whirl into new parents because this one
needs animal              needs   skin
needs   you

### ii. Sister

when sisters frog croaked when        sister
sprayed too     much too much water     dark bark
when the frog lay flat on its belly
legs reaching she          taped it into a box
she used gray duct        tape to shut
the frog and its green          into what turned
to        dirt she shoveled and    dug out the back
            yard threw it in          like some dirty
                    daughter

### iii. Mother

when mother   left      the dog          when
she opened the gate    when she knew          the dog
liked to run     they hated her          they called her
a horrible mother        they    thought she meant to do it
but what kind of daughter     has dogs for arms
what kind      of dog runs              from the
mother

iv. Grandmother

she knew        they kept repeating it to me at
night
she knew what he was doing up there   she      knew
that the dog      was stuck in the utility      room
that her daughter was his favorite        that dog        loved her
that dog wasn't barking        at nothing      he would lock it in
the utility room when grandmother was        the dog
locked in she knew        they kept        repeating
        she knew what he was doing

# A Year or Two

I want very quiet, moneyed pain.
Not to be borrowing enough for bail
and waiting for the tow pound
attendant to unlock the gate.

He suggests you stop by a gas station
to get rid of the empties before
you get pulled over again.
You didn't get pulled over in the first place.

If we get out of East Missoula
in the next year or two
I'll give my anger over
to self-help and sweepstakes.

I'll kick the ass of the boyfriend
that you are far too good for,
then take up Zumba and Pilates.

I won't talk about getting dumped
in a trailer park anymore, begging.

I will lament that my grave plot
is not in the shade,
that my daughter's training wheels
are loose and rattling,
that the cat has a cancerous
growth just beneath its jaw.

Some dark July, when the tomatoes in
my overwatered garden split open,
only then will I blame myself, wonder
if I ever deserved organic anything.

I will fall to my knees
and break whatever delicate
chain I've worn around my neck
for years. I will think of us
at twenty-five, everyone we know
swimming in desire and resentment.

How did we make it out?
How will things have gone
just right enough that the godforsaken
4 A.M. phone call can't be for me.

# Vermont Getaway: Thirteen Gays Looking at a Blackbird

I.  Okay, first off—it's Onyx.

II.  What, are you blind? It's clearly Deep Noir.

III.  Fred was just saying Black Olive or Licorice but I—

IV.  Well, Fred makes everything about food. On our first date, he said my eyes were rum-soaked raisins. Chaaarming!

V.  I should've said they were Blackbirds, darling. Two rum-soaked Black birds who shit on anything I have to say.

VI.  Knock it off, you two. Can't we just enjoy our lovely weekend away from the city?

VII.  I saw a Blackbird once. On Fire Island. Or was it Provincetown? I dunno. But it was definitely at a Black Party—I know that.

VIII.  Remember that drag queen who did pantomime? Wasn't her show called Ballad of the Blackbird?

IX.  She was doing Kabuki, imbecile. And the show was called Memoir of My Last Turd. I'd know, I dated her kimono designer.

X.  Hey, don't Blackbirds have a high frequency of homosexuality? Like giraffes?

XI.  You're thinking penguins. And that's your last mimosa, Danny. You're getting like really loud. You'll scare the little guy away!

XII.  Oh, he split ages ago. Soon as Fred and Jose started going at each other.

XIII.  No! I wanted an Instagram pic. He was so sweet. That's it—next time we drive up, I'm gonna build him the poshest birdhouse you've ever seen.

# reign

selfie-made
buoyed by
a *yas* refrain

identity alchemy
what -isms have done
to us

mean-earned this entry
into the public
[square]

humble-brag liberation
signifying art
everywhere

ideas afterthoughts
of self-
regard

our comeuppance
platformed
heeled

the boosting boon
of the *yas*
immunity

a condition
packaged
as community

flashy fangs
who've made a pact
to Shante

as lifestyle
& status quo
to inherit

the masthead
the ledger
the land

then legislate
for the conditions
of our own material

careful now

be useful
not used

home always
as sheltering outcast

to outlast
the deluge

# THE HOUSE[1] NOT WANTING TO DISAPPEAR, YET

I come home in the afternoons from school and then stay home. Then I turn on the TV to watch the shows I know will while the time away. Eat a bowl of ice cream every day until voices fill the room with their aromas. I don't speak all day and for a majority of the week. The ice cream is disappearing. My grades stay good. The house is quiet underneath the sounds I imagine. I imagine how the others must have each other out there. No one's home. Will I always be this alone? Though I am growing bigger, I have to stay small. I can't get out because I live here.

---

[1] That is, we bought a house but never really cared about silverware. We somehow lived our lives but without completely, as they say, assimilating.

—Christopher Soto—

# The Joshua Tree//Submits Her Name Change

She steps across my chest
      Dragging her shadow & fraying // All the edges.
            My nipples bloom // Into cacti // Fruit & flower.
                  She eats // Then I do // A needle pricks her.

I've only seen this woman cry once // Squeezed like a raincloud.
            She cried because // Two men // Two men
                  Built a detention center // From bone & clay.

The first bone— My clavicle.         The second— Her spine.
          She howls // As the fence // Surrounds her.
              She coughs & combs the floor // My chest shiv-
              Shivering.

Inside the detention center // She's renamed // "Immigrant" "Illegal."
            She loses 15 pounds & Mental health & her feet are
              Cracked tiles // Dirty dishes.

This border // Isn't a stitch // Where nations meet.
            This border's a wound // Where nations part.

—Joshua Jennifer Espinoza—

# What it Takes to Leave a House

First you breathe. This sounds easy,
but trust me—it isn't. The air seems

to get in its own way and your skin
pulls itself taut over your muscles. So

find a window. This can be anything
you want. A soft feeling. A memory

of a youth spent wandering. The
empty space and broken glass where

a window used to be. Now reach
through and feel movement. See the

trees bending and swaying while birds
make the most of things. Observe

the way light changes a scene. Yes,
change, like loss, like fear of a new

reality when you had just finished
learning to survive this one. Hold

the fear. Tear into it and taste it. Let
it dribble in streaks of blue down

your chin and neck and bathe in it.
Your body will do what it will do.

It will accept the air no matter how
thick it becomes. You will reach

for a door and suddenly you'll be
out in the wind touching all the

horribly beautiful things. You'll say
*this moment is not my enemy* and

sometimes you'll believe it.

# Will & Testament

Scatter my bones
on the beach at Manzanillo

where I tried so many times
to heal myself, tried to forget

how we battled one another,
pulled things up by the roots,

brandished them
in our clutched hands.

\*

I had been dreaming
of simple-named places:

Barstow, Duluth;
it didn't matter

so long as I could cut you
from my brain with one

sweet flick of the blade—
but I woke

already headed south,
waiting for your answer,

for the tide—

the green scent it carries,
new and bitter all at once.

*

Look how time
has mellowed us,

worn us thin,
translucent as sea-glass—

see how I savor
this inland landscape,

the tilt and sway
of our tumbledown town,

the way bells sing
through the desert air,

their turquoise collars
oxidized, cured—

but when this particular
dream is done,

won't you scatter me like roses
over Punta Serena,

where the sea-brine
reached up from the sand

into my bones
and softened them.

# One Last Thing: A COVID-19 Afterword

The fire of the sky, reflecting off the low-slung clouds, waves of orange marsh-mallow, and stark dark silhouettes of palm trees and telephone poles—pillars to hold up this hell turned upside down: a California sunset, a sun-set-ed America?

I'm standing on the platform of the Fruitvale BART station. Yes, that Fruit-vale BART station, part of a narrative that feels ever closer to an all-too-com-mon reality. This is the last photo I took before the world pressed its pandemic pause, sandwiched between pictures on my phone of the Austin skyline and my wrecked car in an impound lot. My return home, the rust and steel of the platform, charcoal and churros, a horizon of eaves and sky and skyline. And that sunset fire, glinting in the eyes of the ejected throng. I wanted to be home, to rest on the neck of my husband Marco, to wrap my arms around Lola, our American Bulldog mutt, to speak of books and barbeque, of travels and Texas. But first, this sky.

If I were to scroll further on my phone I would see close-up blooms of my garden, passion fruit curly-cues and mahogany stalks and the blazing tufted canopy of ice plants, because since then there has been nothing more I want to see than life itself.

It is dinnertime in early Spring, where good old Karl the Fog gets cocky, the cold of the Pacific and the simmer of California terrain summoning him to slink past the coast, over San Francisco's Twin Tits, beyond the sparkling Bay and into the Oakland lowlands. The sun has dipped below Karl's chin, and loses its cool in the elliptical path. If Marco were home—which he is not—he would be chopping tomatillos into a tongue-tearing salsa verde, hoping it would be ready by the time I came home, a surprise, for the delight in my eyes that makes him fall in love every time. If he were home—which he is not—I would run into the house and pull him outside to see what's left of the firelight. I would say, "look," the very word a soundtrack of my childhood.

I wonder what my child self would think about this home I've created 30 years later. How would it be written?

An hour later, I am fully unpacked, showered, alone, with a glass of wine held like a gasp of air. I check my email. In one sitting I learn that my book launch and tour are canceled, my car stolen, the college where I teach will close its doors indefinitely come May. I pull from the glass, my lips to rim like the arms of a lover soon left. The bottle is close, and I scan the wine rack for a long night.

Before my discovery on the BART platform, before I run home to share in the delight, I watch the mound of marshmallow cloud come closer from the airplane window as we descend. The sky above spotless. The woman sitting next to me marvels at the sight. She says, "Y'all have the prettiest skies. In Texas it never looks so clean." I nod. She says, "You're very lucky this is home." I nod. She says, "I thought only tech people and hippies lived here." I nod. And all the nods are shades of themselves, like the 1,000 tones of California blue.

I wonder, what will it look like in 30, 50, 100 years? Will it be the same sky? Will luck be the word that comes to mind? And down, into the roads, the backyards. What will be the language of those? What words will build the walls, forge the doorframes, tend the garden? What sort of home will this be, then?

On the streets of Austin the night before, I watch a sixteen-piece Mexican banda practice in the backyard of an old friend's neighborhood taqueria, the swell of brass and tequila buzzing my blood. Between sets Dana sips and fawns, "Remember when we dreamed about our future, those warm Atlanta nights after the club. Did we ever dream this far?" I laugh, "Did we think we'd live this long?" We chuckle into our memories, barely legal, hardly lethal, shiny clothes and sparkling eyes wide with ecstacy, with wonder. She says, "We did okay, yeah?" I nod. She says, "You're very lucky, your life." I nod, and take her hand as the banda blows its return into the Austin night, an orange glow, and the brass floating above us.

And now, the days inside. A small orbit of bed to desk to garden, and back. I walk Lola through the quiet-ed neighborhood, a dog or tree to sniff here and there. I make breakfast, sip my coffee, and sit. I administer the routine of my life through screens. Daylight slurs across the roof above, and it is once again dusk. I walk out to the garden. I talk with it, I prune, I water, flowers and food offer themselves. And there is a bud that blooms from what was a random sprig that I plugged into the ground back in November that has crept and spilled over its container. Parrot's Beak. The flower is forked, three narrow prongs, a feathery talon, in a deep orange the color of a sky on fire.

And it is this, this moment, this writing of memory, of the moments before all of this, that correct me, that discover me, a home for these thoughts. A home of its own. If I hadn't made the choice to write, I would have forgotten. I would have remained sullen, cursing the dearth of inertia, with a mind as closed as a quarantine.

That is ultimately why Arisa, Mo, myself, and the contributors made this book. To celebrate homestead beyond the city, the town, the neighborhood. Beyond the picket fence, the stoop, the kitchen door. And even beyond a state of mind. Shelter crosses all sorts of thresholds. And to shelter-in-place? What do we cross then? Our legs? Some line? A 't'? Perhaps many.

Oh, Mo, Arisa. I cross with you, into gratitude. At least this.

Louis Menand writes, "Writing is a window. It opens onto vanished feelings and vanished words. Often it is the only window there is, the only access we will ever have to those things. It is more than a mere record, like a photograph, because it is also a sensibility, a point of view, a voice. It is the place where, fifty or a hundred years from now, people will go to see — or to hear — what it was like to be alive when we were alive." This book is a collection of queer folx who were alive in 2020. This is what their home was like. This is how they made it. This is how it was made. What will that look like to readers in 30, 50, 100 years?

Before my arrival home, before the reading of emails, before the slurring of days, and this hell turned upside down, I photograph the sky, because it reflects all the joy I feel. I want to share with others, to peel from myself, this gratitude for the beauty of the world, for my home, or perhaps of gratitude itself. When you love something so much, the instances of failure eclipse that which has you understand there has been a failure to begin with. Yes, a blinding dark night, yet before a blazing horizon, and before that a clean shade of blue. I look to my garden. I look at my phone. The photograph tells me: sometimes we need distance to see a thing clearly. Sometimes, clarity can be as simple as writing it down, and putting it away for a bit. I nod, and take the breath that we all know we need. I hit save, and prepare to share:

We are always cultivating the fire, no matter where the sky.

# Acknowledgements

Andrea Abi-Karam: "//CLIMATE CHANGE//" originally appeared in *GUTS Issue 9: Weather.*

Samuel Ace: "The Roads" originally appeared in *Our Weather Our Sea* (Black Radish Books 2019). Reprinted with permission from the author.

Kazim Ali: "Home" originally appeared in *Bright Felon: Autobiography and Cities* (Wesleyan 2009). Reprinted with permission from the author.

Jubi Arriola-Headley: "Leatherback Trantoum" and "& You Shall Know Me By My Lists" originally appeared in *original kink* (Sibling Rivalry Press 2020). Reprinted with permission from the author and Sibling Rivalry Press.

Daniel Barnum: "Would I Change All I Know for Unknowing" originally appeared in *Muzzle Magazine.* "Mansfield Hollow" and "*Sturnus vulgaris*" originally appeared in *The Cortland Review.*

Luke Dani Blue: "Letter to Sly, Bus Roulette" originally appeared as part of the story "Dogs of America" in *Crab Orchard Review.*

Sionnanin Buckley: "Stranger, Brother, Stranger" originally appeared in *Exposition Review* as the winner of the Flash 405 contest, "Underneath the Words."

Marcelo Hernandez Castillo: "Pulling the Moon" originally appeared in *New England Review*, and subsequently published in *Cenzontle* (BOA Editions 2018). Reprinted with permission from the author and BOA Editions.

K-Ming Chang: "Xiaogui" originally appeared in *The Offing.*

Alexis Pauline Gumbs: "Eye of Heaven" originally appeared in *Undrowned: Black Feminist Lessons from Marine Mammals* (AK Press 2020). Reprinted with permission from the author.

Luther Hughes: "Prayer" originally appeared in *Dreginald*; "Culture" originally appeared in *New England Review*.

Kenan Ince: "Chicxulub Köçekçe / Pioneer Species" originally appeared in *Gulf Coast*.

Stacy Nathaniel Jackson: "Kitchen" originally appeared in *Foglifter*.

Michal MJ Jones: "Turnstiles" originally appeared in *Rigorous Mag*; "In the Wake of a Transfer" originally appeared in *Anomaly*.

Bettina Judd: "where you from?" originally appeared in *Because We Come from Everything*, a Poetry Coalition project.

Benjamín Naka-Hasebe Kingsley: "Beautiful Bembé" originally appeared in *Hunger Mountain*.

Afieya Kipp: "Home" originally appeared in *Foglifter*.

Juli Delgado Lopera: "Chapter Nueve" originally appeared in *Fiebre Tropical* (The Feminist Press 2020). Reprinted with permission from the author and The Feminist Press.

Alicia Mountain: "A Year or Two," "Sunday Polarized Lenses," and "Riparian County" originally appeared in *High Ground Coward* (Iowa 2018). Reprinted with permission from the author and University of Iowa Press.

James Penha: A version of the folktale that inspired "Between Towns" appears online in *Folktales for Travelers*, edited by D.L. Ashliman.

Joy Priest: "Dear Aunt Louise, Muh" originally appeared in *Poetry Northwest*; "Blue Heart Baby" originally appeared in *Blunderbuss*; "Rodeo" originally appeared in *Connotation Press*; "American Honey" originally appeared in *Southern Cultures*.

sam sax: "First Will and Testament" originally appeared in *Guernica*, and subsequently published in *Bury It* (Wesleyan University Press 2018); "Everyone's an Expert at Something" originally appeared in *American*

*Poetry Review*; "The Cock" originally appeared in *The Rumpus*.

Kevin Simmonds: "reign" originally appeared in *the system must be tried*. Reprinted with permission from the author.

Christopher Soto: "Home" originally appeared in *The Offing*; "The Joshua Tree // Submits Her Name Change" originally appeared in an earlier draft as "Self-Portrait As Sonoran Desert" in *American Poetry Review*; "All the Dead Boys Look Like Me" originally appeared in *Literary Hub*.

Milo Todd: "Tuesday" originally appeared in *Foglifter*.

Jason Villemez: "All These Cats Have AIDS" originally appeared in *Big Fiction Magazine*.

Yanyi: "THE HOUSE NOT WANTING TO DISAPPEAR, YET" originally appeared in *Open in Emergency* (Asian American Literary Review 2020).

# Contributors

**ANDREA ABI-KARAM** is an Arab American genderqueer punk poet-performer cyborg. Andrea's debut *EXTRATRANSMISSION* (Kelsey Street) is a poetic critique of the U.S. military's role in the War on Terror. With Kay Gabriel, they co-edited *We Want It All: An Anthology of Radical Trans Poetics* (Nightboat).

**SAMUEL ACE** is a trans and genderqueer poet and sound artist. He's the author of several books, most recently *Our Weather Our Sea* (Black Radish). His work has been widely anthologized and recent poems can be found in *Poetry, Best American Experimental Poetry*, and *Vinyl*. He teaches poetry and creative writing at Mount Holyoke College.

**KAZIM ALI** was born in the United Kingdom and has lived transnationally in the United States, Canada, India, France, and the Middle East. He's a professor of literature at the University of California, San Diego. His newest books are *The Voice of Sheila Chandra* and *Northern Light*, a memoir of his Canadian childhood.

**ANASTACIA-RENEE** is a multigenre writer, educator, interdisciplinary artist, and *Deep End* podcast co-host. A 2020 Arc Fellow, she served as the Seattle Civic Poet from 2017-2019. Anastacia-Renee's work has been published in *Furious Flower: Seeding the Future of African American Poetry, Spirited Stone*, and *Ms. Magazine*. anastacia-renee.com

**JUBI ARRIOLA-HEADLEY** is a Black queer poet and first-generation United Statesian. His debut collection of poems is *original kink* (Sibling Rivalry). Jubi's work has been published in *Ambit, Beloit Poetry Journal*, and *Nimrod*. He lives in South Florida with his husband and is probably at the beach right now, wearing as little as possible.

**DANIEL BARNUM** was dreamt up in the desert, raised in the forest, and now lives and writes in Columbus, Ohio. Their poems and essays have appeared in *West Branch, Hayden's Ferry Review, The Massachusetts Review, Pleiades, The Offing, Muzzle*, and elsewhere. Their debut chapbook, *Names for Animals* (Seven Kitchens Press, 2020), was selected for the Robin Becker Prize. danielbarnum.net

Kay Ulanday Barrett aka @Brownroundboi is a poet, performer, and cultural strategist. *More Than Organs* (Sibling Rivalry) is their second collection. Their contributions are found in *The New York Times, Academy of American Poets,* and *Buzzfeed.* Kay lives outside of the NYC area with his jowly dog and remixes his mama's recipes whenever possible. kaybarrett.net

Carson Ash Beker (they/them) is a hybrid storyteller and experience creator, co-founder of The Escapery Pirate Art Collective and Queer Cat Productions Theater Company. Their stories are upcoming or found in *Michigan Quarterly Review, Joyland, Fairy Tale Review, Spunk, Foglifter, Gigantic Sequins,* and on ships and in cemeteries and on stages across the Bay Area. CarsonBeker.com

Britt Billmeyer-Finn is a poet, playwright and social worker living in Northampton, MA. She has published two books of poetry including the meshes (Black Radish Books, 2015) and Slabs (Timeless Infinite Light, 2016). They co- curate the living room reading series, The But Also and are co-founder of Threshold Academy, a future bookstore and current alternative education space in western MA.

Originally from Michigan, Luke Dani Blue is a trans writer of literary fiction and personal essays who has lived across North America and now resides in the Canadian prairies where they work at a public library. Luke's short stories have won the Jack Dyer Fiction Prize and the Nelligan Prize. Luke's work has appeared in or is forthcoming from *Colorado Review,* the New York Public Library's Subway Library collection, *Crab Orchard Review, Catapult* and elsewhere.

Cooper Lee Bombardier is the author of *Pass With Care: Memoirs.* His writing is also published in *The Kenyon Review, The Malahat Review, Ninth Letter, CutBank, Nailed Magazine, Longreads, BOMB,* and *The Rumpus;* and in 15 anthologies, including the Lambda Literary Award-winning anthology, *The Remedy–Essays on Queer Health Issues,* and *Meanwhile, Elsewhere: Speculative Fiction From Transgender Writers,* winner of the Stonewall Book Award. He teaches creative nonfiction in the University of King's College MFA program.

Sionnain Buckley is a writer, editor, and visual artist. Her work has appeared in *Hobart, Winter Tangerine, Wigleaf, Foglifter, Strange Horizons, Autostraddle,* and others. Her flash won first place in Exposition Review's Flash 405 contest. She lives in Columbus, Ohio, where she is pursuing an MFA in Fiction at The Ohio State University. More of her work can be found at sionnainbuckley.com.

MARCELO HERNANDEZ CASTILLO is a co-founder of the Undocupoets campaign. His most recent book is *Children of the Land: a Memoir* (Harper Collins). His work has been featured in the *New York Times, People Magazine,* and *Harper's Magazine.* He teaches poetry to incarcerated youth in Northern California and in the Ashland University Low-Res MFA program.

KJ CERANKOWSKI is a writer currently based in Cleveland, OH. His poetry, short fiction, and essays have appeared in *Short, Fast, & Deadly, Paper Darts,* and *The Account: A Journal of Poetry, Prose, and Thought.* He teaches at Oberlin College.

DOROTHY CHAN is the author of *Chinese Girl Strikes Back* (Spork Press), *Revenge of the Asian Woman* (Diode Editions), *Attack of the Fifty-Foot Centerfold* (Spork Press), and the chapbook *Chinatown Sonnets* (New Delta Review). Her work has appeared in *POETRY, The American Poetry Review,* and *Academy of American Poets.* Chan is an assistant professor of English at the University of Wisconsin-Eau Claire. dorothypoetry.com

K-MING CHANG is a Kundiman fellow and a Lambda Literary Award finalist. Her debut novel is *Bestiary* (One World/Random House). Her poems have been anthologized in *Ink Knows No Borders, Best New Poets 2018, Bettering American Poetry Vol. 3,* and the *2019 Pushcart Prize Anthology.* kmingchang.com

ERICA CHARIS-MOLLING is a lesbian poet, educator, and librarian. Her writing has been published in *Tinderbox, Redivider,* and *Presence.* A Mass Cultural Council Fellow and an alum of the Bread Loaf Writers' Conference, she currently lives in Boston with her wife and works as the education director for Mass Poetry.

JASON B. CRAWFORD is a black, bi-poly-queer writer born in Washington DC, raised in Lansing, MI. His work has appeared in *Wellington Street Review, Poached Hare, The Amistad, Royal Rose,* and *Kissing Dynamite.* He's the chief editor for *The Knight's Library* and the recurring host poet for Ann Arbor Pride.

J DE LEON holds a PhD in performance studies from NYU, where they are also completing their MFA in creative writing.

ROBIN REID DRAKE is a Chicago based writer, artist, and educator from the American South. Drake's written work appeared in *Palimpsest, WUSSY,* and the anthology *If You Can Hear This.* A recipient of the Ragdale Foundation Residency, Drake was named "30 under 30" by Chicago's oldest LGBTQ+ newspaper, *Windy City Times*.

**C.W. EMERSON'S** work has appeared *Atlanta Review, Crab Orchard Review, Greensboro Review, The American Journal of Poetry, Poetry East, Tupelo Quarterly* and others. He received an International Merit Reward in the Atlanta Review 2017 International Poetry Competition. Emerson lives in Palm Springs, California where he works as a clinical psychologist, and studies with poet Cecilia Woloch.

**JOSHUA JENNIFER ESPINOZA** is a trans woman poet living in California. Her work has been published in *The American Poetry Review, Denver Quarterly, West Branch*, and *Buzzfeed*, among others. She is also the author of two poetry collections: *I'm Alive / It Hurts / I Love It* (Big Lucks) and *THERE SHOULD BE FLOWERS* (CCM). joshuajenniferespinoza.com. Twitter/Instagram: @sadqueer4life

**T'AI FREEDOM FORD** is a New York City high school English teacher. Her poetry, fiction, and essays have appeared in *Apogee, Bomb Magazine, Calyx, Drunken Boat, Electric Literature, Gulf Coast, Kweli, Tin House, Poetry* and others. An inaugural erome Hill Artist Fellow, she is the author of two poetry collections, *how to get over* (Red Hen) and *& more black* (Augury), winner of the 2020 Lambda Literary Award for Lesbian Poetry. t'ai lives and loves in Brooklyn.

**SOMA MEI SHENG FRAZIER** recently relocated from California—where she's served as a San Francisco Library Laureate—to New York, for a professorship at SUNY Oswego. Her prose chapbooks include *Don't Give Up on Alan Greenspan* (CutBank) and *Salve* (Nomadic). Frazier is nose-to-grindstone on a novel, but more of her short stories are available in *Hyphen, Glimmer Train*, and *ZYZZYVA*.

**ALEXIS PAULINE GUMBS** is a Queer Black Troublemaker and Black Feminist Love Evangelist and an aspirational cousin to all sentient beings. Alexis's co-edited *Revolutionary Mothering: Love on the Front Lines* (PM Press). *Spill: Scenes of Black Feminist Fugitivity, M Archive: After the End of the World*, and *Dub: Finding Ceremony*, her triptych of experimental works, was published by Duke University Press.

**SUZANNE HIGHLAND** is a writer and educator from Sarasota, Florida. She has an MFA from Hunter College and her poems were published in *Apogee, Nat. Brut*, and *Redivider*. She teaches writing to public high school students and lives in Brooklyn, New York.

LUTHER HUGHES is from Seattle and author of *Touched* (Sibling Rivalry Press). He is the founder of Shade Literary Arts and executive editor for *The Offing*. Along with Gabrielle Bates and Dujie Tahat, he co-hosts *The Poet Salon* podcast. He has been featured in *Poetry, Forbes,* and *The Seattle Times.* He thinks you are beautiful. @lutherxhughes

KENAN INCE is a queer, Turkish-American mathematician, poet, and organizer from Texas living on occupied Shoshone, Paiute, Goshute, and Ute territory. Their work has been featured in *The Iowa Review, Gulf Coast,* and *The Missouri Review,* among others. They are the recipient of scholarships to the Antioch Writers' Workshop and Lambda Literary Writers' Retreat.

STACY NATHANIEL JACKSON was born in Los Angeles and attended Ramona Convent College Preparatory School for Girls in a former incarnation of his life. is the author of the chapbook *Camouflage* (MaCaHu). He's a Cave Canem Fellow and his poems, plays, and visual art have been published in *Black Arts Quarterly, The Georgia Review,* and *Foglifter.* He lives in the District of Columbia with his wife Tammy and their cocker/Frenchie rescue Wally.

MARLIN M. JENKINS was born and raised in Detroit and is the author of the poetry chapbook *Capable Monsters* (Bull City). He received an MFA in poetry from the University of Michigan. His work has found homes in *Indiana Review, The Rumpus, Waxwing,* and *Kenyon Review Online.* marlinmjenkins.com

LAURA JONES was the founding Director of Books for Mondo and currently writes for the *Austin Chronicle.* Her work has appeared in literary journals including *Creative Nonfiction, Foglifter, The Gay and Lesbian Review, The Drum, Wrap-around South, Another Chicago Magazine.* Jones earned her MFA in Creative Nonfiction from Northwestern University, where she also won the 2015 AWP Journals Prize.

MICHAL MJ JONES is a Black, queer non-binary poet and parent living in Oakland, CA. Their work is featured or forthcoming at *Kissing Dynamite, Rigorous Mag,* & *Borderlands Texas Poetry Review.* They are currently the Community Engagement Graduate Fellow in the MFA program at Mills College. michal-jones.com

BETTINA JUDD is an interdisciplinary writer, artist, and performer who is an assistant professor of Gender, Women, and Sexuality Studies at the University of

Washington, Seattle. Her Hudson Book Prize-winning collection of poems, *patient.* (Black Lawrence), tackles the history of medical experimentation on Black women. bettinajudd.com

DONIKA KELLY is the author of *The Renunciations* and *Bestiary.* Donika is a Cave Canem graduate fellow and member of the collective Poets at the End of the World. She has received a Lannan Residency Fellowship and a summer workshop fellowship from the Fine Arts Work Center.

JAHAN KHAJAVI writes "wildly amusing & explicit queer poetry" informed by classical Persian traditions. When not in South Bend, Jahan lives, works, and performs in Rome. Other poems by Jahan can be found in *Lotus-eater, Flash Cove, Split Lip,* & *The Recluse.*

BENJAMÍN NAKA-HASEBE KINGSLEY belongs to the Onondaga Nation of Indigenous Americans in New York. He is the author of *Not Your Mama's Melting Pot* (University of Nebraska), *Colonize Me* (Saturnalia Books), and *Dēmos* (Milkweed Editions). Ben is recipient of the Provincetown Fine Arts Work Center, Kundiman, and Tickner Fellowships, among others. He is Assistant Professor of Poetry and Nonfiction in Old Dominion University's MFA program.

AFIEYA KIPP is a creative and founder of Pink Composition Media, a publishing company that believes in the sincere, enthusiastic championing of underrepresented voices. Afieya lives in northern New Jersey where they carry poems in their wallet and is an MFA candidate at Lindenwood University. @AfieyaK or afieyakipp.tumblr.com

KEEGAN LAWLER's work has been published by *Foglifter, 5x5, Washington Poetic Routes, Homology Lit,* among others. He's currently an MFA candidate from Western Washington University and lives in Washington State with his partner, their two basset hounds, and their cat.

JULI DELGADO LOPERA is an award-winning Colombian writer, historian, speaker, and storyteller based in San Francisco. They're the author of the *New York Times*-acclaimed novel *Fiebre Tropical* (Feminist) and *¡Cuéntamelo!* (Aunt Lute), an illustrated bilingual collection of oral histories by LGBT Latinx immigrants. Juli is the former executive director of RADAR Productions.

JOEY MANCINELLI was born in Milwaukee, WI, in 1996. He studied History at

UW-Madison and was a student of Aria Aber.

MAYA MARSHALL is the author of *Secondhand* (Dancing Girl Press), and co-founder of *underbellymag.com*, the journal on the practical magic of poetic revision. A Cave Canem fellow, she lives in Chicago where she works as a manuscript editor for Haymarket Books. Her debut poetry collection is *All the Blood Involved in Love* (Haymarket). @mayaAmarshall

AIREA D. MATTHEWS is the author of *Simulacra* (Yale University), selected by Carl Phillips as the winner of the 2016 Yale Series of Younger Poets. A Cave Canem Fellow and a Kresge Literary Arts Fellow, Matthews is a founding member of the Riven collective along with Marissa Johnson-Valenzuela and Cynthia Dewi Oka. She is an assistant professor at Bryn Mawr College, and lives in Philadelphia, Pennsylvania.

CLARA MCLEAN lives and teaches in the San Francisco Bay Area. Earlier poems have appeared in *Rattle, Cider Press Review, Terrain.org, West Trestle Review, Bird's Thumb,* and other publications.

KATE ARDEN MCMULLEN received her MFA in fiction from the University of North Carolina at Wilmington. Her work has appeared in *Paper Darts, The Boiler*, and *Foglifter,* among others. *The Girls of Indigo Flats and Other Stories* was the 2015 recipient of the Colbert Chapbook Award. She is the assistant director of Hub City Press.

GABRIEL JUAN MEMBRENO is a queer, latinx writer from Long Island, NY. They studied English at SUNY Oneonta, worked with the poetry slam team, and was editor-in-chief for the college's literary magazine. They can be found on Instagram as pseudo.boy showing the lovely mess of some moments.

RAJIV MOHABIR is the author of *The Cowherd's Son* (Tupelo) and *The Taxidermist's Cut* (Four Way Books), and translator of *I Even Regret Night: Holi Songs of Demerara (1916)* (Kaya), which received a PEN/Heim Translation Fund Grant Award. His memoir just won Reckless Books' New Immigrant Writing Prize and is forthcoming 2021. He's an assistant professor of poetry in the MFA program at Emerson College and translations editor at *Waxwing*.

TOMAS MONIZ's debut novel, *Big Familia*, was a finalist for the 2020 PEN/Hemingway, the LAMBDA, and the Foreward Indies Awards. He edited the popular

*Rad Dad* and *Rad Families* anthologies. He's the recipient of the SF Literary Arts Foundation's 2016 Award and the 2020 Artist Affiliate for Headlands Center for Arts. He teaches creative writing at Berkeley City College, Ariel Gore's Literary Kitchen, and the Mendocino Coast Writers Conference. He has stuff on the internet but loves penpals: PO Box 3555, Berkeley CA 94703. He promises to write back.

MICHAEL MONTLACK is editor of the Lambda Finalist essay anthology *My Diva: 65 Gay Men on the Women Who Inspire Them* (University of Wisconsin) and author of two books of poetry, most recently *Daddy* (NYQ Books). His poems have appeared in *North American Review, Cincinnati Review, Poet Lore, The Offing, Hotel Amerika, Court Green,* and *Los Angeles Review.* His prose has appeared in *Huffington Post* and *Advocate.com.* He lives in NYC.

ALICIA MOUNTAIN's debut collection, *High Ground Coward* (Iowa), won the Iowa Poetry Prize. She is also the author of the chapbook *Thin Fire* (BOAAT). She is a lesbian poet, scholar, and teacher. Her work has appeared in *The Nation, American Poetry Review, Prairie Schooner, Poetry Northwest, Guernica* and elsewhere. @HiGroundCoward

GALA MUKOMOLOVA is a Moscow-born, Brooklyn-raised, poet and essayist. Her full-length poetry collection, *Without Protection,* is available from Coffee House Press. She's a recipient of the 2016 Discovery Prize. Gala writes astrology for *NYLON Magazine* and is the co-host of *Big Dyke Energy* Podcast. She's a founder of The Cheburashka Collective.

MEL NIGRO is a queer writer from California in search of a place to call home. They live in Minneapolis, where they do graphic design and volunteer at Boneshaker Books. They are a 2018 Lambda Literary Fellow and their fiction has appeared in *The Knicknackery.* melissanigro.com

ROMEO ORIOGUN was born in Lagos, Nigeria. He is the author of *Sacrament of Bodies* (University of Nebraska). His poems have appeared in *Prairie Schooner, American Poetry Review, Harvard Review, McNeese Review, Bayou,* and others. He is an MFA candidate for poetry at the Iowa Writers' Workshop.

HOLLY PAINTER has published two books of poetry: *Excerpts from a Natural History* (Titus Books) and *My Pet Sounds Off: Translating the Beach Boys* (Finishing Line). She teaches writing and literature at the University of Vermont. Her poetry has been published in *Barrelhouse, The Cream City Review, Bombay Gin*, and *Spork*. hollypainter.com

Born and raised in Brooklyn, Shelagh Patterson is a poet, scholar, and activist. Shelagh has an MFA in creative writing from CUNY Hunter College, a PhD in English from the University of Pittsburgh, and is a Cave Canem fellow. Ze teaches at Montclair State University and lives in Newark.

A native New Yorker, James Penha has lived for the past quarter-century in Indonesia. Nominated for Pushcart Prizes in fiction and poetry, his verse appeared in *Headcase: LGBTQ Writers & Artists on Mental Health and Wellness*, and *Lovejets: Queer Male Poets on 200 Years of Walt Whitman*. Penha edits *The New Verse News*, an online journal of current-events poetry. @JamesPenha

Baruch Porras Hernandez is the author of *I Miss You, Delicate* and *Lovers of the Deep Fried Circle*, both with Sibling Rivalry Press. He was awarded an artist-in-residence at The Ground Floor at Berkeley Rep, and his solo show *Love in the Time of Piñatas* earned a "clapping man" rating from the *San Francisco Chronicle*. Baruch lives in San Francisco.

Joy Priest (she/her) is the author of *HORSEPOWER* (Pitt Poetry Series), winner of the Donald Hall Prize for Poetry. Her work has appeared or is forthcoming in *Poetry Northwest, Gulf Coast,* and *Mississippi Review.* She is a PhD candidate in literature and creative writing at the University of Houston.

Claudia Rodriguez is a grassroots oriented poet/writer/performer, dedicated to creating accurate and empowering representations of marginalized communities and raising awareness of social issues through her art. Her first collection of poetry, *Everybody's Bread*, was a 2016 Lambda Literary finalist. She is a PhD candidate in Chicana/o and Central American Studies at UCLA.

Sam Sax is a queer, jewish, writer, and educator. The author of *Madness*, winner of The National Poetry Series, and *Bury It*, winner of the James Laughlin Award from the Academy of American Poets. He's a 2018 Ruth Lilly Fellow and currently a Wallace Stegner Fellow at Stanford University.

Maureen Seaton has authored twenty-one poetry collections, both solo and collaborative. Her most recent collection is *Sweet World*. Her awards include the Iowa Prize, Lambda Literary Award, Audre Lorde Award, the NEA, two Pushcarts, and the Florida Book Award. Seaton is a professor of English and creative writing at the University of Miami. @mseaton9

**J.G. SIMIŃSKI** is a writer, poet, and audiobook narrator. Simiński is also the writer of the TV pilot, "ProvinceLands," about the disappearances of young, queer men on Cape Cod. He has been the host of the podcast *talkin' 'bout Our Generation* since 2019 and most recently narrated the promo for the new Widdershins Role-Playing Game.

**KEVIN SIMMONDS** is a writer and musician originally from New Orleans. His full-length poetry collections include *Mad for Meat* and *Bend to it*, the anthology *Collective Brightness: LGBTIQ Poets on Faith, Religion & Spirituality*, and, most recently, the chapbooks *the system must be tried* and *The Noh of Dorian Corey*. He lives in San Francisco.

**BENNY SISSON** is a trans poet. She is a library assistant, adjunct instructor, and MFA candidate at Adelphi University. Her poems have been featured with *rinky dink press, Crab Fat Magazine, Lunch Ticket*, and elsewhere. She currently lives in Mineola, with her partner and her pug, Gertrude.

**CHRISTOPHER SOTO** is a poet based in Los Angeles, California. He works at UCLA with the Ethnic Studies Centers and sits on the Board of Directors for Lambda Literary. Soto's poems, reviews, interviews, and articles can be found at *The Nation, The Guardian, Los Angeles Review of Books, Poetry, American Poetry Review, Tin House*, and more.

**TRAVIS TATE** is a queer, black playwright, poet and performer from Austin, Texas. Their poetry has appeared in *Borderlands: Texas Poetry Review, Underblong, Mr. Ma'am, apt*, and *Cosmonauts Avenue*, among other journals. *Maiden*, their debut poetry collection, is out on V.A. Press. They earned an MFA from the Michener Center for Writers. You can find more about them at travisltate.com.

**MICHAEL TODD** is a writer and ESL teacher currently living and working in Madrid, Spain. They obtained their BFA in sculpture and extended media from Virginia Commonwealth University. Their current work engages queer identity, bodies and intimacy, and notions of free will and inheritance. IG: @babyvangogh Twitter: @michaeltodd92 FB: https://www.facebook.com/toddmrt

**MILO TODD** was a Pechet Fellow in GrubStreet's Novel Incubator Program, Lambda

Literary Fellow in Fiction, and is a regular presenter at the Muse and the Marketplace and the Boston Book Festival. His writing has appeared in *Writer Unboxed, Dead Darlings, GrubWrites, Everyday Feminism, Emerge: 2019 Lambda Fellows Anthology*, and more. @todd_milo or on milotodd.com.

JASON VILLEMEZ is a biracial gay man born to an American father and Filipino mother. His fiction has appeared in *Joyland, Foglifter, F(r)iction*, and other journals. Jason writes about LGBTQ history for the *Philadelphia Gay News,* the *Bay Area Reporter* and *Seattle Gay News*. He lives in Philadelphia with his husband and their dog. jasonvillemez.com or Twitter @jasonvillemez.

YANYI is the author of *Dream of the Divided Field* (One World Random House, forthcoming 2022) and *The Year of Blue Water* (Yale University), winner of the Yale Series of Younger Poets Prize. His work has been featured in NPR's *All Things Considered, Tin House, Granta*, and *A Public Space*. He is poetry editor at *Foundry* and a poetry review editor at *Public Books*. yanyiii.com

# Editors

Miah Jeffra is author of *The Violence Almanac, The Fabulous Ekphrastic Fantastic!*, the chapbook *The First Church of What's Happening,* and the forthcoming novel *American Gospel.* They are co-founder of Foglifter Press, and faculty at Santa Clara University. miahjeffra.com

Monique Mero-Williams is a professor at Chabot College. She has worked as an editor and book designer for *Fourteen Hills, Red Light Lit,* and Foglifter Press. Monique currently sits on the board of directors for Foglifter.

Arisa White is an assistant professor of creative writing at Colby College and a Cave Canem fellow. She is the author of *Who's Your Daddy* and co-author of *Biddy Mason Speaks Up.* She serves on the board of directors for Foglifter and Nomadic Press. arisawhite.com

Rooted in the San Francisco Bay Area, **Foglifter Press** is a platform for LGBTQ+ writers that supports and uplifts powerful, intersectional, and transgressive queer and trans writing through publication and public readings to build and enrich our communities as well as the greater literary arts.